AF291174

PIRATES

AND

PRIVATEERS

OF THE

ATLANTIC

AND THE

CARIBBEAN

HUNT JANIN & NICOLE SHEEHAN

PIRATES

AND

PRIVATEERS

OF THE

ATLANTIC

AND THE

CARIBBEAN

HUNT JANIN & NICOLE SHEEHAN

PEN & SWORD HISTORY

AN IMPRINT OF PEN & SWORD BOOKS LTD.
YORKSHIRE – PHILADELPHIA

First published in Great Britain in 2026 by
Pen & Sword History
An imprint of
Pen & Sword Books Ltd
Yorkshire – Philadelphia

ISBN 978 1 03614 519 4

Typeset in INDIA by IMPEC eSolutions
Printed and bound in England by CPI Group (UK) Ltd, Croydon, CRO 4YY

The Publisher's authorised representative in the EU for product safety is Authorised Rep Compliance Ltd., Ground Floor, 71 Lower Baggot Street, Dublin D02 P593, Ireland. www.arccompliance.com

For a complete list of Pen & Sword titles please contact:

PEN & SWORD BOOKS LIMITED
George House, Units 12 & 13, Beevor Street, Off Pontefract Road,
Barnsley, S71 1HN, UK
E-mail: enquiries@pen-and-sword.co.uk
Website: www.pen-and-sword.co.uk

or

PEN AND SWORD BOOKS
1950 Lawrence Rd, Havertown, PA 19083, USA
E-mail: uspen-and-sword@casematepublishers.com
Website: www.penandswordbooks.com

An Invitation to all brave Seamen and Marines, who have an inclination to serve their country and make their Fortunes. The grand Privateer Ship DEANE, commanded by Elisha Hinman Esq., and prov'd to be a very capital sailor, will sail on a cruise against the enemies of the United States of America, by the 20th instant. The DEANE mounts thirty carriage guns, and is excellently well calculated for Attacks, Defence and Pursute. This therefore is to invite all those Jolly Fellows who love their Country, and want to make their Fortunes at One Stroke, to repair immediately to the Rendezvous at the Head of His Excellency Governor Hancock's Wharf, where they will be received with a hearty welcome by a number of Brave Fellows there assembled and treated with what excellent Liquor is call'd Grog [a mixture of water and rum, served warm] *which is allowed by all true Seamen to be the Liquor of Life.*[1]

Contents

Preface

To keep this text as free-flowing as possible, explanations of the nautical and historical concepts mentioned here – some dating from the Middle Ages – have been kept short and simple.

A good example of this is that the guns (the cannons) carried aboard ships are mentioned frequently in the text and in more detail in Appendix 2 on Naval Gunnery in the Age of Sail. However, since naval gunnery in that era was a complicated subject which is now probably of most interest chiefly to experts in that field, the comments here are only introductory.

Piracy is an important topic, too, but it is discussed here in its relationships to privateering. By the same token, privateering in the West Indies was also an important undertaking. It has already been covered in scholarly studies, however, and the limitations of space here mean that I will touch only lightly on some of its many interesting highlights.

To define a sea-going term when first used in the text, it will be explained very briefly in parentheses. Some complex nautical matters are discussed at more length in the endnotes or in the appendices. There are eight short appendices in the latter pages of the text. They all make useful points that are relevant and interesting, but which probably do not merit stand-alone positions.

Also included are some contemporary comments on the most important political, economic, or social conditions prevailing in the areas most directly or indirectly involved in privateering.

Unless stated otherwise, currency values in this book are given as being valid in the year then under discussion. Precise figures do not exist now, but a reasonable guess is that, during the Revolutionary War alone, American privateers captured about 1,600 to 1,800 British ships which had a cumulative total value of between $1.4 billion and $1.6 billion in today's dollars.[2]

To the best of our knowledge, this is one of the very few modern books, and certainly one of the most broadly-based in historical terms, which is devoted entirely to American and other forms of privateering. It includes, for example, Marc Russon's excellent 2004 study, in French, on *Les Côtes guerrières: France – Façade océanique au Moyen Âge* (*The Warring Coasts: The Oceanic Theatre of Combat in the Middle Ages*). This area of privateering covered the Atlantic coastline of France and thence through the English Channel northeast up to what is now Belgium.

Readers' comments – whether pro, or con, or otherwise – on any of the points made in it are most welcome. They can be emailed to the authors c/o the publisher, Pen & Sword Books.

Introduction: Setting the Stage

Because very little of this complicated subject will be understandable to readers who are not familiar with at least a few parts of it, a broad-based introductory survey will be offered now. It will be much more useful here rather than being embedded in bits-and-pieces in the body of the text.

The inherent complexity of eighteenth- and nineteenth-century sailing ships can best be seen in historic line drawings that carefully describe twenty-seven of their sails; 131 of their spars and rigging; sixty parts of their frames (the hulls of the ships); and the more than ten different major categories of different types of ships that were built and outfitted for very different assignments.[3]

Virtually all the officers and crews of privateer vessels were *men*. As will be explained later, while there were in fact a very small number of *female pirates*, no women were ever known to have been part of any privateering crew. The male owners, the male officers, and the male crews of privateer ships would simply not have invited any female crew member aboard because of the contemporary belief that their presence would have generated discord.

The term "privateer" can be confusing because it had three equally valid but overlapping meanings:

- The first meaning was that of a privately owned ship outfitted and staffed to capture or to sink an enemy ship, under the auspices of an official commission issued by a national government or by a powerful local authority. In the Age of Sail, the word "ship" technically meant a full-rigged sailing ship with three or more masts, all of them square-rigged. As used in this book, however, "ship" often simply means "a large seagoing vessel".

- The second meaning of "privateer" was that of an officer or a seaman who was serving aboard a privateering ship. A few of these men were probably self-serving individuals who went into this business only in hopes of making money from capturing enemy ships, which were known in the trade as "prizes". Most of the privateersmen, however, were most probably decent men who simply wanted to combine patriotism, profit, and adventure.
- The third meaning of "privateer" was that of an investor or a consortium of investors who took the sizeable financial risk of financing privateering expeditions, both for patriotic reasons and, equally important, to make money for themselves.

In most cases, privateering was a joint entrepreneurial endeavour, undertaken by a group of ship-owners who shared the considerable costs of outfitting and staffing a privateer ship. There was a very good chance – but of course no certainty! – that they would profit considerably from this risky investment. Local governments, for their parts, usually encouraged privateering: it cost them nothing at all to commission privateer ships, and they would impose stiff taxes on them when they were built.

In even broader terms, however, the sea itself was long judged by medieval thinkers to be "a zone beyond the boundaries of civilization" – in other words, as a "perpetually lawless environment where land-based rules could never be applied and was inherently dangerous".[4]

In part for this reason, in some circumstances, the English and other rulers actively encouraged shipowners and shipmasters to set out to sea with the express intention of attacking enemy ships – in order to keep for themselves and their crews a sizeable portion of the value of any prizes thus taken. The surplus inherent in this process would of course go to the rulers.

This point of view remained dominant in the public's mind for many generations. Indeed, it finally faded away only with the much later arrival of well-navigated, iron-hulled, heavily armed, and steam-driven ships.

During the early formative period of 1688 to 1815, however, the vigorous growth of both the British economy and of the British Empire itself depended on successful international maritime trade. These early years ultimately changed how Britain governed itself: Parliament would be given more power over the monarchy, and seeds would be planted which would eventually blossom into the beginnings of political democracy in Britain.

During this long, slow, process, the British, and to some extent the French as well, habitually kept very well-equipped naval units stationed overseas, not so much to defend their homelands against European enemies as to protect their own far-flung colonies and their extensive patterns of international trade. This meant that they had to be prepared to cope with the interrelated maritime threats posed by privateers, pirates, smugglers, foreign coastguards, policy changes by foreign countries, and big storms at sea.[5]

Guerilla warfare, also known as unconventional or irregular warfare, is now usually thought of only as involving land-based fighting, but in historical terms it also flourished quite well at sea, too. Its name comes from the diminutive form of the Spanish word *guerra* ("war") and literally means "little war".

Whether on land or at sea, guerilla warfare involved many small groups of well-trained and well-armed men pitted against much larger, better organized, and much more powerful military forces. "Guerilla warfare at sea" is a very good description of international privateering, involving as it did numerous small-scale but ultimately, over time, very effective hit-and-run maritime attacks, set in many of the world's oceans by land-based participants.

Effective as it was, however, guerilla warfare at sea has never received the full extent of scholarly attention it deserves, probably because written details on it are generally lacking. The fundamental reason is that the officers engaged in such combat never had the time or the legal need to keep accurate logs of their ship's activities. Any informal notes they may have made after combat were probably ignored and were eventually destroyed.

For this reason, the official canon (written body) of naval history in both Britain and the United States tends to ignore privateers/guerilla warfare at sea, favouring instead the more exciting, more dramatic, "big screen" events that took place afloat with big fleets at sea supporting big armies on land.

In point of fact, however, the crews of privateer ships, setting out in their small but well-armed vessels (usually schooners in the 200-ton, 150-foot-long range) pitted themselves, often successfully, against much bigger commercial cargo ships that were either unarmed or were only very lightly armed.

A schooner is a type of sailing vessel defined by its rig (the arrangement of its sails). It has two or three masts, with the foremast generally being shorter than the mainmast. A schooner is fore-and-aft rigged, which means that the sails run down the centre of the ship and are hoisted on the gaff and boom. Such a ship had a great advantage in combat over a less agile square-rigged merchantman or man-of-war. Square-rigged ships have their sails and rigging mounted on heavy horizontal spars, which take effort and more time to handle.

The schooner rig was used in vessels designed for a wide range of assignments. Today it is still said to be the best, the safest, and the handiest rig for large yachts, particularly those with long, narrow hulls and sharp bows. It is also, arguably, the most beautiful rig. For all these reasons, real and fictional schooners have often starred in films and in novels.

Since schooners often had fast hulls and a very good ability to sail to windward (to sail close to the direction from which the wind was blowing), they were much favoured for service as privateers.

Because they were designed for speed, they were too unstable to be reliable gun platforms for use in actual combat. Other and more suitable uses for them, however, were as blockade runners, slave ships, opium clippers ("clipper" was a generic name for any large, fast sailing ship), pilot boats, vessels transporting perishable fruits, and fishing boats.

Schooners were durable and were very popular on both sides of the Atlantic in the late 1800s and early 1900s for many different purposes. The Norwegian polar schooner *Fram*, for example, was used by both Fridtjof Nansen and Roald Admunsen in their explorations of the polar seas. These all had the advantage of spreading their total sail area over several smaller sails, thus making it much easier for crews to man-handle them at a time when mechanical assistance aboard ship was rare.

Brigs (slightly larger ships than schooners) were favoured, too, for both official naval duties and for privateering. These were smallish warships featuring two masts, with square rigging on the foremast and fore-and-aft rigging on the mainmast. In a square rig, the sails are bent (that is, they are attached) to the yards that extend across the width of vessel.

Ranging in length from about 75 feet to 120 feet, brigs were cheap to build and easy to maintain; quite manoeuvrable; and, armed with ten to eighteen guns, ideal for privateering, naval combat, reconnaissance, and raiding.

With crews of about 100 men, brigs were known for their speed and agility. For this reason, they were often assigned to chase down other vessels in order to board them if need be, or to escort larger but slower ships that were part of a fleet.

A good example of a brig was the nimble *Swift*, built and based in Charleston, South Carolina during the American Revolutionary War. She was only 75 feet long with a 20-foot beam and had an 88-ton displacement and was the first ship officially commissioned by South Carolina.[6]

Privateering soon became the ideal weapon of warfare for the weak to use against strong, e.g., for the feeble American colonies to use against the world-straddling mighty British Empire. Usually funded by only private non-official/non-governmental contracts, privateer officers and men eagerly volunteered to fight for the United States in the Revolutionary War, the War of 1812, and the Civil War.

During the Revolutionary War, many American privateersmen cruised the Atlantic Ocean hunting for British ships they could capture, staff with prize crews and then legally sail to a port for a quick sale, or barring that, simply loot and burn at sea. Their "happy hunting grounds", as it were, ranged from Nova Scotia to the West Indies (the Caribbean), and from the North Sea all the way to the coasts of Africa.

A privateer was a flexible private individual or a private company authorized by a country's central government or by a regional authority to attack local and international shipping on the oceans at times and places of its own choosing – both for its own profit and to inflict substantial damage on an enemy country for political or economic reason. It was a long-running, well-developed, respectable, prosperous and very popular line of work.

Indeed, its first recorded appearance dates from the fourteenth century, when the Victual Brothers, a loosely organized Germanic guild of maritime brigands led by a warrior named Klaus Störtebeker (whose skull has now been reconstructed by modern means) raided ships at sea, but without any formally documented authorization to do so.

In 1449, an international incident occurred near the Isle of Wight. The salt trade between England and France was very important then, salt being needed to preserve all the fish being shipped to markets.

This incident arose when English privateers captured the "Bay Fleet", which consisted of sixty Hanse ships (the Hanse was a trading alliance in northern Germany and along the North Sea coast) and fifty ships from Holland and the Low Countries. The privateers released the Holland and Low Country ships, but nevertheless kept the salt owned by the Hanse.

English privateers captured the Bay Fleet again in 1458, but this time diplomacy smoothed out the issue, to the extent that in 1471, the English king, Edward IV, was restored to power with Hanseatic support, and in 1474 a treaty was negotiated between England and the Hanse.[7]

Nevertheless, privateering proved to be so attractive that it continued unabated until 1856. In that year, as we will see later, seven European nations agreed to the Paris Declaration. This treaty renounced privateering in terms that effectively ended its wide-spread practice, initially by the seven signatory states, and then, later, by many other countries as well.

The treaty, however, did not put privateers into any new category of international criminals, but rather made it a treaty obligation of all signatory states that they must refrain from ever commissioning privateers in the first place.

The United States, however, declined to ratify this agreement – in order, said the Americans, to preserve the rights of any weak nation, e.g., the young United States, against the better-armed maritime powers of the day, such as Great Britain, France, and Spain.

The activities of privateers often exceeded the legitimate boundaries set forth in their commissions. When this happened, it was impossible for outsiders to distinguish between men who looked, acted, and dressed much alike and who were also known by a large number of often-overlapping terms.

These terms included:

- Privateers: This word can refer to the men themselves, to their backers, and to the ships they used. Formal written permission was legally necessary to practise this trade, which has sometimes been described, only half-jokingly, as "officially approved piracy". Privateering and piracy were both very important efforts, together with official trading and settlement policies, in the push for English expansion overseas.[8]

- Pirates: In times of war, privateers were often licensed by a government or by a local ruler to attack enemy shipping. Wartime profits enticed many seamen to become privateers, but as soon as peace broke out, if only for a short time, many of them were forced to turn to piracy simply in order to make a living.

After about 1800, however, piracy was almost unnecessary, at least in the Caribbean, because any men so inclined could easily legitimize their calling and protect themselves legally by obtaining letters of marque (these will be discussed in later pages).[9]

It must be remembered that piracy occupied a shady and very ill-defined area falling somewhere in the broad spectrum between outright theft, semi-official raiding, lawful but cutthroat commercial competition, and government-approved reprisals. The story of pirates was largely a French one occurring between 1500 and 1559; an English story from 1560 to 1600; and a Dutch story from 1600 to 1648; but privateering always remained a continuing story until it was finally internationally outlawed in the mid-nineteenth century.[10]

For example, many of the claimants involved in legal cases and in incidents referred to in Britain's Patent Roles and similar legal sources were certainly not, by their own lights, pirates or robbers at all. They were more likely to be honest citizens simply asking for legally sanctioned fair payments for the damages or losses they had suffered at sea or somehow involving ships.

In the Middle Ages, and in fact until privateering was formally banned internationally in the mid-nineteenth century, three distinct kinds of maritime violence took place:

The indiscriminate, persistent and criminal pursuit of maritime robbery; officially authorized reprisals by merchants for loss of ships or goods; and government-commissioned but privately promoted action against enemy shipping and goods in time of war.

Or, to put it more simply, piracy, reprisals, and privateering. Of these three different forms of private maritime violence, only the first – piracy – was illegal, but in fact all three were very much alike in motivation and methods.[11]

- Corsairs: This term was derived from the French word for privateer (*la course*). Classic examples of corsairs were (1) the Barbary corsairs, who were Ottoman and Beber pirate-privateersmen operating out of North Africa, and (2) the French corsairs, who were privateers working on behalf of the French crown. Until the end of the Middle Ages, the terms "corsair" and "pirate" were very often used interchangeably.

Some were locally famous. In 1144, for example, the French bishop Jean de Châtillon gave to local privateers-pirates the 44-acre fortified town of Saint-Malo in Brittany, France which they turned into a base from which they could attack ships coming into the Iberian Peninsula. They were so well-known that the local residents proclaimed Saint-Malo to be an independent, if very short-lived, republic. This was its bold motto, translated into English: "Neither French nor Breton, but a Corsair am I!"

In 1235, King Henry III of England authorized Geoffroy de Clamorgan to undertake privateering against Count Pierre of Brittany, up to the value of all the English goods destroyed by the Count's ships. Any value over and above this sum would then be sent directly into the King's treasury.[12] This is one of the earliest examples of the English monarchy being willing and, indeed, eager to profit from privateering.

As early as 1525, the Spanish government required its treasure-galleons to travel in convoys. Privateer and privates could always pick off a few of the ships that were lagging behind, but these losses were not very high and the fleets usually made it home more or less intact.[13]

- Buccaneers: These were Caribbean-based pirates whose name came from their subsisting chiefly on smoked dried beef (*buccan*). They did not have big ships but used instead numerous small sailing boats, such as sloops (a sloop has only one mast), to attack Spanish shipping in the Caribbean.

A lovely painting by the modern artist Howard Pyle shows several buccaneers in a small sloop, secretly sailing at night toward a huge Spanish galleon in order to attack and board her from the stern.[14]

The most famous account of seventeenth-century buccaneering was published in Dutch in 1678 by Alexander Olivier Exquemelin. It ran through five English editions, and was also translated into French, Spanish, and German. Its title (in English) was *The American Sea-Rovers*.

- Freebooters: This name came from the small, fast *flibotes* ("fly boats") used by some French desperados. After falling out of use before the nineteenth century, it was revived then as "filibuster", which meant a smuggler or a blockade runner. In the United States, this revived term now means "the delaying tactic of a time-consuming speech made in the Senate to prevent the passage of a bill or an amendment".

Moreover, many of the above men also sailed under false or imaginary commissions, thus blurring the defining terms even further. For example, after the War of 1812 between Britain and the United States, the pejorative term "Cartagenian privateer" referred to any semi-pirate Latin American ship that had nominally been commissioned by the corrupt government officials of what is now Columbia. In point of fact, most of these ships were nothing more than pirate ships carrying worthless documents.[15]

At first, the rebellious American colonies had no ability to challenge Britain's Royal Navy during the Revolutionary War. It was by far the most powerful naval force in the world, and the Americans had no organized navy of their own and no way to build one quickly.

It is estimated that in 1776 there were only about 100 ships of various shapes and sizes and in various locations in the service of the American colonies.[16] The Americans' creative solution to this problem, however, was to modify their existing ships or to build specialized ships that could easily be constructed without delay, namely, privateer ships.

Privateer ships were the key players in what has aptly been called "the prize game".[17] Derived from the Old French word *prise*, (taken, or seized), this meant the capture, by privateers, of enemy ships in wartime and then either selling them and their contents in neutral or welcoming ports, or alternatively (and only if there was no other option), burning them at sea, after first having removed both the crew and the most valuable parts of the cargo.

Such arson usually occurred only after, as happened during the War of 1812, it simply became too dangerous, due to an effective British blockade of some parts of the 2,000 miles of America's porous coastlines, with all its thousands of bays, river mouths, and harbours, to risk asking an American prize crew try to deliver a prize to a port where it could easily, legally, and safely be sold.[18]

Resolving legal disputes over prizes could be a very tedious process. For example, Captain Gideon Olmstead, who at the age of 20 had commandeered a British sloop during the Revolutionary War, spent the next thirty years of his life pursuing a legal case on this issue. He was finally successful in 1809 when the Supreme Court ruled in his favour.

Today, it is impossible for historians to determine how many prizes were actually condemned, that is, how many claims by privateers were formally approved. The British colonies in what is now the United States licensed at least forty-four privateers – some taking no prizes at all, some having only modest successes, but one capturing about fifty ships. In addition, many more American ships seized by privateers were condemned in the Vice-Admiralty courts located in Newfoundland, the Caribbean, and in England.[19]

It is also impossible to say how the privateers fared financially. Some of them moved into licensed trade. The need to restock British forces in Spain, Portugal, the West Indies, and British North America, for example, led to the issuance of hundreds of licences to unarmed, and now-unnamed, American ships to deliver food and non-military supplies to these forces. Thomas Jefferson himself argued that since the British government had to pay someone to carry supplies to its troops in Spain, it might as well be the Americans themselves.[20]

In addition, privateer captains could always turn their hands to smuggling, which had long been honed to a fine skill by merchants on both sides of the Maine-New Brunswick border. Privateers were, it was said, among the most active people in this illicit trade.

A sign of these troubled times was that in 1814 the American Secretary of State, James Monroe, had to order American tax collectors not to issue letters of marque (formal permission) to any ships manned by fewer than twenty men. The reason was that, with such small boats, the smugglers could, quite undetected, slip in and out of the many harbours dotting Maine's border region and thereby avoid customs duties or other legal issues.

To avoid the danger of battle with a more powerful adversary, privateers tried hard to get very close to a prize before making their move. Their crews did not wear uniforms and often flew false flags to confuse an enemy. (A false flag was flown to disguise the true identity or affiliation of a ship.)

In addition, privateers captured by one side in a conflict could quickly and easily be redeployed against their previous owners. For example, eighteen captured American privateers were turned against their former owners as New Brunswick and Nova Scotia privateers.[21]

That said, however, it is not easy to distinguish between the privateering programmes of the Americans and of British during the War of 1812. The goal of both sides was much the same: not to wage an all-out, death-or-glory, war but simply to drain the enemy's wealth by slowing or, ideally, even by halting most of its key exports.

During this war, there were about 600 American privateers at sea versus about forty-four British privateers. At the end of the day, however, their net impact was probably much the same for both countries.

What is most clear, however, is that for every captain, mate, sailor, or cabin boy who made his fortune as a privateer, far more men came back home empty-handed, or perhaps they did not come home at all. Many privateersmen were lost at sea through capture, storms, accident, disease, combat, or died unsung as prisoners of war.[22]

The United States Constitution, in Article 1, Section 8, paragraph 11, still allows Congress to authorize letters of marque and reprisal, which will be discussed later. However, Congress has not done so for more than 150 years and is not likely ever to do so again in the foreseeable future.

This is true even though some conservative American politicians have suggested it as a way to deal with terrorist or pirate attacks on American cities, on big cargo-carrying or oil-carrying ships, or even to seize yachts owned by Russian oligarchs. For better or worse, however, Congress has never seen fit to enact any of these ideas into law.

Privateering was a very big and a very attractive business. American privateers are believed to have captured up to 300 British ships during the Revolutionary War, although some of these may later have been recaptured by the British, released, ransomed, or sent in to ports as cartels.

Ransoming, in the context of privateer life, meant that the victor would allow his prize to depart unharmed, provided that the captain of the prize signed a document promising that the owner of the vessel would pay a given fee for its safe return to him. Cartels, on the other hand, were agreements between sellers and buyers of ships to collude in order to improve profits by dominating markets.

In that era, in the big port of Liverpool, England, there were said to have been about 120 privateer ships, crewed by nearly 9,000 seamen.[23] Privateering was a huge and quite profitable business both in England and in America.

In England, it was, at least in theory, officially governed by the Admiralty. The owners of the privateer ships may not themselves all have been very greedy or very cruel men, but they had no direct control over what their officers and crewmen did when out of sight of land.

They thus could never, even if so inclined, try to punish any men who went to excessive lengths just to stay alive themselves or to capture enemy ships that were then in the process of resisting them very violently. Their job was to stay alive themselves, not to dispense mercy.

In North America, there was no theory of centralized national direction and by the end of the Seven Years' War, privateering was widely being hailed there as an essential element in maritime warfare. Many Eastern Seaboard ports – for example, Halifax, Salem, and Newport – had become successful privateer bases.

The men who were daily engaged in this line of work were not necessarily monsters of depravity but, when at sea, the need to "kill or be killed" was their common belief.

One of the most successful privateers was the Englishman Fortunatus Wright, whose popular exploits in the Mediterranean during the War of the Austrian Succession (1740-1748, known in the American colonies as King George's War) and in the Seven Years' War (1755-1763) made him a celebrated hero. For better or worse, however, he vanished at sea with his ship in 1757.[24]

Chaired by its "First Lord", the British Admiralty Board provided both convoys for the American colonials, and Royal Navy "guardships" stationed in the colonies to protect them against enemies and pirates and to enforce Britain's Acts of Trade.

The Admiralty also authorized the issuing of letters of marque to privateers; provided passes to help protect English merchant ships from Barbary corsairs; and encouraged the production in the colonies of important maritime items such as rope, pitch, tar, turpentine, and tall masts for ships.

Moreover, it also served as the final court of legal appeal in admiralty cases – via the High Court of Admiralty.[25]

Liverpool was also a bustling centre of the slave trade, one reason being that it was relatively remote from the main areas of British official activity.

Moreover, the skippers of slave ships were much less likely to be stopped for inspection there than they might well have been on the English Channel or on the River Thames. This makes the point that, in practice, the officers and men on duty in the privateer ships docking in Liverpool were certainly not saints: the most aggressive of them were in fact hardly better than full-time pirates.[26]

In the American colonies, on the other hand, privateer ships, officers, and seamen enjoyed a much better reputation. Indeed, they were so familiar and so important that they were hailed on the street by the public as "the militia of the sea".[27]

Moreover, the phrase "privateer-built" was used by experienced seamen to note with approval how the running rigging of a ship (the moveable lines and tackle used to hoist and lower sails and to adjust them once underway), as well as the fixed blocks and cleats, could all be installed on the *outside* of her bulwarks, that is, on the extensions of a ship's sides, raising them above the level of the deck. This would keep the desk itself entirely clear of ship's gear and thus always ready for immediate combat action.

Remarkably, it was private investors, and not colonial government entities, that financed American privateers during the three major wars discussed in this book, namely, the Revolutionary War, the War of 1812, and the Civil War. The ships and the crews these investors paid for fought in many different war theatres of the world, e.g., off the Carolinas and among the islands of the Caribbean.

The crews of privateer ships presented a very mixed picture. At their best, they could be "cheerly" responsive, that is to say, quickly and with good will obeying all the orders coming from their officers.

At their worst, however, as one English official complained, "To govern and command the dissolute mariner from his riot" taxed virtually all of a good officer's powers of command. Drunkenness, brawls, violence, and insults were commonplace aboard privateers, where "no disciple is used, nor authority obeyed".

It was even said of a typical privateer captain that "though he be styled the captain, yet they [the crew] do not use to obey him so strictly as him that has power from a General ... for they receive no pay [they received no pay apart from their own share of prizes] whereby to oblige them, but everyone goes upon his own adventure [everyone does just as he pleases]."

The imperative need for what we might well call "gentleness in command" was stressed on privateer ships. This was because privateer captains, as free-lance individual businessmen, could never profit from the Royal Navy's long tradition of rigid discipline aboard ship – a tradition which ultimately relied on the presence of armed and intelligent royal marine officers on the ship, who were assigned to back up the captain's orders if need be.

The owners of the Boston privateer *Despatch* made all this very clear in their instructions to Captain Nathaniel Ingersol, given here verbatim:

> We are Sencible the Minds of Weak people require the nicest judgment in Manageing them where a Command is not altogether Absolute, and as the Success of our Enterprize depends very much on preserving a good Harmony between ... the Offices and people [the crew of the ship]…
>
> That task we must submit to your Skill and Shall only Say that the most judicious way of Governing is always to preserve the Dignity of Command, and at a proper season a Mild and Somewhat Familiar but still distant behaviour will win Harts and Steal the affections of those in Subjection [namely, the crew].[28]

One of the most difficult problems on privateer ships was the distribution of booty from prizes. As soon as a prize was docked at port, the crew began to pillage and steal the cargo of that ship. At the same time, the owners also began to cheat the men out of their pay and their prize money.

One partial solution was the use of birdlime: "all these sea-goods [the ship's cargo] are mixed with birdlime; for no man can [then] lay his hand on them, but is [thereby] limed ... [Their officers were warned:] Watch and look ever so narrowly, [the men] will steal and pilfer."

This was a long-standing problem. Of the prizes brought back by English ships in 1589:

Two thirds of all the lading [the ship's cargo] were spoiled and embezzled by the men of war and mariners of the sea before they were brought into [the port of] Plymouth and ... one half of that third remaining was purloined and scattered abroad since the arrival of the ships in that haven, so that nothing was left aboard the ships but that which was too cumbersome or heavy to carry away...[29]

Mutinies were also not unknown on privateering voyages. Although privateering was not anything as egalitarian as pirate life, where the captain was elected by the men, who could depose him and choose a new captain any time they wished, the captain and the crew of any given privateer had to work very closely together – for their own safety, for the safety of their ship, and to have any chance of capturing lucrative prizes.

Punishments for misbehaving sailors were clearly laid out in 1627 and included the following:

- 24 hours in irons for missing a watch (for example by failure to be ready for duty when summoned), gambling, lighting candles after the watch had been set for the night, or overstaying leave; three buckets of water poured over the head for sleeping on watch three times.
- For striking or fighting another man the offender was to be ducked three times (being dropped into the sea from a yardarm) and then discharged without pay.
- A thief received five lashes from every man in the ship and was also discharged without pay. Drunkards were usually put in irons.
- Shore leave for the men was regarded by officers as normal and, indeed, quite essential for a contented crew. Even the best officers, however, found it impossible to control the "extravagant lewdness" and "dissolute wildness" of the seamen ashore.[30]

At the same time, historically, these maritime actions were also part of broader human interest stories that lose nothing in the retelling today. These accounts include the unsung but nevertheless quite important supporting roles played by racial minorities and by women directly or indirectly involved in the business of privateering.

The sole difference between the pirate and the privateer was that the pirate acted only in pursuit of his or her own interests and only on his or her own authority. In contrast, the privateer acted, in theory at least, under the nominal authority of some official entity which accepted responsibility for or was at least believed to hold responsibility for all his actions at sea.[31]

Sometimes, however, national definitions were based chiefly on international politics. For example, during the Revolutionary War, many British lawmakers considered the American privateers, whose considerable success in looting and seizing British ships at sea greatly angered wealthy British merchants and drove up costs to British consumers, to be nothing more than pirates.

As a result, Parliament passed the Pirate Act of 1777, which allowed the British to hold American privateers without trial and to refuse to treat them as prisoners of war, which meant that they could not be exchanged for other prisoners of war.

These draconian measures, however, stimulated the anti-war movement among some parts of the British public. It led these citizens to protest that such actions were compromising Britain's traditional moral values in its treatment of American prisoners of war. Protestors also denounced Britain's decision to license its own privateers and to revive the forced conscription (known as "pressing") of British citizens into the Royal Navy.

Pressing was very unpopular among the working class of England. Most of these men, if ever themselves inclined to go to sea, much preferred to work on privateer ships. These paid very well when prizes were taken, were not exceptionally dangerous to serve on, and were administered under a more relaxed form of discipline than that practised by the Royal Navy.

Another result of the Pirate Act was that the Royal Navy captured or destroyed hundreds of American privateer vessels at sea. In addition, most of the 12,000 American seamen who died in British prisons during the Revolutionary War were privateers, and these heavy losses left in their wake a whole generation of widows and orphans in New England seaports.

It was said that in Newburyport, Massachusetts, for example, the loss of twenty-two privateering ships involved the deaths of 1,000 men in their crews. By the same token, Gloucester, Massachusetts lost all twenty-four of its registered privateers, which during the course of the war cut the population of adult males in that port by 50 per cent.[32]

Chapter 1

The Historical Background of Privateering

It has always been very expensive for a country to have a good navy. For example, in the 1330s, England went to war with France when England had a national income, using contemporary figures, of somewhere between £18,000 to £33,000 per year. This was only about one third of the national income of France.

These estimates, however, fall very far short of the real costs of all the ships and trained officers and men needed to staff them in a war.[33] Indeed, they were much more than the English king, shipowners, or the taxpayers were able or willing to pay for on their own.

A workable solution to this vexing problem, however, was found by using "prize money" (the income generated by selling captured ships), to help fund an English navy. The realization that keeping a fleet of royal ships, e.g., a prototype navy, right at hand and ready to defend England was only slowly being accepted by the English Crown as a pressing need in the late fifteenth century.[34]

English privateering is thought to date from the 1200s, when the king ordered the vessels of the traditional "Cinq Ports" of England, namely, Hastings, Hythe, Dover, Sandwich, and Romney, to attack France.[35] In England, privateering was often considered the best way to make profitable use of a nation's shipping. At least during the time of the Tudor dynasty, for example, it was said of privateering that "those who knew what they were doing usually ended up better off than they had started".[36]

What is most clear, however, is that, from early times, the English kings claimed a large share of any prize captured in English waters, and 100 per cent of any prize captured by one of their own ships.

In 1243, King Henry III issued the first privateering commissions, which provided that he would receive one half of the value of any prize taken by his ships, while in 1319 Edward II became the first king to give his whole share to English ships. Letters of marque were issued for the first time in the war of 1543-1546 in order to lure private enterprise into the service of the government.[37]

In time, this gradually evolved into a much simpler and more widespread process, by which some English ships were given "letters of marque", which formally turned them into privateers. It can safely be said that, to use a modern Wall Street phrase, privateering was always a business based on a calculated assessment of "fear versus greed".

In the medieval era, the essence of the phrase was much the same: "risk versus revenue." As long as there were good profits to be made at sea, courageous privateers would continue to try their luck there. In so doing, however, these men were also strongly motivated by a long-established legal process which was quick, clear, accurate, conclusive, and, of course, which favoured the privateer rather than his prey.[38]

Privateer ships constituted a large part of all the military forces at sea during the seventeenth, eighteenth and early nineteenth centuries, and were duly authorized by all the major naval powers. Long before then, however, we heard news of medieval privateering.

The matter of "safeguarding the sea", or as the British traditionally put it of "keeping the sea", was of the utmost concern to all coastal dwellers, especially in England, where this historical issue is so well documented. There, beginning by about the year 1400, coastal men and women suffered, directly or indirectly, from the attacks directed by raiders against commercial shipping off the English coasts.

Seakeeping patrols organized by the English Crown showed the determination to exert the nation's control over the English Channel and English maritime waterways. These patrols hoped to ward off attacks ranging from simple robbery on the high seas; to local or regional piracy; or even to thefts carried out under some kind of official blanket permission from a ruler, in other words, an early form privateering.[39] None of these abuses, however, lent themselves to quick or easy correction.

From the English point of view, one of the most despised but colourful French villains was the French privateer-pirate Eustache Busquet (ca. 1170-1217), who is better known to history as Eustache the Monk.

He was variously a monk, a knight, a sorcerer, an outlaw, an excellent sailor, a mercenary, and a turn-coat. A wonderful manuscript, written between the years 1223 and 1284, blending fact and fiction and written in Old French, recounts his many adventures in France, Spain, England, and the Channel Islands.[40]

All of these adventures stemmed from the fact that, after his father was murdered by a local nobleman, Eustache first tried to avenge his father by hiring a champion (a "hired gun", to use a modern term) to fight a judicial duel on his behalf. Such a duel was considered at that time to be the most sure-fire way to determine God's will on any given issue.

However, in this fight Eustache's champion was soundly defeated, which clearly meant that God did not support Eustache's case. The net result was that, later on, Eustache was still so persecuted by the evil local nobleman that he felt driven to become an outlaw.

Many of his outlaw-adventures strongly resemble the folklore tales surrounding the mythical Robin Hood. In 1205, however, Eustache became a real-life privateer and was always quick to change sides, variously supporting either the French or the English, as seemed to him most promising at any given time. He was so good as a privateer, however, that for some time he was actually in total control of the English Channel.

During the Barons' War, he transported King Louis from France to the Isle of Thanet, the most easterly point of Kent, England. At the battle of Sandwich in 1217, however, his good luck finally ran out.

His own ship was attacked and was one of the French ships seized in that battle. Possibly because Eustache himself was such a formidable fighter, however, the English sailors did not try to board the captured French ships at once, but decided to resort instead to a clever strategy which would keep their own casualties to a minimum.

They therefore hurled big pots of finely ground lime onto the decks of the French ships. When these smashed against the railings, they released such great clouds of dust that the French crews were immediately blinded, could not fight, and were thus forced to surrender.

After the English attack, Eustache was found cowering in his ship's bilges (the lowest, wettest, and smelliest parts of a ship), where he offered his English captors great sums of money if they would only spare his life. Because of his long career as a turn-coat privateer, however, they refused to do so.

The best they said they would do for him was to offer him, as his place of execution, a choice between the rail on one side of his ship, or the edge of a catapult stowed on the other side of the ship. History does not record which side Eustache chose, but he was certainly beheaded right then and there.

During the Middle Ages, many armed private ships sailed with their sovereign's tacit approval, but not always with his or her explicit royal commission. The practice of well-organized sea-raiding under official auspices dates only from 1243, when the English king, Henry III, issued the first formal privateering commissions. These were licences he granted to specific individuals authorizing them to seize the king's enemies at sea – provided that he would always receive half of the proceeds from the sale of the seized ships and their cargos.

Privateering thus flourished in England during the early years of Henry III's reign (1216-1272), but the term "privateer" itself did not come into widespread use until after the mid-seventeenth century. A brief and very selective glance at some of the history of privateering reveals some interesting facts which are mentioned below in rough chronological order.

We must first remember, however, that – unlike the often well-organized official records of a national government – the lack of any centralized historical record and documentation of privateering's successes means that they were probably underreported over the years.

In any case, beginning in 1342, in what is now France, the English king, Edward III's advisors, trying to cope with the problems posed by the Breton privateers and pirates, allowed the Duchess of Brittany to license privateers herself during England's war with France at sea in Britanny.[41]

These early French privateers were not paid anything for their dangerous work but instead were authorized to attack and to capture enemy ships in Breton waters. One third of their profits would go directly to the duchess, which was a good deal for them because usually one half of their profits would be earmarked directly for the king.

As a result, a number of pirate/privateer barges (small flat-bottom ships usually propelled by oars) quickly gathered in Breton waters and preyed upon the Norman ships that were moored there, then relatively undefended, because their Norman crews had been sent ashore to fight.[42]

Between 1401 and 1406, Henry IV, the French, and other nautical powers all pursued a "proxy warfare" by using privateers to avoid direct state-to-state and royal ship-to-ship conflict. A real problem in this policy, however, was that it was all-too-easy and so attractive for privateers to slip into fully fledged piracy.

If this happened, the king was then, to use an old American expression, "between a rock and a hard place". To win naval expeditions and wars, he was obliged to rely on his very best seamen – who were often, in their off-duty hours, as it were, also the very best pirates.[43]

This fact was certainly not a plus for royal public relations, however, so it is not surprising that, when Henry V took charge of the royal council in 1410-1411, one of the things he did was to make efforts to revive the king's own ships as an effective naval force.[44]

When in 1544, for example, King Henry VIII, during a war with France, gave blanket permission for English privateering with no legal safeguards, he also, for the first time, allowed his privateers to keep all of the loot they seized. Not surprisingly, his sailors immediately extended the range of their potential targets from French ships to any neutral vessels that carried the rich and tempting traffic between Spain and Flanders.

Again, not surprisingly, many of these English privateering operations were the handiwork of the courtiers and the other hangers-on of the king himself. The most impressive haul was made by the wealthy Southampton merchant Robert Renegar, who captured the Spanish treasure ship *San Salvador* when she was off Cape St Vincent, homeward bound from Hispaniola with a valuable cargo worth nearly 20,000 ducats.[45]

In their medieval wars with France, English kings mobilized their navy and requisitioned both merchant and private ships. English ship–owners who had no other immediate assignment were issued licences and were ordered to go to sea in order to "annoy [to attack] the King's enemies" as privateers.[46] Needless to say, the very fine line here between "privateer" and "pirate" must have been quite invisible to their enemies at sea!

The downside of this edict, however, was that, although wages for seamen went up, the competition from the influx of privateersmen reduced the number of other seamen. In fact, it was reported from Devon and Dorset in

1545 that men were so scarce there that women had to crew the fishing boats. It was estimated that in 1548 some 5,000 seamen would need to be recruited. They were not available, so the authorities had to "press" (forcibly conscript) the needed men.[47]

This new-found freedom of action encouraged privateers to expand their range of maritime targets from French ships alone to any neutral shipping they happened encounter during their cruises, e.g., the rich and tempting ship traffic between Spain and Flanders. All of this constituted a new, unique, and profitable way of waging war at sea: in effect, drafting English private enterprise into the unpaid service of the English state.

Improvements in naval warfare, notably faster ships with three masts instead of only two, plus an increased supply of cannons, meant that privateering ships no longer had to form big squadrons to accomplish their objectives. Instead, they either sailed alone or in twos or threes, relying on their greater speed and better armament to force transport vessels to surrender without the necessity of dangerous hand-to-hand fighting.

Many a merchant captain at sea, well-aware of the futility of fighting or running away from a determined privateer who had a better-armed and faster ship with a much bigger crew (which he needed in order to have enough men to put a prize crew aboard a prize), would simply fire a gun to windward (away from his enemy) in order "to save his honor", and then "strike his colours" (hauled down his ship's flag as a sign of his surrender.)[48]

Privateer crews were not paid in cash but did get a good share of the booty, with one third of its value going to them. Moreover, they also had the right to seize any valuables from the passengers they found on a prize, and probably to strip-search both men and women, too, for any hidden loot.

Perhaps the best news from this era was that, as a modern historian tells us, "It was all very rough and ready, but we do discern a more civilized attitude than in the medieval centuries: far less wanton killing and the blackguardism of throwing men overboard to drown."[49]

The goal of Henry VIII's policy was to increase the incentives for English privateering and thus to boost the national wealth. This approach had helped to enrich the nation, but it was now becoming less attractive in royal eyes because privateers were being forced to share their profits with a host of lesser but nevertheless still-rapacious English officials.[50]

During a period of continuing warfare with Spain, the French kings famously authorized their privateers to attack both Spanish galleons at sea and Spanish colonial cities located in the Caribbean.[51]

The galleons were big, heavy, slow-moving ships. They were thus quite vulnerable to attacks from the much faster and more nimble English and Dutch privateers that cruised the Caribbean Sea, hoping to get their hands on some of the Aztec gold or the Inca silver that these galleons were believed (often correctly) to be carrying.

As a result, the galleons were ordered to sail together in an annual, large convoy, known as a *flota*, which gave them a higher degree of protection. Any galleon which for one reason or another lagged too far behind the pack, however, risked being seized and boarded by one or more of these prowling privateers. From a privateer's point of view, a *flota* represented the greatest collection of plunder that he and his crew could possibly imagine.

Sir Francis Drake (c. 1540-1596) was an English explorer and privateer best known today for his circumnavigation of the world in a single expedition between 1577 and 1580.

He was also one of the English ferocious privateers ("sea dogs", as their Spanish enemies called them) who, with the consent and financial support of Queen Elizabeth I of England, plundered Spanish colonial settlements and treasure ships in New World during the second half of the sixteenth century. During the war years of her reign (1585-1603), the English invested an estimated £2,000,000 in privateering ventures.[52]

It was said that "Privateering was second nature to Elizabethan sailors, especially if their victim was a Spanish or Portuguese ship", since these were likely to be full of treasure.[53] Such men could easily be legal privateers at one time and free-lance pirates at another time.

In 1572, for example, Drake obtained a privateer's commission from Queen Elizabeth I. This was basically an official licence to steal any property belonging to King Philip II of Spain or his subjects. Probably on the basis on this commission, Drake demanded – and received – huge sums of money from some Spanish colonial cities, simply by threatening to burn them if they did not pay him. He did, in fact, destroy three Spanish cities.

Drake's privateering achievements against the Spanish led them to denounce him as a pirate and to nickname him *El Draque* ("The Dragon" in

Old Spanish). The English, however, always hailed him as one of their greatest national heroes. Nevertheless, one modern British scholar has concluded that his attacks on Spanish ports and his captures of Spanish prizes at sea really amounted only to a "quasi-legal privateering war he claimed was fought in the name of his queen".[54]

In any case, working together with the French privateer Guillaume Le Testu, Drake ambushed a Spanish silver train in 1573. They captured 20 tons of silver and gold – so much loot that they had to bury most of it because it was simply too heavy for their small party to carry away. It now seems quite possible that this single event was the seed from which sprang so many later and repetitive stories of buried pirate treasure.

During the intercolonial wars of the seventeenth and eighteenth centuries, the imperial governments of Britain, Spain, and France all encouraged their businessmen to invest in, fully equip, and man their own privately funded warships in order to attack rival merchant ships in the North Atlantic Ocean.

Even before then, however, the advent of open warfare between England and Spain had resulted in a "privateering war" between these two powers, known as the Anglo-Spanish War of 1585-1604. The flourishing of English privateering during this time was seen by its seamen as one of the few boons of the conflict. The boundary between the fishing community and other seamen, e.g., the privateers, was very porous, so many seamen could look for jobs both in England's merchant marine and in the privateers so active during this war.

In any case, the net result of blanket-encouragement of privateering was that thousands of private men-of-war set sail looking for enemy ships to attack. Capturing enemy ships and their cargos weakened an enemy's economy and thus its ability to wage war. Moreover, it also enriched both investors in privateers and their officers and crews. An added plus was that since privateers were privately funded, they did not drain the national treasury of any privateering country.[55]

By 1600, the English merchant fleet had grown to become twenty times larger than the royal fleet. Much of the English privateering effort was then focused on the eastern Atlantic and around the British Isles.

These privateering attacks on Dutch, Danish, Hansard, Scottish, Polish, Swedish and other neutral ships that were transporting to Spain much of the grain, timber, copper, and naval stores on which it depended did a great deal of damage. Twenty years of incessant ship losses by Spain to the English, coupled with the ship-building expenses imposed by the Spanish Crown, bled white the merchant fleet of Spain.

This was especially true in the Basque and Cantabrian ports, which had provided most of Spain's ships and seamen. Indeed, it is said that, due to English privateers, 300 years later the Spanish merchant fleet had still not yet recovered the strength it once had in the 1570s.[56]

One major consequence of this long-running struggle was the growing belief of the English merchant fleet – and of the London merchant class and politicians who financed it – that England's wealth and glory could now best be won, maintained, and expanded by more wars at sea. As a contemporary English commentator put it, since the 1540s "Our shipping and sea service [including privateering] is the best and safest as being the only fortification and rampart of England".[57]

By about 1595, privateers were swarming all over the oceans, trying to capture ships off the Spanish coast, around the Azores, and in the Caribbean. Many of them were owned by the great men of England, such as senior officers of the Royal Navy, the Privy Councilors, the leading merchants of London, and lesser men from the smaller ports of England.[58]

The Dutch have always been very good at sea, so they responded to a 1598 Spanish embargo on their trade by declaring unrestricted commerce raiding, that is to say, by unrestricted privateering. A modern scholar, Peter H. Wilson, tells us that:

The move was equivalent to the German submarine campaign of the First World War and just as controversial. Small vessels were licensed as privateers to intercept enemy trade, disguising themselves as harmless fishing boats, or as friends in distress, to deceive merchantmen…

The Dutch assuaged their pious burgher consciences by issuing regulations to distinguish patriotic privateers from godless pirates, but turned a blind eye to their frequent infringement of these. Privateering was not only a lucrative weapon of war but was also deeply embedded in Dutch culture.[59]

In the years 1626 to 1649, the privateering war, which in Queen Elizabeth I's day had brought the English so many spectacular successes, now fell upon hard times. The English Parliament, the king, and even the Irish rebels all commissioned privateers, who spread European conflicts more broadly because they accepted commissions from their foreign friends to justify attacking neutral countries.

Between 1626 and 1630, perhaps as many as 1,000 prizes were taken by the English, but most of them were only small French, Spanish, or Portuguese coasters or fishing boats of very little value. Moreover, about 15 per cent of the prizes captured turned out to be owned by neutral or friendly powers. This meant that they had to be set free at once to avoid any diplomatic problems.[60]

The Dunkirk privateers, who were working for the Spaniards, are said to have captured nearly 1,500 ships and to have sunk in combat more than 300 others. The English are also thought to have lost more than 450 merchant ships to the Barbary privateer/pirates of North Africa, while some 160 English ships were seized by privateers sailing out of Algerian waters between about 1677 and 1680.

In 1670, the Treaty of Madrid between England and Spain outlawed privateering in European waters, but the most enterprising pirates then began to focus instead on capturing treasure ships navigating the Indian Ocean and the Pacific Ocean off North America.

Woodes Rogers (c. 1679–1732), an English privateer and slave trader, was later the first Royal Governor of the Bahamas.[61] He hired privateers to attack the Spanish ships that were threatening these islands. On a more positive note, however, he also took great pride in insisting on his crew's respectful behaviour toward women who happened to be passengers aboard any of the ships he captured. For example, he ordered his men only to grope these women for any jewellery hidden in their outer clothing, rather than undressing them publicly, either in whole or in part!

For a few years after the Peace of Utrecht in 1713, many former wartime privateers, most notably "Blackbeard", whose real name was Edward Teach (or Thach), turned to piracy as the only way they knew to make good money very easily once a lasting peace had broken out.

A contemporary nautical writer, who published his fact-and-fiction accounts of privateer and pirate life in 1734 under the pen name of "Captain

Charles Jackson", explains why, after the Peace of Utrecht, so many privateers became pirates. This, in his own words, is what he has to tell us:

> The multitude of men and vessels employ'd this way [as privateers], in time of war, in the West Indies, is another reason for the number of pyrates in a time of peace: this cannot be supposed to reflect on any of our American governments, much less on the King [of England] himself, by whose authority such commissions are granted, because of the reasonableness of the thing, and absolute necessity there is for doing of it; yet the observation is just; for so many people employing themselves in privateers, for the sake of plunder and riches, which they always spend as fast as they can get, when the war is over, and they can have no further business in the [privateering] way of life they have been used to, they too readily; and, indeed, too naturally engage in acts of pyracy: and this being but the usual practice without a commission, they make very little distinction betwixt the lawfulness of the one, and the unlawfulness of the other.[62]

Blackbeard is one of history's most colourful and most famous privateer/pirates and was a master of what today we might jokingly call "negative public relations".

Our reason for labeling him thus is that he terrorized his potential victims by his heavy black beard, from which issued diabolically-looking-and-smelling black smoke, generated by the smoldering tapers he had wired into it; and by his fearsome personal armament: six single-shot pistols holstered in two cloth sashes strung across his shoulders, plus one heavy broadsword in his leather belt.

Blackbeard apparently never killed anyone who was not trying to kill him, but he did inflict some heavy if only localized losses on colonial merchantmen, both in the Atlantic and the Caribbean.

Local officials in Charleston, notably Tobias Knight (the provincial secretary) and possibly Charles Eden (one of the most senior political figures) may have provided Blackbeard with harbour facilities and even helped in the sale of his booty.

By the early 1720s, however, the joint efforts of the colonial governments, backed up by the powerful British Navy which now had a truly international reach, had effectively ended this pirate menace. Blackbeard himself, for example, was finally cornered and killed on the Albemarle outer banks near Ocracoke Inlet in 1718.[63]

The main threat to British trade in its wars with France came between 1689 and 1815, due to the large numbers of French privateers that were based in Saint-Malo, Dunkirk, and many other ports along the French coast.

These men took full advantage of the watery wars that seriously disrupted England's normally flourishing trade in the Atlantic and in the Mediterranean. This issue probably encouraged some local English merchants to invest in privateers instead of, or at least in addition to, their usual stock-in-trade of local products.

After emigrating from their ancestral home in the Channel Islands, the Cabot family became highly successful shipping merchants in Boston during the eighteenth century, operating a fleet of privateers carrying opium, rum, and slaves.

Much of the War of Spanish Succession, known as Queen Anne's War in the Americas, from 1702 to 1713 was fought at sea. The English offered pardons to any pirates who would be willing to fight for the British government in its war against the Spaniards. This gave numerous pirates the opportunity, which they seized, to begin new and semi-legitimate careers as privateers.[64]

A very unusual privateering conflict of 1739 to 1748 is known to history as the "War of Jenkins' Ear", which provoked a British conflict with Spain. Its remarkable name was coined in 1858 by the British historian Thomas Carlyle, 110 years after hostilities had ended. In broad terms, this conflict formed only a tiny part of the bloody and far-ranging War of the Austrian Succession between Britain and Spain. Its story, however, marks the beginning of privateering in American waters and runs along the following lines:

- This event took place off the coast of Florida when the British brig *Rebecca* was boarded by an armed Spanish party from the Spanish patrol boat *La Isabela*.
- The Spanish vessel was commanded by a Spanish coastguard privateer officer named Léon Fandiño, who believed that the British ship was engaged in smuggling. As punishment, he therefore is said to have cut off the left ear of Robert Jenkins, the captain of the *Rebecca*. Fandiño

then ordered Jenkins to tell the king of England that he would also cut off the king's ear if the king ever dared to do the same thing.

- In 1738, Jenkins was ordered to testify before Parliament and to repeat his story to the House of Commons. It is said that Jenkins produced his severed but now dried ear at the hearing as part of his dramatic testimony, although no proof of this event exists.

- Nevertheless, the incident was considered by some Britons as a grave insult to their country's honour; for them it was thus a legitimate reason to go war. Modern historians believe, however, that foreign trade issues were in fact only one of several very divisive problems stemming from British expansion into North America. For example, British merchants, who were unable to make any dents in Spain's monopolies in the New World, were ready to try war instead.[65]

- That said, however, this insignificant war would eventually leave in its wake, on the British side, some 20,000 dead and wounded (chiefly due to disease,) and, on the Spanish side, about 4,500 dead and 5,000 wounded.

During and after the War of Jenkins' Ear, moreover, violence afloat became much more widespread.[66] For example, British colonial privateers were armed for attacks against the Spaniards. France joined the conflict in 1744. American privateers began chasing prey in the Gulf of Saint Lawrence and off the islands of the West Indies at the same time, while French Canadian privateers looked for ships to capture off New England.

In this era, the residents of New England turned their near-by sea into a peaceful asset through maritime trade of all kinds. This ranged from the products of the cod and whale fisheries to exports of timber, "naval stores" (pitch and turpentine), and rum, made by importing and then refining sugary West Indies molasses into potent New England rum.

On the privateering front, in 1745 British privateers helped the British army by landing troops ashore and into good positions to attack successfully the French fortress of Louisburg.

A number of Irish privateersmen were also then very active at sea. Many of their officers were Irishmen who held commissions from the kings of France or Spain to attack British shipping wherever they could.

In times of peace, moreover, these Irish lived as merchant seamen and as smugglers who could use their nautical skills, their knowledge of the coasts, and their fluency in English (and often in French, too) for Irish privateering forays. Many Irishmen also held commissions in the French navy, notably some members of the Macnamara and MacCarthy families.

Saint-Malo in Brittany became an important centre for Irish privateers. One of the members of a leading family there, Anthony Vincent Walsh, even used his own brig to bring the pretender to the throne, "Bonnie" Prince Charlie, to Scotland in 1745.[67] For this feat, he was rewarded by the prince's father, the exiled King James III, with an Irish earldom – notwithstanding the fact that he was also a slave-trader on a large scale.[68]

In 1746, two American privateers based in New York seized a French prize worth over £11,000. The next year, the twenty-gun American privateer *Shirley* captured eight French ships in Canadian waters. In 1746, the courts of New York also chronicled the distribution of cargos taken from French Caribbean provinces.

Every war waged by Britain in the early to mid-1700s, and especially the Seven Years' War of 1756 to 1763, which the British won decisively, and which spelled the end of the French colony of New France in Canada, set loose at sea large numbers of British privateers who were under orders to attack Britain's enemies at sea.

During the Revolutionary War, the residents of Canada's Atlantic region constantly had to be on the alert for privateers, who captured large numbers of ships there. Newfoundland, for example, had long been dependent on provisions from New England. Privateering generated famine-level food shortages there (and in Ireland as well). Privateer attacks on the fishing fleets made off-shore fishing so expensive and so dangerous that it collapsed during the war.[69]

Such wars tended to overlap. For example, the War of Jenkins' Ear that began in October 1739 eventually merged into the War of the Austrian Succession from 1740 to 1748. These conflicts were never fought in a vacuum, however, but were lightly regulated by a battery of unenforced but well-understood rules and customs. These were generally followed – out of national self-interest, not due to any international authority – by Britain, France, and Spain in their continuing efforts to extend their own spheres of influence in colonial North America.

The British, for instance, sent out numerous instructions to their fleets in order to promote privateering and to direct the activities of their warships. These regulations defined the rules for privateers and specified which enemy ships could be seized as prizes.

Without wading too deeply into very complicated historical details, it is clear that privateering did enjoy a great deal of popular and governmental support in both England and in America in the eighteenth century. At the same time, there were also some vexing problems associated with it in practice. The British, for example, eventually found it impossible to control their American colonies, in part because of London's firm adherence to its political doctrine of mercantilism.

This widely accepted school of thought held that Britain must rely chiefly on its own private capital, and not on government support funded by politically unpopular higher taxes, to increase its own sea power. In practice, this meant that the owners of private men-of-war (privateer ships) were expected to do their utmost to maximize their own profits, cutting corners wherever feasible. In these efforts, they were protected both by insurance from Lloyd's of London and by the might of the Royal Navy.

Even though Parliament and royal spokesmen in London tried to slow the cost-cutting trend, the British colonial courts in America were always quite happy to bend the imperial rules and regulations in order to encourage British privateering and to reward the many well-connected investors in this business.

This whole procedure held out the pleasant prospect for all players, private and public alike, of the possibility of high profits – without any onerous higher taxes, and at very tolerable levels of economic risk. As one modern scholar tells us:

Attracted by the possibilities of windfall profits, merchants in London, Bristol, Dunkirk, Bayonne, Cadiz, and San Sebatian in Europe; and in Newport, New York, the British West Indies, Havana, St. Augustine, Martinique, and Cap François in America, all sent out thousands of vessels during the conflicts of the 17th and 18th centuries. Naval prize money motivated officers and men alike in the service of European monarchs. It provides additional testimony to the enormous influence of prize actions on all hands.[70]

At about the same time, Parliament also spelled out its own rules for the conduct of British privateers, setting out a very complicated procedure defining which enemy vessels were legitimate prizes, and insisting that British ships comply with some basic rules. In effect, by doing so, London tried ineffectively to govern American privateering in much the same way that it tried to regulate American colonial trade, even to the extent of using the same British courts for both purposes.[71]

So it was that privateering became a key part of maritime strategic planning and of maritime warfare. Harbours such as Halifax, Salem, and Newport all found lucrative new roles as privateer destinations. Many of these privateers sailed from New England's American colonies, most notably from New York, which soon became the leading centre of American colonial privateering; from Rhode Island and from Massachusetts.

The American colonies were held to be essential for Britain's continued prosperity and for its future growth. Transatlantic trade significantly enriched the mother country, increased government income, and provided a ready reserve of well-trained highly disciplined sea-going officers and men (the best maritime force in the world) to serve in the Royal Navy and in the merchant marine, both in times of war and of peace.

That said, however, the American colonies also caused many difficult problems for Britain. For example, the colonial legislatures always dragged their heels when asked to provide funds to recruit more British troops and to make sure they were well-trained and well-led.

Even more importantly from London's point of view, however, the Seven Years' War had been ruinously expensive. As a result, successive administrations in London were under great political pressure to limit government spending and to find new sources of revenue.

The results were a series of very unpopular Acts – on sugar, legal documents, newspapers, playing cards, dice, and items for British troops – the income from which was expressly designed to help pay for keeping these troops in North America.[72]

Privateering was always a chancy business, however: wind, wave, and enemy action could all take a heavy toll on ships. In retrospect, though, it is now thought that "today's losses would be usually more than balanced out by tomorrow's profits".

The bottom line was therefore that most of the American leaders in the runup to, and then during the Revolutionary War itself, were very familiar, directly or indirectly, with the dangers, the technology, the practice, and the strategic and financial rewards of privateering.[73]

Even before the Revolutionary War began, they had some experience in destroying British ships, e.g., in 1772 the British armed revenue schooner *Gaspée* ran aground near Providence, Rhode Island, and was burned by local American residents infuriated by its enforcement of anti-American trade legislation.[74] In the process, the ship's commanding officer was wounded; both events "caused outrage in British government circles".[75]

The American colonies actively supported privateering during and after the Revolutionary War, and in the War of 1812, too, chiefly because they had no standing navy of any size and did not have the time or the money needed to develop one themselves quickly. Thus, they had little choice but to turn to privateering, in the hope that it would bring such financial and political pressures on British merchant shipping that these merchants would begin to pressure their government to end the war.

A literal translation of the historical French definition of privateering – *la guerre de course* – is "the war of the chase" or "the war of the hunt". This captures perfectly the exciting spirit of this fast-moving and dangerous enterprise, which also had the added attraction of being virtually self-supporting and costing a government nothing at all to launch. A less colourful but more appropriate translation for our use in this book, however, is simply "the war of commerce-destruction".[76]

Remarkably, privateering continued for a very long time. For example, writing in 1899 and stretching his point considerably for literary effect (because formally commissioned naval vessels were not in fact privateers), the American journalist and historian Edgar Stanton Maclay (1863-1919), whose 519-page book on this subject will be quoted often here, claimed that although the traditional form of privateering had legally been outlawed by an international treaty in 1856:

> privateering ... still exists today. The essential feature of privateering
> is commerce-destroying. Our [commissioned] commerce destroyers of
> the navy today [and here Maclay names three powerful American naval

ships of his time] take the place of our earlier privateers and are capable of doing the work far more effectively ... and are equally efficient when needed for the regular service [that is to say, when they are needed for the regular duties of a naval vessel].[77]

In any case, at sea the distinction between peaceful trade, privateering, and piracy was often very elusive. As the British historian Susan Rose pointed out in her *Medieval Naval Warfare, 1000–1500*:

It is perhaps unsafe to say that ships engaged in aggressive activities were always clearly acting with knowledge of a ruler. The distinction between outright piracy and the actions of privateers, conveniently described by the phrase 'guerre de course', was blurred and [a ship's officer at sea] might be a respected renowned naval leader at one point in his career and the leader of at least quasi-piratical raids at another.[78]

There are therefore copious records of cases of violence, robbery and general mayhem at sea. Some of those involved were, at other times, in the king's service and were respected members of their communities.

A prime example of the difficulty of drawing the line between legitimate reprisals (that is to say, privateering) and brigandage (piracy) can be found in the careers of the two John Hawleys, father and son.[79] Moreover, in some cases, as in about 1700, seamen who had been gainfully employed as sailors suddenly lost their income if their king made peace.[80]

In addition, the privateering trade and its derivatives lent itself to all sorts of legal complexities and disagreements. A case from 1441 is a good example of the kind of incident which peppers the shipping records.[81]

An English ship, named *Christopher of St Servan*, was carrying a French cargo of wine and salt from La Rochelle, France to England. This was the property of two Breton (French) merchants, but the English ship was captured off the Isle of Wight by two balingers (small sea-going ships powered by either sails or oars) from Falmouth, England and was forced to moor at the harbour of Newport on the Isle of Wight. The wine could thus be considered to have been stolen wine.

This was a familiar fact of maritime life then. The English royal records contain frequent mention of cases brought in the courts or petitions to the king himself or from commission of inquiry to ferret out, if ever possible, just what happened to missing wine or other shipped goods. Some of these must have been the work of shore-side robbers; others were due to men who could flaunt some kind of legal cover. Taking them all in all, however, these losses never reached a level where traditional patterns of trade were in any danger.[82]

So far, so good but, later on, other men who bought the allegedly stolen wine claimed that the wine had in fact been seized quite lawfully – on the grounds that it was not in fact the property of the Bretons (who at that time had a trade agreement with England), but was instead the property of the Dutch, who were then the enemies of the king of England.

As if that was not enough, the ship itself was from the French port of Dieppe and, as such, was said to be lawful prey. The Bretons argued, however, that the tuns (namely, the barrels) in which the wine was stored carried their own markings and were clearly in their own possession. Alas, the historical record does not tell us whether they were eventually successful in getting the wine back or somehow being compensated for their loss.

What is very likely, however, is that these men, and many others like them, had very close financial and kinship ties to privateers, pirates, and dealers in stolen goods all along the western reaches of the English Channel. This had become such a problem in 1432 that a delegation of the unhappy merchants in western France volunteered to meet with the Chancellor (a very senior English official).

> They wanted to prove to him just how well-protected the wrongdoers on the sea-coasts of Devonshire [western England] were: when they had taken [captured] any vessel or goods or merchandise of the king's friends, they sent at once for the deputy of the admiral of England and induced him [persuaded him] to empanel a jury of twenty-four or twelve men, who were for the most part the relatives and friends of the same wrongdoers and the victualers [food merchants] and owners.

> [These men] gave their verdict that the vessels, goods, and merchandise taken from the king's friends belonged to the king's enemies, and then the wrongdoers caused the deputy to be in league with them, and to

enroll and record the verdict so given, by giving him half the goods and merchandise for his trouble.[83]

Looking further ahead, however, by 1856 we will see that scores of well-armed nations with faster ships and improved cannons and much better navigation capabilities had made privateering an unprofitable investment in most cases.

The net result of these changes was a binding international agreement, known as the 1856 Declaration of Paris, which effectively banned privateering by the seven major signatory states. This one action effectively ended successful, protracted, and large-scale privateering. It was not signed by the United States, but since the Americans formally agreed to respect its provisions, their signature was not necessary.

The last official privateering documents anywhere in the world were those issued by the Confederate states (the states of the American South during the Civil War of 1861 to 1865). These privateering expeditions, which will be discussed later, were not a success and were soon replaced by lightweight seagoing blockade-running steamers for the rest of the war.

Historians today tell us that the Union blockade of Southern ports had two major impacts:

First, it reduced by 95 per cent the export of cotton, the most important product of the South; devalued the South's currency; and seriously hurt its economy.

Second, the 2,500-mile-long blockade from Virginia to Texas was very porous. It did not prevent at least 600,000 good-quality British Enfield rifles from being smuggled into the South, about half of them via the Gulf ports. This influx of British weapons is believed to have extended the Civil War for up to two years.

In the end, of course, the South totally lost the war, which it never had much of a chance of winning. Not only was this because the North had many more men to pour into the conflict, but it also had a much more highly developed economy geared toward manufacturing, e.g., of war materials, and not toward simply growing more cotton and trying to maintain slavery.

It must be kept in mind, however, that none of the three wars discussed in this book occurred in any political, economic, or cultural vacuum. Limitations of space, however, prevent us from exploring most shore-side events here. However, the following historical points can safely be made:

- The Revolutionary War itself extended from 1775 to 1783 but it was preceded by the deeply unpopular Stamp Act in 1765 and was followed by the warm public support for the ratification of the Constitution in 1790.
- The Civil War of 1861 to 1865 arose after more than eighty years of heart-felt American disagreements over the proper reach of the Federal government and, most significantly, over the role of slavery in American society.
- The War of 1812 to 1815 between Great Britain and the United States developed in large part because Britain needed more sailors to keep its extensive naval fleets well-manned. To meet this demand, the British began to intercept American ships at sea and to "press" (to conscript forcibly) some of the American seamen aboard them.

This process involved capturing them by force, removing them from their own ships, and compelling them to work on British ships instead. These actions led to what has been termed "the second war of American independence" from 1812 to 1815 between Great Britain and the United States. It is thought that more than 15,000 American sailors were impressed by the British for various periods of time to flesh out the British fleets.

In any case, for many generations, privateering was a legitimate, well-established, and common practice undertaken by many of the countries bordering the sea. More rarely, it was also resorted to by a few countries that traded along the major inland waterways of the world.

Formal legal permission to engage in this often lucrative and almost always dangerous enterprise was traditionally conveyed in the Western world only through what was termed "a letter of marque and reprisal".

In legal terms, this document automatically promoted a privateer vessel into becoming the temporary warship of the ruler who had issued the document. This single and easy step authorized the vessel to attack and capture the ships of a nation that was at war with the issuer. Good examples of such ships, as will be mentioned in later pages of this book, are the privateers sailing out of Salem, Massachusetts during the American Revolutionary War.

During the Revolutionary War, Congress issued over 2,000 letters of marque, which licensed American privateers to attack British ships. There was nothing clandestine about this process, but its impact cannot be denied. The net result of the Congressional decision was this: by the end of the war, Lloyd's of London had estimated that these privateers had captured or destroyed 2,208 British merchantmen.[84]

The term "marque", which derives from the Germanic word *mearc*, ("boundary marker"), also refers to the medieval "marcher law". This law could be invoked whenever the legal ownership of a given piece of land was in serious dispute – for example, in a region in which there was no clear legal governance or where there were overlapping legal jurisdictions.

"Reprisal", on the other hand, meant the right of a private party to resort to violence to correct a wrong allegedly done to him or to his ship or goods after all peaceful efforts to get redress had failed.

More broadly and most remarkably, such a private party could also legally seize the goods of an offender's country and from his countrymen, although both might be many hundreds or even many thousands of miles away and have had no direct involvement in the matter.

An English military campaign in France, for example, marked the first extensive use of letters of reprisal.[85] These provided the legal basis, if only a very flimsy one, for privateering by English, French, or other powers to attack merchant shipping at sea.

Widely known in French as a *lettre de marque* or as a *lettre de course*, a letter of marque authorized a private person, who was now defined as a privateer or, somewhat less accurately, as a corsair, to attack, capture, sell, or destroy ships of a nation that was at war with the issuer of the letter.

Once a ship was captured, under admiralty law (maritime law) both the ship and her cargo became known as a "prize" (as a prize of war), and were regulated under the provisions and customary procedures of "prize law".

A modern British scholar has written that "Prize law made naval warfare a kind of gigantic wartime lottery. Though the profits were distributed with gross inequality in favour of the officers, it was reckoned that nothing did so much for recruiting [the common sailors] as the prospect of a Spanish war with its promise of Peruvian plunder" [this refers to the flow of silver coins from the mines of Peru].[86]

The gold and silver from the New World was minted into coins before being shipped toward Spain via the Camino Real, known as the Gold Road, in Panama. The two chief coins of this trade were the gold doubloon and the silver piece of eight. Huge quantities of doubloons were ferried across the Atlantic in the holds of treasure galleons.

Many of these coins found their way, sooner or later, into the hands of pirates and privateers. They thus became part of the fact and fiction of pirate and privateer lore. Indeed, in Robert Louis Stevenson's celebrated 1883 novel *Treasure Island*, an ex-pirate's tame parrot repeatedly squawks the phrase "Pieces of eight, pieces of eight!"[87]

Less heady prizes included the ship herself and all the equipment, personal valuables, and cargo aboard her. If an admiralty court judged that a captured ship was not, in fact, a valid prize, then her captors would have to return it to the owners if possible and to pay damages for their mistake.

A privateer captain was required to deliver the ship, her cargo, and her gear to an admiralty court in a neutral country, first for formal condemnation as a valid prize (the initiation of a prize case was technically known in legal terms as a "libel") and then for the formal transfer of ownership to the privateer.

An admiralty court was a tribunal with jurisdiction over maritime law, including cases involving shipping, oceanic matters, and laws of the sea. Prize proceedings were held in an admiralty court *in rem*, which means "against the thing", that is, against the vessel itself – not against the owners of the vessel, who were unlikely to be present, either during the actual capture of the ship or in the admiralty court itself.

For this legal reason, decisions in prize cases state only the name of the vessel involved, as in *The Rapid* [a U.S. Supreme Court case involving contraband goods], rather than using the typical legal case format of "Jones v Smith".[88]

The letter of marque and reprisal also gave a privateer formal legal permission to cross international borders and, on the other side of them, to take punitive action to retaliate against any attack or any injury allegedly inflicted on the privateer or, more broadly, on his company or on his nation. Some privateer ships alternated between officially identifying themselves both as a privateer and as a letter of marque ship. For our purposes here, however, there was no significant difference between these two designations: they were clearly both privateers.

Since most large merchantmen already carried some guns to protect themselves from pirates, the transition from trader to privateer did not take very long. All that was required was to reinforce the deck to support additional guns; increase the size of the crew and provide some living space for them; and make sure the powder magazine was well-protected from sparks and, of course, from fire.[89]

The earliest recorded use of letters of marque and reprisal was in an English law of 1354 during the reign of King Edward III, although these letters were actually issued by England for the first time in a war of 1543-1546. It has been estimated that under its provisions as much as £2 million – an enormous sum at that time – was invested in privateering during the war years of Queen Elizabeth I's reign (1585-1603).[90]

She herself had issued a proclamation in 1563 reaffirming her own support for general privateering by English ships – a process through which the English Lords Admiral stood to profit personally because they were entitled to 10 per cent of the proceeds. The net result was that this move caused even more problems for English diplomats posted in foreign capitals, and made more enemies at a time when England really needed more friends instead.[91]

Elizabeth's radical legal procedure would become a very effective new way to encourage private investors to play an active role in helping finance the many wars and military actions approved by their governments. It strongly appealed to governments because it cost them nothing at all to issue many such privateering letters and because the financial returns from them could be quite substantial. As a result, these governments could now rely on privateers to help them fight their wars and could thus avoid some of the enormous hassle and great expense of creating and maintaining hefty navies of their own.

One of the first British privateering ventures was led by the warrior-merchant James Lancaster, who had fought for England against the Spanish Armada in 1588 and who commanded the East India Company's first venture abroad in 1601. In a very modest success, Lancaster's seamen boarded a lone

Portuguese carrack (cargo ship) which was outward-bound from Lisbon. They seized 164 butts of wine, 12 barrels and 176 jars of oil, and 55 hogsheads and vats of meal. One of the merchants on the conquering English ship happily reported that these provisions were "a greate helpe to us in the whole voyage thereafter".[92]

During the Revolutionary War, for example, by the end of the summer of 1775 the Continental Congress first began to use armed shallow-draft schooners against the British. George Washington called these vessels his own "privateers" but, technically speaking, these were not in fact privateers at that point: Congress did not officially authorize privateering until the very end of the year. These vessels did, however, set the stage for later privateering developments. Under international law, they were in fact nothing more than pirates, but the American public overlooked this small detail and happily always referred to them simply as "Washington's Navy".[93]

In March 1776, Congress finally began to issue over 2,000 "letters of marque and reprisal", which will be discussed later, and American states would issue many hundreds more. Privateering thus became a very well-regulated business, not a fly-by-night "get-rich-quick" operation generated only by private enterprise.

In fact, privateering became so popular and was so well-regarded that the Continental Congress even began to hand out pre-printed and preauthorized privateering commission forms, with blank spaces thoughtfully provided so the names of ships, captains, and owner could easily be written in.[94] Such commissions sometimes also had an embossed seal depicting a seaman holding an unsheathed sword in his right hand and what may have been a copy of his commission in his left hand. Nevertheless, there were in fact some constraints already in place.

For example, Americans seeking privateering commissions were first required to post bonds of up to £5,000 per ship in order to make sure they would not mistreat any enemy seamen they captured, and that they would never knowingly attack any American or neutral ship.[95]

A letter of marque was the only valid distinction between the men who were privateers, on the one hand, and the men (plus the very few women) who were pirates, on the other. While in legal terms this distinction was always crystal-clear, in real life at sea the dividing line between privateers and pirates was often fuzzy indeed.

It could easily depend only on the chosen point of view of the observer – much like the distinction between freedom fighters and terrorists today. During the Revolutionary War, for example, the British officially considered all American privateers to be pirates simply because they could not produce any letters of marque acceptable to their British captors.

After the Peace of Utrecht of 1713 ended the War of the Spanish Succession, an anonymous English nautical writer noted that many former privateers turned to piracy only because "they make very little distinction between the lawfulness of privateering with a commission and piracy without one".[96] When and if peace broke out, as was the case after the end of the War of the Spanish Succession, these ex-privateers felt that they had no other choice but to become pirates.

Since privateering itself was always considered to be an entirely lawful undertaking, it was never subject to the modern revisionist criticism that it was simply piracy in a slightly different form: that it was really only state-sponsored piracy.

In point of fact, however, privateering was always governed by the provisions of international "prize law". The structure of this important body of law was first laid out by the Dutch scholar Grotius in 1604 and will be discussed later in this book.

Pirates, of course, never had any kind of official approval at all. Their actions were always illegal and, when captured, these men were usually publicly hanged. However, the very few female pirates could, if pregnant, "plead their bellies", as the saying had it, and could thus by law always escape the death penalty.

In general, by the time of the American Revolution, anti-pirate law had become much more widespread and more effective in American colonial waters. Thus there were far fewer incentives for mariners there to slide into criminal activities. So, almost by default, colonial mariners were now strongly inclined to follow the detailed rules and regulations set forth by the American Continental Congress.

One technical nautical point can usefully be made here. A "letter-of-marque ship" was not, technically speaking, a privateer ship at all.

A privateer ship was very likely to be a fast, weatherly, fore-and-aft rigged ship that was very well-armed and carried the very large crew needed to handle any "prizes" (enemy ships) that the privateer might capture, while at the same time being able to watch over any prisoners the privateer might have to seize in this process.

This latter point could well pose nutritional problems at sea: in many instances, privateering ships did not carry enough food for both crew and prisoners.[97] Since reprovisioning at foreign ports could be impossible or too dangerous to attempt, and since privateers usually wanted to remain at sea as long as possible in order to take prizes, probably only the ship's senior officers always had full rations. Indeed, during one privateering voyage in 1591, the crew of the ship *Bark Hall* rebelled against their rations being cut and demanded instead that the ship return at once to England.[98]

When all else failed, vital provisions could always be seized by force – a method of resupply used both by privateers and by pirates. In one of several cases that could be cited here, the English privateering vessel *Alcredo* forced the Danish ship *Alexander* to heave to (to come to a stop) in 1595. The English crew came aboard, took some of the Danes' food supply, and also made off with their ship's boat.[99]

Any prizes taken had to be sailed by a reliable crew to a port where they could legally be sold. A fore-and-aft rigged ship was one that had its sails, also known as the "ship's clothing", set along the line of the ship's keel. This made it easy to adjust, fast, manoeuvrable, and able to sail closer to the wind with minimum leeway (very little sideways drifting).

In clear contrast, a letter-of-marque ship was typically a heavy, slow, lumbering, square-rigged freighter designed to carry cargo. Square-rigged ships were entirely in their element in deep water with constant trade winds in the tropics, but it was slow and difficult for them to tack because it was hard for them to change direction quickly.

A letter-of-marque ship, however, had the legal authority (via its letter of marque) plus a modest amount of firepower, to capture prizes whenever this was possible or necessary. Taking prizes not only weakened an enemy's ability to wage war but also profited the privateer's own investors, officers, and crew at the same time.[100]

This was important because, unlike Royal Navy ships where the men had modest but regular and reliable earnings, the income of the men of a privateer depended entirely on the skills of the captain. If he could take many lucrative prizes, they, too, would prosper; if not, they were out of luck.

Privateering made a few Americans very rich indeed. By 1780, for example, the Philadelphia statesman, investor, and later U.S. Senator William Bingham, who helped to broker the Louisiana Purchase of 1803, was held to be the richest person in the United States, thanks to his joint ownership of privateers and to his business trading skills.

Bingham died in 1804 in Bath, England and was interred in Bath Abbey, but his considerable estate remained in his family and was not finally settled until 1964. Some of the following chapters will trace how American privateering arose and flourished.

At this point, however, it is worth taking a broader view and learning something about privateers in action.[101] In practice, this was often a three-stage sequential operation: first, locating a likely prize; second, chasing her; and, finally, boarding her and making her surrender.

Finding a lone ship underway in mid-ocean was not very likely. For safety reasons, cargo ships tended to form big convoys. The bad news was that these convoys were often so large (sometimes as many as 600 merchant ships) and so slow that some captains decided to take the risk of sailing independently. In so doing, however, they might well be intercepted by one or more prowling privateers and could lose everything, possibly including their own lives.

It was precisely for this reason that the captain of one New England ship gave such firm advice to any ships sailing by themselves. It is repeated here verbatim, with some explanations provided in brackets. He told them:

Keep a good lookout from your masthead every half hour for your own safety ... if any vessel should give you chase, then make from her with all heart [that is to say: then sail away from her as fast as you can.] Don't speak with any vessel about your safety if you can help it. [Don't discuss your sailing plans with any other ship.] Don't trust to no one at the danger times. [Don't rely on anyone else in times of danger.] Don't run [don't sail] after night, as night has no eyes [you can't see anything at night.]

It was the use of large British convoys during the American Revolution that finally forced the Americans to use from two to eight ships to attack a given convoy. If, however, a convoy became strung out due to darkness, fog, or very bad weather, this gave American privateers a much better chance of breaking up a convoy and of capturing one or more prizes.

A sharp-eyed lookout posted on the mainmast of a privateer schooner in good weather could first see an enemy ship at sea up to 15 miles away. If so, he would usually stand to earn a £100 bonus from his captain.

As soon as a potential prey was sighted, the privateer would chase it; identify it; and, if it was indeed a valid prize, would then demand that it surrender at once or face being boarded.

Since privateers were designed and manned to be much faster than cargo ships, the odds were much in the privateer's favour once the chase began. Moreover, if the wind died, the privateer's large crew could "man the sweeps". This meant that they could insert oars through the oar-ports especially designed for just this purpose, and then begin to row hard toward the prize. Since their prey would not have any oar-ports, all it could probably do was to surrender as quickly and as gracefully as possible.

The best time for a privateer to attack a prey was at night or in fog. It was then most vulnerable because it was "blind". Alternatively, a privateering captain could disguise his own ship by concealing its gunports; using ratty old sails to imply that this was an old, poor, and hopelessly-slow vessel; or even by towing empty barrels behind it to slow it down even more.

Once the prize was within range, the privateer might then fire one cannon-shot over its bows. This would probably encourage the prize to surrender, rather than engaging in a fire-fight which it was very likely to lose.

Chapter 2

Privateering and British North America

The term "British North America", as used in this book, refers to the colonial territories of the British Empire in North America from 1606, when King James I established the Colony of Virginia in North America, to after 1783, when thirteen of Britain's colonies in North America split off from their mother country to form the United States of America.[102]

Privateering played a key role in the history of British North America. Transatlantic trade and migration there was disrupted from time to time by both privateering and by piracy, but never enough to have major adverse effects on the ever-growing patterns of settlement.

Indeed, they stimulated the colonists to improve their own defence by forcing them to pay for most of it themselves. This was the case despite the hard fact that many of the governments of that era were unwilling to tax their citizens heavily enough in order to finance large powerful navies, packed with costly ships that demanded constant maintenance and crews.

Moreover, these governments also faced a shortage of the experienced officers and seamen needed to use these ships effectively in combat. For all these reasons, it is not surprising that privateering became so popular: the costs were borne by private investors and not by the state.

At the same time, however, merchants also demanded protection from enemy fleets and from enemy privateers. In 1708, for example, the British Parliament passed Acts to regulate privateers in America, to condemn piracy, and to establish the value of specific foreign coins used in the colonies. As amended, the 1696 Navigation Act strengthened royal control that protected customs revenues.[103]

The large number of American ships and men that eagerly chased prizes proves the continuing popularity of privateering. For example, more than 300 privateer ships were built, equipped, and manned from the British colonies alone (others came from France) in what is now the United States during the mid-eighteenth-century wars of 1739 to 1748. American privateering ships often hailed from Newport or New York, but the British West Indies ports were not far behind them because of the large number of British plantations and personnel there.

Privateers were clearly financially successful in overall terms, but how well an individual privateer ship fared is somewhat less clear. Windfall profits were possible if several prizes were captured, but even seizing one very lucrative prize might pay off both the owners and the crews quite handsomely.

Moreover, in more personal and subjective terms, both the American investors and the American privateersmen were very proud of the patriotic sprit they showed. They also appear to have relished the dangers and the excitement of the chase itself.

Losing the thirteen colonies in North America

It is worth reviewing this story now because, in retrospect, it clearly had such huge impacts on the United States and, later, on much of the rest of the world.

The British mercantilist code, which claimed that colonies existed solely for the benefit of the mother country, imposed many restrictions on Britian's thirteen American colonies. An early and onerous of these was the Molasses Act of 1733, which was designed to restrict the colonies' freedom to trade and to manufacture products. The increasing roles of the British Treasury and of Parliament in governing the American colonies, presaged in the Molasses Act, were central to the eventual arrival of the American Revolution.[104]

The goal of this Act was to limit trade between the American colonies and the West Indies in order to protect the imperial market for British sugar.[105]

By 1700, sugar had become the dominant agricultural commodity pouring into Europe from the New World. The production of sugar was perfectly suited to the tropical climate of the Caribbean; to its slave labour-plantation-based economy; to its easy access to the sea; and finally, but by no means least, to the political stability and military protection afforded by the Royal Navy.

There were about 1,800 sugar plantations in the British West Indies on the eve of the American Revolution.[106] Sugar fortunes allowed an increasing number of British planters to send their children off to be educated in Britain, where they were brought up to support, and often to play leadership roles themselves in, the vast water-borne British Empire overseas.

During the 1760s and early 1770s, the political and economic tensions between these colonies and Britain itself became increasingly tense as the British Parliament increasingly tried to rule and to tax these colonies without their formal consent.

This struggle was immortalized in the colonists' now-famous slogan: "No taxation without representation!" In other words, no more taxation imposed by Parliament until and unless the colonies themselves can have a much greater say in the workings of Parliament.

The American Revolution stemmed from the rejection of Parliamentary authority and from the colonists' own steps toward independence. These in turn prompted the British to send troops to reimpose direct rule from London, a move which sparked the outbreak of war in 1775. It was during that war that American privateers played such a central role.

The next year, 1776, the Americans' Second Continental Congress issued the Declaration of Independence, which separated the colonists' sovereignty from that of the British Empire and created a new entity known as the United States of America. By 1778, from the British point of view, the American war was not going very well.

What they denounced as "legalized piracy", namely, privateering, was putting increasing pressure on British trade. This proved to be impossible for the British to suppress effectively: witness the successes of the sometimes-privateer and later-day famous American naval hero John Paul Jones, who operated more as a privateer than a commissioned naval commander. Moreover, the war was proving to be financially very costly to Britain and politically increasingly controversial.

As soon as French and Spanish forces joined the war on the American side, the military balance clearly turned in favour of the colonists and, after Britain's clear defeat at Yorktown in 1781, peace negotiations began and were successfully concluded at the Peace of Paris in 1783. The continuous shipping losses that it suffered from American privateers was one of the major reasons why, after Yorktown, the British decided not to continue what had clearly become a losing fight.[107]

Some modern historians believe that this unexpected loss of such a big chunk of British North America was a major turning point. After it, the British decided to refocus their attention on other parts of the world, e.g., on Asia, on the countries of the Pacific Ocean basin, and, eventually, on Africa itself.

The major international impacts of the American Revolution were two-fold:

- The widespread broadcasting of "radical" democratic ideas – for example, the right to more freedom, to more social equality, and to more political representation – influenced leaders and peoples all around the world.
- These ideas also inspired anti-monarchial democratic independence movements in many other countries, e.g., in France, the Netherlands, Poland-Lithuania, Ireland, and Haiti.

In terms of British-American relations, the growth of trade between the new United States of America and Great Britain in the wake of the Revolutionary War was seen as clear proof that dominant political control by one country was not necessary (in contrast to the earlier dogma of mercantilism) for economic prosperity to flourish between countries.

Tensions between these two countries soared again, however, during the War of 1812. This fight also saw a heavy use of privateers, but peace was soon reestablished (and no lasting damage was done to either side) in the Treaty of Ghent in 1814.

In Britain itself after the war, there was a tendency to avoid repeating the mistakes of the past and perhaps even a growing sympathy for British subjects who now lived in distant lands. Nevertheless, as a modern scholar has noted, "The sympathy and humanity for which Americans looked in vain [from the stay-at-home British people] were much more likely to be granted once the Americans had actually left the empire".[108]

Chapter 3

The Impacts of American Privateering

This chapter focuses briefly on the impacts which occurred during the Revolutionary War, the War of 1812, and the Civil War. Later chapters will elaborate on all these points.

Four different kinds of ships served the American cause during the American Revolution. These were:

1. The heavy cruisers commissioned by George Washington in 1775 to attack British shipping, plus the flotilla of ships assembled in 1776 by Benedict Arnold (who was later a traitor to the American cause) for Washington in order to oppose the use of Lake Champlain by British ships.
2. The small navies established by eleven of the thirteen American states.
3. The very modest national Continental Navy between 1775 and 1785, which is said to have had only thirty-one ships in it during the Revolution.
4. Last but certainly by no means least: the many privateers commissioned both by the Continental Congress and by the state governments. It is believed, for example, that during the Revolutionary War about 1,151 to 1,607 American privateers were in action.[109]

The keystone in the arch of American privateering was a resolution of 20 June 1775 by the Massachusetts Provincial Congress. Technically speaking, the first armed ships used by the American colonists were not in fact truly privateers, because Congress did not formally authorize privateering until the very end of 1775. Nevertheless, for our purposes here – and this how they were understood by the American man in the street – they can, in fact, be considered to have been "proto-privateers".

In any case, the Massachusetts Provincial Congress had authorized its assembled delegates to purchase:

> a number of armed Vessels, not less than six, to mount [each ship was to be equipped with] from eight to fourteen carriage guns [deck guns], and a proportionate number of swivels [anti-personnel guns mounted on swiveling bases so they could be aimed in any direction] ... to be with all possible dispatch provided, fixed, and properly manned, to cruise as the Committee of Safety, or any other person or persons who shall be appointed by Congress for that purpose, shall from time to time order and direct, for the protection of our trade and sea-coasts against the depredations and practices of our enemies, and for their annoyance, capture, or destruction.[110]

The famous insurance firm Lloyd's of London estimated that, by the end of the war, these and other American privateers had captured or destroyed about 2,208 British merchantmen.[111]

Both the Continental Congress and some of the most highly motivated colonial state governments offered in 1776, by enlisting the services of vibrant commercial sector of the colonial economy, to issue privateering licences to skippers of all American merchant ships who wanted them. The resulting mini armada was not huge. It had only about 2,000 vessels of widely varying shapes, sizes, and armament, ranging from simple whaleboats[112] from 27 to 31 feet long and carrying less than twenty men, up to fully rigged ships at least 140 feet long with very large numbers of men. Nevertheless, it was still quite effective in combat.

Calling up privateers was a very wise decision and, in point of fact, given the great weaknesses of the American colonies when weighed against the enormous power of the British Empire and its Royal Navy, this was really the only sensible choice open to leaders of the rebellious colonies.

The Americans urgently needed to have their own ships at sea for two reasons. First and most importantly, for their national defence they had only a tiny number of commissioned naval vessels at their own disposal and could not afford to risk losing many of them in combat against the Royal Navy.

Second, any formal exchange of prisoners of war captured at sea by the ship of one government and then transferred to the ship of another government was inherently a very slow and complicated process. The colonists would have to have at least a handful of ships afloat make this transfer possible at all.

The British steadfastly refused to recognize American independence, insisting instead on treating American captives not as prisoners of war but merely as misguided and rebellious Englishmen. On the American side, the slow-motion pace of prisoner exchange was due in large part to the fact that only the federal government, and not any of the individual states, had the power to negotiate prisoner exchanges.

During the Revolutionary War and in the War of 1812, a privateering licence permitted American captains to seize "prizes" (enemy ships and their contents) from both the Royal Navy and from the loyalist pro-English Tory privateers who were supporting continued British rule over the American colonies. These prizes were seized legally under the widely accepted provisions of international maritime law, which dated from the work of the young Dutch scholar Grotius in 1604.

Grotius was an exceptionally brilliant 20-year-old lawyer. He was hired by the Dutch East India Company (not to be confused with the bigger and much better-known English East India Company, often informally referred to as "John Company", which will be discussed later in this book) to provide legal and public relations backup in the Dutch East India Company's dispute over ownership of the *Catharina*, a large and rich Portuguese carack (a cargo ship).

In 1604, a Dutch privateer ship holding a commission from the Dutch government had captured the *Catharina*. In due course, a prize court (a court set up to adjudicate nautical matters) made an award for this ship to the Dutch East India Company, which by then had become a part-owner of it.

However, some of the company's shareholders were committed pacifists and refused to accept their share of the prize money for the ship, since it had been seized by naval force. Indeed, they even threatened to set up a new shipping company based on their own pacifist principles. The Dutch East India Company thereupon hired Grotius to write a legal brief to support its position on this controversial and difficult issue.

The final result of Grotius' research was three now-famous works: *De Jure Praedae* (The Law of Prize and Booty), *Mare Liberum* (Freedom of the Seas), and *De Jure Bellis ac Pacis* (On the Law of War and Peace). Taken collectively, these studies synthesized and restated Greek, Roman, biblical sources, and the maritime law of his own time, into a durable legal blend that had a profound and long-lasting impact on international maritime law.[113] One key result of Grotius' work was that, in the future, privateering and prize money issues would be decided only by admiralty (nautical) courts, not by the captains of the ships at sea who actually captured enemy vessels.

As an additional historical note here, it can be suggested that during the eighteenth century, privateering – bloody as it could be – actually may have been a more humane form of warfare than what had gone on much earlier, for example, during the Middle Ages.

The reason is that it was now much to the advantage of privateers not to destroy the ships and the goods that they captured, and not to kill any enemy seamen unnecessarily.

Ships and goods could easily be sold at welcoming ports; killing enemy seamen, however, whether by gunfire, by swords and axes, or simply by throwing them overboard while still alive, could never be done safely without the probability of heavy losses to the victor's own crew, who would have to do all the dirty work.

Returning now to the Revolutionary War, although only rough estimates are available, it is thought that as many as 55,000 seamen of various nationalities willingly and eagerly signed up to serve aboard the American privateers. These men were motivated both by their hope for excellent pay if their ships captured any rich prizes and by their anti-British political sentiments. They quickly divided up their profits from prizes, sharing them by agreements both with the persons or company financing them, and also with the local American colony or state.

For skilled and lucky commanders, profits from prizes could be considerable. Here are some examples:[114]

- Captain Abraham Whipple of Rhode Island may well have seized more British vessels than any other privateer during the American Revolution.
- On one cruise, for example, he took twenty-three prizes valued at more than $1 million. In 1779, he joined forces with two other privateers, and in several weeks he and the two other captains brought into Boston harbour eight prize merchantmen valued at more than $1 million.

- One 14-year-old novice sailor on a similar privateering cruise, said to be "fresh from the farm", received as his own share of the profits: 20 pounds of cotton; 20 pounds of valuable all-spice, ginger, and logwood; 1 ton of sugar; between 30 and 40 gallons of strong Jamaica run; and $700 in cash.

Indeed, these profits were so great that famous Continental Navy commanders such as John Paul Jones always railed against the proliferation of privateers. One reason was that privateers were quite reluctant to take enemy prisoners: such men were very dangerous to capture and then had to be kept on board, carefully guarded and given food and water, until they were finally (and hopefully) exchanged for some captured American sailors.

Moreover, and more importantly to Jones and other senior commanders, the privateers also enticed many seamen to leave the navy and join them on privateers in return for much better pay, shorter periods of enlistment, and less dangerous fights with unarmed merchant ships, rather than with the very heavily armed and very aggressive warships of the Royal Navy.[115]

At a time when the best American sailors are said to have earned only about $200 a year, a privateer seaman's share of a single prize might have been up to twenty times his yearly pay. It was not unheard-of for a successful privateer ship to take as many as six prizes during one voyage.

Privateer captains did not pay their crews monthly wages as all the merchant ships did, but wanted instead to capture enough prizes to be able to pay off all hands very handsomely at the end of a voyage. The downside of this arrangement, of course, was that "no prize = no pay"!

It is now thought that American privateers captured up to about 300 ships during the Revolutionary War, though often a captured British ship was later recaptured by the British and reinstated into the British fleet. Such was indeed the case with the British ship *Jack*, which was captured by the Americans and became an American privateer – only to be recaptured later by the British in a naval battle off Halifax, Nova Scotia.

One of the most active sites for American privateering during the Revolutionary War was Long Island Sound, the 110-mile-long marine sound and tidal estuary that lies mainly between Connecticut to the north and Long Island in New York in the south.

Long Island Sound was considered to be a virtual hornet's nest of privateering activities because most of the flow of cargo to and from New York had to pass through it. The port of New London, Connecticut was also one of the chief privateering ports for the American colonies – to the extent the Royal Navy found it necessary to send Royal Navy ships to blockade this port from 1778 to 1779 to prevent British ships from being sunk by American privateers patrolling these waters.

Other Revolutionary War privateering ports included Boston, Salem, New Haven, Bridgeport, and, of course, New York. A modern line-drawing map of the American and Canadian East Coast shows numerous privateering ports sprinkled between Charleston in the south to Halifax in the north.[116]

A good human interest story about "whaleboat privateers" during the Revolutionary War is set in Long Island Sound. It is the tale of Ebenezer Jones, a privateersman from Stamford, Connecticut. He was the captain of one of the dozen whaleboats that had been commissioned by the American colonists to attack British shipping in the Sound and to pillage the loyalist properties in those sections of Long Island itself under British control.

Jones had only three small boats in his tiny fleet: *Rattle Snake* (perhaps also spelled *Rattlesnake*: there were at the time several vessels by this name), *Viper*, and *Saratoga*. Each vessel, crewed by ten men well-armed with knives, cutlasses, and probably a few single-shot pistols, also had a swivel gun (a light cannon that could be aimed easily) mounted on the ship's rail. It could be turned to sweep the enemy decks with a charge of musket balls or even sharp-edged scrap-metal pieces.

It is thought that Jones and his whaleboats did manage to capture numerous British vessels. However, there is no record to back up the following account, which must be considered as a tall tale happily making the rounds of waterfront bars.

The story is that Jones and his men rowed up to a British sloop of war that was simply bristling with guns. He came aboard her, claiming that he was a British official, and strongly criticized the captain of the sloop for keeping such a poor watch when there were so many American whaleboats in these waters, simply waiting to pounce upon any British ship that was not completely on guard.

The captain of the sloop, now very much taken aback, apologized at once and at length. During their conversation, however, Jones' own men were silently climbing aboard the sloop and getting ready for action. When Jones suddenly gave them the signal by stamping his foot hard on the deck, they drew their hidden pistols and quickly captured the sloop.[117]

Not all the whaleboat privateers were angels, however. In 1781, Lieutenant Colonel Caleb Brewster, a member of the American spy ring that collected information for George Washington on British army operations in New York, reported that two whaleboats had landed at midnight on 14 August 1781 at a home owned by Captain Miller and his brother Andrew, both of whom had fought against the British for the American cause.

While the whaleboat men were stealing Captain Miller's firearms, they made so much noise that Captain Miller's son William opened his bedroom window to look outside. One of the privateers raised his gun and fired, killing William instantly.

Another privateer burgled Andrew's house, seriously wounding Andrew in the process. Both houses were then ransacked. As a result of these incidents, the privateering licences of such whaleboat privateers were cancelled, but scattered incidents continued to occur from time to time because of "freelance" whaleboat privateers[118] who were nothing more than petty criminals.

During the Revolutionary War, George Washington was known to pay close attention to his own business interests as well as to national and international issues. He invested in at least one privateer.

On 14 November 1777, he wrote the following letter to John Parke Curtis, his stepson, regarding his ownership of this privateer:

It is perfectly agreeable [to me], too, that Colonel Baylor should share part of the privateer. I have spoken to him on the subject. I shall therefore consider myself as possessing one fourth of your full share [of the privateer], and that yourself, Baylor, Lund Washington, and I are equally concerned in the share you first held.[119]

[Baylor was Washington's former aide de camp and an escort of Martha Washington. Lund Washington was Washington's cousin and his business manager.]

The War of 1812

During this war both the British and the American governments used privateers. The U.S. Congress specified that in this conflict the President was empowered "to issue to private armed vessels of the United States commissions of marque and general reprisal ... against the vessels, goods, and effects of the Government of the said Kingdom of Great Britain and Ireland, and the subjects thereof."

As a result, President Madison issued 500 letters of marque authorizing the hiring of privateers, and Congress is said to have issued about 1,100 letters of marque during the War of 1812.

The cost of buying and fitting out a big privateer was as much as $40,000. This considerable investment, however, could hopefully be quickly repaid by the capture of just a few good prizes, the most valuable of which might possibly be worth as much as $100,000. It seems to have been a rare occasion when an American privateer captain returned from a long voyage with nothing at all to show for his efforts.

Between the end of the Revolutionary War in 1783 and during the War of 1812, about 200 American privateers took prizes under the authority of their letters of marque. In this same era, however, the Americans also lost a great many ships as well. Roughly 2,500 American ships were captured by various opponents of the United States at various times and places, namely, by Britain, France, Naples, the Barbary States of North Africa, Spain, and the Netherlands.

One of the most famous and most successful privateer captains during the War of 1812 was the newsworthy Irish-American Captain Thomas Boyle. He will be mentioned frequently in this book because he captured more than fifty British merchant ships when commanding two very fast sailing ships himself – first, the Baltimore schooner-rigged privateer *Comet*, and then the Baltimore clipper schooner-rigged privateer *Chasseur*.[120] This latter ship is said to have inflicted about $1.5 million worth of damage on Royal Navy vessels.

Captain Boyle was always an extremely able privateersman. Twice "worsting a cruiser" (defeating a much bigger and more powerful ship) and also ably defending his own small ship in fights against other larger British warships, he was described by a man who knew him well as a quiet, unassuming man "who said very little but did very much".

Captain Boyle, was, this man tells us:

> always annoying [always attacking] the enemy wherever he chanced to steer, sometimes on the coasts of Spain and Portugal, and, anon, in the British and Irish Channels, carrying dismay and terror to British trade and commerce, in defiance of their fleetest frigates [fast, manoeuvrable ships that could operate independently at relatively long range] and sloops of war, which strove again and again to capture him, but were never able. He appeared frequently to tantalize and vex them as if for mere sport, and at the same time convince them that he could out-manoeuvre and outsail them in any trial of seamanship.[121]

In the winter of 1813-1814, Captain Boyle took twenty prizes in the Caribbean before returning to Beaufort, North Carolina, where he sold *Comet* and then moved to New York. There he became co-owner of the *Chasseur* (French for "Hunter"), which had also been built in Baltimore, where the fastest privateers of that era were being constructed.

The *Chasseur* was armed with sixteen 12-pound guns (each of the sixteen cannons on the ship fired an iron ball weighing 12 pounds), and this ship could also carry a very strong complement, namely, a strong and well-trained crew of up to 160 men.

Once he left New York, Captain Boyle decided to sail directly to the British Isles and to attack local shipping there. His first prize as a privateer was a British ship of little value known as the *Marquis of Cornwallis*. He ordered that she be sailed to the nearest port for use as a prisoner exchange vessel. In fact, however, Captain Boyle also had an ace up his sleeve.

He posted a message in Lloyd's Coffee House in London, the nerve centre of the entire marine insurance industry in Britain and the predecessor of Lloyd's of London, the modern insurance giant of our times.

Angered by the many and quite meaningless British declarations of "blockades" against the United States (which, had they ever been enforced, would have prohibited British ships from calling at any American ports), Captain Boyle unilaterally proclaimed, entirely on his own volition and without any official approval, a "strict and rigorous blockade" against "all the ports, harbours, bays, creeks, rivers, inlets, islands, and seacoast of the United Kingdom of Great Britain and Ireland."

The gist of his proclamation, as reported by the naval historian Maclay in 1899, runs along the following lines:

> Whereas it has become customary with the admirals of Great Britain, commanding [only] small forces on the coast of the United States ... to declare the [entire] coast of said United States in a state of strict and rigorous blockade, without possessing the power to justify such a declaration or stationing an adequate force to maintain said blockade, I do therefore, by virtue of the power and authority vested in me declare all the ports, harbors, bays, creeks, rivers, inlets, outlets, islands, and seacoast of the United Kingdom of Great Britain and Ireland in a state of strict and rigorous blockade

Since Boyle himself had only one ship, this boldly proclaimed blockade existed only in his own mind and on paper. What was most important, however, was that news of it travelled very fast along shipping circles by word of mouth. Indeed, within a short period of time, British merchants were even petitioning their own king to protect them from "the number of American privateers with which our channels have been infested".

The king heeded their request and assigned fourteen sloops of war and three frigates (these latter were bigger and stronger ships than mere sloops) to protect the British Isles against this lone American ship, which only had the very feeble firepower of less than 100 pounds. This meant that the total weight of all the cannonballs that could be fired at the same time in a broadside from the ship was under 100 pounds.

Captain Boyle took eighteen prizes during this cruise and then returned to New York, where he was given a hero's welcome and where his ship was hailed as "The Pride of Baltimore".

It was during his last cruise in the War of 1812 that Captain Boyle earned his most impressive reptation for boldness, daring, and success on the high seas. This story is such a classic of its time and place that it must be recounted here at some length.

On 26 February 1815, Captain Boyle was about 36 miles windward of Havana, Cuba and 12 miles from land, when he saw another schooner not too far from his own ship. This turned out to be the English war schooner *St Lawrence*, a former American privateer that had been captured by the British in 1813, renamed, and then put into the British fleet. At the time, the ship was carrying both important dispatches and British troops as part to the British war effort against New Orleans.

Captain Boyle promptly began to pursue the British ship, because Captain Boyle's lookout in the masthead of his ship could see in the distance that the English vessel was actually a warship protecting a convoy of other British ships.

Since Captain Boyle's ship was faster than the *St Lawrence*, he soon got close to her. Wanting to find out the nationality of the vessel, he fired a gun and showed his colours (meaning that he fired a cannon-shot as a warning and also raised an American flag). The *St Lawrence*, however, paid no attention to this summons but instead raised so much more sail that her foretopmast was carried away (that is, the top of one of her masts broke off due to the great force of the wind on it).

Repairing this damage forced the *St Lawrence* to slow down to the point where Captain Boyle was now close to her. The *St Lawrence* then fired a stern gun (a cannon pointed toward Captain Boyle's ship) and hoisted the English colours (she raised a British flag).

Since Captain Boyle could only see three gun ports on the side of the *St Lawrence* closest to him, and since he saw only a few men on the deck of this ship, it seemed to him that the ship was probably only a poorly armed and lightly manned cargo vessel bound for Havana. He therefore redoubled his efforts to get alongside, confident that she would be an easy prize, and therefore he had not "cleared his own ship for action" by making full preparations for battle.

Suddenly, however, when his own ship was very close (within pistol shot, that is, about 50 yards) of the enemy ship, he was very shocked and very surprised to see her reveal her full armament, namely, ten gun ports, each with a loaded gun in it. Moreover, suddenly, too, her decks were now swarming with British sailors in uniform, proving that she was really not a helpless cargo ship after all but was actually a fully equipped British man-of-war.

It took the British sailors only about five seconds to give three cheers, to run out their guns (they opened their gun ports so that the muzzles of the loaded cannons protruded from them), and to pour a whole broadside of round shot (cannon balls), grapeshot (small balls designed to spread out in flight and thus hit a number of men), and musket balls (the equivalent of rifle bullets) into Captain Boyle's ship. For once, at least, this famous American privateer captain had been caught napping!

Captain Boyle had only two choices: surrender or fight. He decided to fight, and therefore quickly, using both his cannons and musket fire from his crew, returned the enemy's fire.

Believing that his best chance in this engagement was to fight at very close quarters, Captain Boyle manoeuvred his ship to be within 10 yards of the English ship; both ships were now firing at the same time at very close range and thus doing a great deal of damage to each other. Captain Boyle seized the initiative, however, and, just as the two ships touched, W.N. Christie, the prize master of Captain Boyle's ship, jumped onto the deck of the English ship, immediately followed by some of his men.

A prize master was one of the best sailors on a ship and was the man put in charge of any prize captured in battle. Christie and his men were ready for a bloody fight, but before they could strike a single blow, the English ship surrendered.

According to American accounts, during this battle, which lasted only fifteen minutes, the English had six men killed and seventeen wounded, several of them mortally. The Americans had five men killed and eight men wounded, among the latter being Captain Boyle himself. The masts of the English ship "went by the board" (that is, they were so weakened by cannon fire that they toppled overboard) and the ship was a total loss. Its officers and crew became prisoners of war for the Americans.

After the fight, and back on land again, an officer of the captured English ship voluntarily issued a certificate praising Captain Boyle for "his obliging attention and watchful solicitude to preserve our effects and render us comfortable during the short time we were in his possession".[122]

When the war was finally over, Captain Boyle carried cargo between Baltimore and ports of the Caribbean and South America. He was also one of the War of 1812 captains who was a privateer during the Spanish American

Wars of Independence. Captain Boyle finally died at sea en route from Alvarado, Mexico to Philadelphia, in 1825.

Turning now to a new subject; the American privateer schooner *Decatur*. She hailed from Charleston, South Carolina and saw action during the War of 1812 under the command of Captain Diron.

In the summer of 1813, he went into battle against a British war schooner near Bermuda. A summary of this dramatic clash, highlighted by verbatim quotes from Maclay, runs as follows:[123]

- Captain Diron knew that the British schooner had much heavier armament (more cannons) than his own ship, but he believed that he had more men aboard his ship. This persuaded him to fight at very close quarters and try to subdue the British ship by boarding her.

- As first steps, Captain Diron cleared for action (got his ship ready for action by removing anything from the decks that might get in the way of hand-to-hand fighting), sent his men to their battle-quarters, and hoisted the American colours. He also had, right at hand, all the necessary ammunition, water, and sand (the latter being used to give men better foot-grips on wet or bloody decks).

- To make sure that no man could leave his post and run below to hide from the gunfire, he also ordered that all the hatches be closed. His plan was to get as close to the enemy as possible before firing a shot, first by using grappling irons (iron hooks attached to ropes to pull the ships close together); then to deliver a full broadside from his cannons, plus a volley from the crew's muskets; and, finally, to order his boarders onto the decks of the enemy ship.

- Captain Diron began by damaging the enemy ship heavily by opening fire on her with his own ship's most powerful long-range gun, known as a "long tom" because of the length of its barrel. Soon the two vessels were so close to each other that the Americans could clearly hear the British officers shouting at their men to make even greater efforts. Captain Diron then ordered his own men to leave their cannons, to arm themselves with muskets and cutlasses, and to be ready to leap onto the enemy's decks as soon as he gave them the order to do so.

- The British at this stage of the battle now realized that they were now in very grave danger: their officers could be heard shouting to the gunners not to continue to fire at the American ship's rigging (which, if cut, would have slowed the ship considerably), but instead to aim at her wooden hull in order to sink her outright.
- The British crew quickly followed the new orders, and their next broadside killed two of the American crew and seriously damaged their ship's sails and rigging. This prevented Captain Diron from immediately boarding the enemy ship: some of their ropes having been cut by cannon fire, his sails were flapping and were unmanageable for the moment.
- The two ships then in effect raced each other, virtually sailing side-by-side, but Captain Diron "had the satisfaction of seeing his craft gradually overhaul [go faster] than the Englishman" because the American ship could sail better than the British ship.
- Captain Diron then called on his men to be ready to board the enemy ship – just as, in a planned manoeuvre, he ran his bowsprit over the stern of the enemy ship. It pierced her mainsail and, as will be seen, provided a convenient "walkway" for his borders to use.
- The Americans at once opened a heavy fire with their muskets, while two of the very best men on their ship – Vincent Safitt, the prize master, and Thomas Wasborn, the quartermaster – led the borders along the bowsprit, from which they sprang onto the decks of the British ship.

> Then began a terrible scene of slaughter and bloodshed. The two crews were soon intermingled in an inextricable mass, which the narrow deck of the schooner kept compact as long as the struggle lasted. Nearly 200 men and boys, armed with pistols, cutlasses, and muskets, were now shouting, yelling, and cheering, while slashing at each other in a space [on the deck of the ship] not more than 20 feet wide and 80 feet long.

- The final result of what was called "this battle royal" was a clear American victory: the British lost sixty men killed or wounded, out of a total of the eighty-eight men on their ship.

- On the American side, five privateersmen were killed and fifteen were wounded. This lower figure of American losses was said to have been principally due to the better seamanship of Captain Diron and to the better marksmanship of his crew, both with their cannons and with their muskets and pistols.

Shifting our focus now to the fast and famous Baltimore clippers, their design dates from 1789, when a one-page drawing of "His Majesty's Arm'd Schooner *Berbice*" later found its way into the holdings of the National Maritime Museum in London, where it can still be seen today.

It is the earliest draft of what would later become known as the Baltimore clipper. These were very good ships indeed and lasted a surprisingly long time. For example, one of them – the schooner *Vigilant*, which was built in the 1790s – traded successfully in the U.S. Virgin Islands until she was finally sunk there by a hurricane in 1928.

A clipper was a type of mid-nineteenth-century merchant sailing ship chiefly designed for speed while carrying very perishable cargo, e.g., fresh fruit or captured slaves, which did not take up much space in the hold of a ship. Clippers had relatively narrow hulls and very large total sail areas. A schooner-rigged ship had fore-and-rigging on all her masts. When she had a square topsail (known as a topgallant) on her foremast, she was called a topsail (pronounced "top-sl") schooner.

From an historical point of view, however, such ships were variously known as Chesapeake Bay pilot schooners; as pilot-boat schooners; as schooners, pilot-boat built; or, less commonly, simply as Baltimore schooners.[124]

In any case, a Baltimore schooner/clipper was a very fast and very beautiful schooner built in the port of Baltimore, Maryland. It was said of this type of ship that she was "A long, slim, graceful vessel with a projecting bow, a streamlined hull, and an exceptionally large spread of sail on three tall masts."[125] This is indeed a good description of the lovely replica of an 1847 Baltimore Clipper, named *Californian*, which was built in 1984.

Chapter 4

Letters of Marque and Reprisal

Ships sailing in wartime conditions or in dangerous waters were traditionally entitled, without the need for any government authorization, to carry lethal weapons both for self-defence and to capture any enemy ship that might attack them.[126]

As part of this process in Western Europe, from the late Middle Ages through the long Age of Sail, which ended only in the mid-nineteenth century, the proceeds of any prizes taken by such armed ships went, in part, to the ruler of the country whose ship made the seizure. These proceeds could include the ship itself, its cargo, and the ransom of any rich prisoners able to pay for their own release.

However, if before the voyage began the captor had taken the precaution of obtaining from the ruler certain documents allowing him to attack enemy vessels on behalf of the ruler, the results would have been much more favourable to him.

Such letters, known as letters of marque and reprisal (usually shortened in official documents to simply "letters of marque"), permitted governments to fight their wars by enlisting what, in modern terms, essentially amounted to "maritime mercenaries" or "legalized pirates". That is to say, governments could save a great deal of time, money, and trouble simply by hiring private captains, private sailors, and private ships, rather than having to invest in and to maintain a very expensive national navy. The ruler would often happily waive his own share of the proceeds of privateering as a bargain price for obtaining a competent navy virtually free of charge.

In the case of a warship, her commissioning papers would prove she was a vessel of the national navy and not just a mere pirate craft. In the case of a privately owned ship, obtaining letters of marque and reprisal before the voyage automatically and legally transformed her into a privateer. This important change saved her from the possibly fatal consequences of being mistaken as a pirate ship at some remote port and attacked and destroyed there.

An early letter of marque issued in England in 1400 tells the recipient what he could do or not do:

> Commission to William Prince, master of a barge [sailing ship] called *le Cristofre* of Arundell, to take mariners for the same, to go to sea on the king's service; provided that neither he nor any liege [any subject of the king] in his company on the barge take any ships, barges, or other vessels, merchandise, goods or chattels of any of the realms of France, Spain, Portugal or other parts of the realm except only the realm of Scotland.[127]

Another version of such a letter, written in Dutch and now very faint and badly charred around as a result of a fire, was issued by Maurice, Prince of Orange in what is now the Netherlands, on 1 June 1618 to Captain Johan de Moor from Vlissingen in the Netherlands, authorizing him to sail his ship to South America in order to trade there.

Another letter of marque, this one in faded French script and also impossible to read now, was given on 27 February 1809 to Captain Antoine Bollo from the shipowner Dominique Malfine of Genoa. Malfine was the owner of the 15-ton privateer *Furet*.[128]

Vessels documented as privateers enjoyed numerous benefits. The most important of these were two-fold. First, as noted above, the ruler often waived his share of the proceeds in order to encourage private investors to gamble by betting their hard-earned money on a privateer. Second, both the officers and the crews of privateers might well earn sizeable bonuses if they could capture valuable enemy ships.

The crew of privateers typically included four categories of men, listed below in order of their increasing expertise and thus of their present incomes and future prospects:[129]

1. "Landlubbers" – This group consisted of a very wide range of men, e.g., country boys fleeing from the drudgery and dead-end quality of rural life; failed doctors, ministers, lawyers, farmers, and shopkeepers;

runaway slaves; and sometimes even a local Indian who hoped for a broader life beyond the confines of his tribe.

As soon as they got their sea legs, all were trained and set to some of the ceaseless tasks aboard ship. One of the largest uses of these men was as prize crews, each of which needed between twelve and twenty men who were unlikely to return to their "home ship" once they left to take a prize to a port where it could be sold. They then had to look for other jobs ashore or afloat there.

2. Marine guards – These men were not members of what we now consider to be the U.S. Marine Corps but were instead "Gentlemen Volunteers" who came from well-connected families and who probably wanted a little bit of adventure before settling down into boring provincial lives as members of the local gentry.

They held an intermediate social status aboard ship because they were neither officers nor crewmen. In practice, however, they were all intelligent, well-schooled, good shots with muskets and pistols, and could easily back up the officers' orders to the crew.

Moreover, in combat, they were also the sharpshooters posted high in the rigging of their ship to give them a clear field of fire; the leaders of the groups of seamen assigned to board enemy ships; and the men put in charge of guarding the prisoners captured from these ships.

3. Seamen – About one third of the crew were salty "tars" (experienced seamen so-called because of their custom of putting tar on their jackets, trousers, and hats to waterproof them). These men constituted the bulk of the crews of privateers and were very conservative in evaluating themselves.

For example, none of them would ever presume publicly to put himself forward as an "AB" (Able Body) seaman unless it was perfectly clear both to his coworkers and to himself that he had virtually all of the experience and ability needed to "reef, hand, and steer" (to manage the sails and to steer the ship) in all weathers. If he did not have all these skills, in an emergency he would be a real threat to his teammates, to his officers, and to the ship himself. He was therefore much more inclined to understate his own abilities rather than to trumpet them.

4. Officers – Chosen very carefully by the captain himself, these men came up through the ranks by beginning as ordinary seamen.

Needless to say, those with the most intelligence and most training and best family background would rise through the ranks most quickly. Besides their maritime expertise, however, officers also had to win the respect of the crew. Cruel, lazy, or stupid officers would result in a surly crew that would never respond "cheerily" (pleasantly and quickly) to all orders, no matter how dangerous.

Although privateering, like all other forms of gambling, had both its winners and losers, a few lucky privateersmen would manage to return from the sea with comfortable fortunes. Windfall profits were always possible, though unlikely. If, however, a privateer ship captured a prize of even only average value, the owners of the privateer stood to earn profits of more than 100 per cent, while its crew would have more than enough in their pockets for some jolly flings ashore.

Their personal stories – losing nothing of course in the telling and retelling – would circulate in waterfront bars, in ships' forecastles (the living quarters of the crews), and, most probably, in port brothels. Such exciting tales could only encourage other ambitious young men to want to try their own luck aboard privateer ships.

Historically, letters of marque and reprisal were issued in Britain by the Admiralty in the name of the king or queen. In the United States, during the American Revolution both state governments and Congress issued them at first, but after the Constitution was adopted in 1781, the power to issue privateer commissions passed to Congress, which in turn delegated it to officials of the State Department or to the customs collectors of the Treasury.

These commissions had to specify the sailing rig of the ship, its tonnage (the cargo-carrying capacity of the ship), the name of the ship, the names of the owners and of the captain, the number of its guns, and the size of the crew. An interesting historical footnote here is that the "long ton", or "imperial ton", of 2,240 pounds derives from the fact that one "tun" of wine typically weighed this much.

In addition, privateers had to post sizeable bonds to ensure their compliance with relevant laws and had to comply with detailed sailing instructions known simply as "Instructions to Privateers". Failure to heed all these guidelines could result not only in the loss of a valuable prize but also to the forfeiture of their bonds and to their liability for legal damages.

During the American Revolution, although the historical documentation is very incomplete, it is thought that roughly some 2,000 letters of marque were issued, on a per-voyage basis, after the Continental Congress had formalized in 1776 the commissioning and the bond-posting processes.

In total, about 800 American vessels were commissioned as privateers and are credited with seizing or destroying about 600 British ships.[130] It is estimated that the total damage done to British shipping by these privateers was about $18 million at that time; about $302 million in today's figures.[131]

Chapter 5

Prize Law in Action

Most privateering efforts took place out in the open sea beyond any country's territorial waters, which were usually defined as beginning 3 miles (the traditional range of a muzzle-loading cannon-shot) from nearest neutral shore.

The territorial waters of a given state, however, could also include any big rivers, river mouths, bays, and estuaries located in Europe, North America, or in the islands of the Caribbean. All these areas were potentially ripe for privateering but presented some important challenges to the officers and crews of these ships.[132]

The first step was for the privateer to inspect any distant newly detected ship, first seen by the privateer's lookout, at closer range. This new ship on the privateer's horizon would technically be known as the "chase". The privateer first signaled the chase to turn into the wind, to come to a stop, and then to wait for the privateer to inspect her. This well-rehearsed process was known as "bringing the chase to", or simply, in the usage and spelling of the time, as "bringing her too".

The privateer then lowered a ship's boat[133] and sent an officer, who could be accompanied by only one other man (in addition to the crew rowing the boat), over to the chase. This officer had the right to demand to see all the documents aboard the chase, to inspect the ship itself, and to require that its crew tell him if anyone aboard had destroyed any documents or thrown them overboard.

If the chase was believed by the privateer to be an enemy vessel, then the captain of the privateer could do one of five things, which show how well-regulated privateering could be:

1. Transfer the entire crew to his own ship, place them under armed guard, and burn or sink their ship or use it for target practice by his crew.

2. Seize any of the food, water, ship's tackle, weapons, or ammunition he wanted for his own ship.

3. Create a "sea cartel" by putting aboard the chase any prisoners he might have been carrying on his own ship, making them sign a document promising not to fight any more in the war until they were formally exchanged for prisoners of his own nation.

4. Sign a ransom agreement with the captain of the chase, agreeing that the chase would be free to leave the scene – but only in exchange for a legally binding promise to pay a ransom later on.

5. Decide to abandon the chase entirely due to bad weather or the threat of imminent enemy action.

It was up to a maritime court to decide, as quickly as possible, whether the chase was in fact a valid prize. This question would be answered by the judge based on the chase's documents and after an interrogation of the crews of both ships. If the judge decided that the chase was not a valid prize, it had to be released at once.

If it was a valid prize, however, then the ship and her cargo were sold as quickly as feasible. The proceeds were distributed by the court to the several possible claimants, e.g., the shippers of the cargo, the privateer's sovereign, and the officers and crew of the chase itself, in accordance with the Parliamentary or Congressional rules then in force.

One of the thorniest questions involved in this whole process was what the naval historian Donald A. Petrie aptly described in his book *The Prize Game* as the neutrality and the nationality of the ships involved in legal disputes at sea.

The law of nations (an earlier term for what we now call international law) was initially drafted by Emerich de Vattel in 1758. It did not, however, automatically equate nationality with citizenship, as was often done much later.

For example, a merchant or a ship-owner who continued to reside in a nation that was at war; who accepted its protection, and who contributed to its economy by his own business activities; was – but only for the purposes of prize law – no longer a neutral but was instead a national of that country.

As Lord Stowell, a famous jurist on prize law, summed up the matter, "The character of the goods [aboard a given ship] is taken from the character of the person [who sent them]; the character of [that] person is taken from the Place of his Inhabitancy".[134]

Another way to put this is to say that, under prize law, if a man lived in England, he was considered to be English, and the merchandise he shipped by sea, no matter what other claims may have been made about it, was legally considered to be English, too.

When dealing with a potential prize, the privateer captain and his officers had to be very careful not to "break bulk", as the phrase had it, in other words, to meddle with the cargo in any way.

A textbook (Upton on *Maritime Warfare and Prize*) written in 1863 made the following points in dense legal language:

Embezzlements of the cargo seized, or acts personally violent, or injuries perpetrated upon the captured crew, or improperly separating them from the prize-vessel, or not producing them before the prize-court, or torts injurious to the rights and health of the prisoners, may render [may result in] the arrest of the vessel or cargo as prize, defeasible, and also subject the tort feasor for damages thereof.

This meant in simple terms that they were forbidden to disturb the cargo of any prize, no matter how alluring it might be to them, without the prior approval of a prize court.

The one exception to this rule was if a true emergency suddenly arose – for example, if the captain decided that he had to jettison part of the cargo at once in order to keep his ship afloat and to keep the crew safe.

Historically, the colourful and often-violent international prize game did not come to a total halt for the Americans until 1899, when Congress officially ended the programme after the Spanish-American War. It did not end for the British, however, until 1948, when Parliament finally discontinued it.

Today, under the provisions of international law and relevant treaties, enemy ships that have been captured in a war can probably still be sold, but it seems unlikely that the officers and men of the ships who captured them would be entitled to any part of the proceeds.

Chapter 6

Financing American Privateering

As early as 5 July 1775, Thomas Jefferson, then a member of the second Continental Congress, wrote to a friend reporting on what he had learned from his recent travels in Massachusetts and other nearby colonies. He explained that:

> The New Englanders are fitting out privateers, with which they expect to be able to scour the seas and bays of everything below ships of war [that is, everything smaller than the biggest vessels of war]; and may probably go to the European coasts, to distress [attack] the British trade there. The enterprising genius and intrepidity of these people are amazing.[135]

Americans were fitting out these privateers for two reasons. First, although this was considered to be a rather risky investment, it was one that might pay big dividends. Second, it was clear proof of their personal and patriotic confidence in the long-term prospects for the American Revolution.

In 1776, for example, the two owners and other investors in the privateers *Chance* and *Congress* made a considerable profit of at least £5,000 each. British pounds are used here because the American "continental dollar" was not of much value then: in fact, there was a contemporary saying to the effect that an allegedly valuable item really "was not worth a continental".

This was at a time when men in other lines of work took home the following sums:

- A prosperous merchant had a net income of around £6,000 per year.
- A carpenter in Rhode Island earned £82 per year.
- A common labourer earned about £40 per year.

-   A captain of a merchant ship earned £10 per month.
-   A common deck hand (that is, sailor) earned £3 per month.

The £5,000 earned in 1776 by the privateer-investors mentioned above would have been worth about $900,000 today.[136] However, this was not a line of work suitable for timid souls who wanted to put all their eggs in the same basket: success often depended largely on wide diversification.

Because of the key role France played in helping the Americans to win the Revolutionary War, the French were always very interested in developments in the United States.

For example, a French visitor to the United States commented in 1782:

It is scarcely to be credited that, amidst the disasters of America [such as the Revolutionary War], Mr. Morris, the inhabitant of a town just emancipated from the hands of the English [namely, Philadelphia], should possess a fortune of eight million [French] *livres*, worth between £300,000 and £400,000 sterling. It is [true], however, that it is in the most critical times that great fortunes are acquired ... [Mr. Morris] is in fact so accustomed to the success of his privateers that, when he is observed on a Sunday to be more serious than usual, the conclusion [to be drawn by his friends] is that no prize has arrived in the previous week.[137]

Although financing privateers always had ups and downs, it was their own self-interest that pushed both seagoing and shoreside men to be willing and, indeed, to be eager, to put down their money on the risky business of underwriting privateers. This was also the basic reason why prize courts did such good business and attracted such good legal talent.

These courts injected an invaluable but previously long-missing element of certainty into the business of financing privateers. If the financial rules of this game were in fact very clear, simple, and legally enforceable, then businessmen and shippers alike could first buy insurance and could then export their goods with confidence. Moreover, the cost of insurance could also properly be passed on to the consumer.[138]

There were many lucrative opportunities for sea-borne trade in American waters during the eighteenth century, and privateers tried to make the most of them. A wide range of potential cargos was available to privateers.

All that was required to profit from this potential bounty were (1) privateer captains who had a great deal of personal courage and nautical skills; (2) well-trained and well-disciplined crews who were willing to risk their lives for the high pay that would flow from capturing lucrative prizes; and (3) a great deal of good luck.

Some of the cargos were as follows: cane sugar; bales of raw cotton and finished linen; North and South American spices; while a vast amount of tobacco was shipped east from the Americas to Western Europe. At the same time, the ever-growing and very lucrative slave trade carried large numbers of Black men, women, and even children from West Africa to the Americas.

The sizeable numbers of indentured male and female European servants, plus all the free European women recruited for the colonial wedding market, led to growing demands for more consumer goods and for some luxury items, e.g., the latest Paris fashions and the best teas.

On the commercial front, and almost always by sea, cotton was exported; rum was shipped from the Caribbean; beer and wine flowed in from Western Europe. American and European multi-shot rifles and pistols were much in demand, while edged weapons and tools all found ready markets, too.

This ceaseless flow of imports and exports offered endless opportunities for adventure and for profit.[139] Even during the worst days of the American Civil War, for example, blockade runners like the dashing but fictional character Rhett Butler in *Gone with the Wind* did a colourful and thriving business.

Chapter 7

Privateers in the Revolutionary War

The American Revolution was a political and ideological upheaval ultimately based on the philosophic principles of what is now termed the American Enlightenment.

Its most important provisions were reliance on the consent of those governed, on a domestically drafted and domestically approved constitution, and on a liberally based democracy. This revolution was influenced by both the seventeenth- and eighteenth-century Age of Enlightenment in Europe and by domestic American philosophy.

In more down-to-earth terms, the American colonists increasingly objected to being forced to pay the onerous taxes being imposed on them during the 1760s by the distant British Parliament, an institution in which they had no direct representation.

That is to say, Parliament had no American members: American interests were considered by the British government to be adequately represented by other members of this hallowed institution. For his own part, King George III feared that any leniency toward the rebellious Americans would merely be seen by them as conclusive proof of his own weakness and would therefore incite them to even further rebellious thoughts and actions.

Moreover, the king was also convinced that he was only doing his royal duty by upholding Britain's threatened monarchy against these usurpers. In his view, purely for their own selfish interests, his distant and ungrateful American subjects wanted to overturn violently the ancient, God-given, sea-based British way of life which had made the British Empire so very strong.

The net result of his stubbornly held views was that the Revolutionary War would eventually involve both France and Spain as belligerents against Britain. It would rage not only in North America but also in the Caribbean and the Atlantic Ocean.

The war would end only when Britain finally accepted its defeat by signing the Treaty of Paris with the United States in 1783. This treaty was the high-water mark of the British Empire in North America.[140]

Today there is a general consensus among historians of the Revolutionary War that, during this war, the rebellious American colonists decided to follow a creative maritime strategy of relying chiefly on privateering to offset the Royal Navy's vastly superior power at sea.[141]

Privateering, therefore, played an important role in the evolving history of colonial America. Indeed, it even dominated American naval thinking until the 1890s, when the most important naval expert of his time – Alfred Thayer Mahan – raised the Americans' strategic sights and began to call for a new naval policy based on destroying an enemy's fleet, not just its commerce.[142]

The role of privateers in the American war effort can be seen in a wide range of historical facts. Perhaps the most significant of these are:

1. About 55,000 seamen (many but no means all of them American) are estimated to have served aboard American privateer ships.
2. During the war, the American colonies had about 1,697 privateer ships but only about sixty-four official Continental Navy ships.[143]
3. The American privateer ships mounted (were equipped with) a cumulative total of about 14,872 guns, whereas the sixty-four Continental Navy ships mounted to only a total of about 1,242 guns.[144]
4. It is not entirely clear whether the balance sheet of privateering during this war actually produced a net advantage for the Americans. A British historian, for example, has even argued that in the American war their "losses and gains more or less cancelled each other out".[145]

That being said, however, it is evident that privateering was an extremely popular enterprise during the years of the American Revolution. This can most easily be seen by citing the gist of some comments from knowledgeable contemporary observers:[146]

- 1776: "In the eastern states, [local citizens are] so intent in privateering that they mind little else."

- 1778: "Privateering was never more in vogue than at the present, when two or three privateers sail every week from this port [Boston], and [privateersmen] seem as plenty as grasshoppers in the field; no vessel is detained an hour for want of them."
- 1778: "Privateering still flourishes, and although some individuals are losers, yet the bulk are great gainers and may make amazing fortunes."
- 1779: The demand for privateering commissions was so great that colonial officials had to beg Congress to send them more. Thomas Jefferson, then Virginia's second governor, claimed that "for want of the pre-printed letters of marque our people have long and exceedingly suffered [because they had not been able to send out their privateers]."

In any case, the best single summary we have seen of the complicated privateering aspects of the first two years of the Revolutionary War comes from Edgar Stanton Maclay, who we have quoted earlier. His most notable work was *The History of the United States Navy*, which he probably wrote while working in relative poverty, loneliness, and boredom as a lighthouse keeper in New York.

Maclay tells us:

When the American colonists finally realized that they must open hostilities [with Great Britain] in order to maintain their rights, they became exceedingly active in fitting out vessels at private expense.

Every seaport soon had its quota of privateers scouring the seas or hovering on the coasts of the enemy. Merchant ships that were no longer able to ply their usual trade were hastily fitted with a few guns and were sent to sea with a [privateering] commission.

Fishing smacks were divested of their cargoes and were transformed into belligerent craft, and even whaleboats ventured out, and in many cases succeeded in making valuable prizes.

... a total of one hundred and forty-two privateers [were] fitted out by the colonists in the first two full years of the war. 'The people have gone mad a-privateering,' said one of the writers of the day, and in some cases the expression 'the enemy coasts are swarming with our armed ships' was literally true. This was especially the case off Halifax [Nova Scotia] and in the Gulf of St. Lawrence, where so many American privateers had collected that they, in truth, very much interfered with one another.[147]

In overview, the first American privateer was a ship named the *Boston Revenge*, which received its letter of marque from the British colony of Massachusetts on 7 December 1775. This soon prompted other colonies, e.g., New Hampshire and Rhode Island, to follow suit.

Even before the Revolutionary War, however, some commercial fishing boats from New England, known as Marblehead schooners (these schooners were fast and relatively shallow-draft vessels), which had been captured by the French were then used by them against their British enemies.

During the American Revolution, schooners were being used by Canadian-based British privateers to attack American ships because they were considered to be such "prime sailers". The American colonists had no standing navy and no privateers in stock when the Revolutionary War began. Even so, they were able make some initial attacks on British ships by resorting to their own jury-rigged (temporarily modified) merchant ships.

These were assisted by the own colonists' privateer boats, which were crewed by very lightly armed men, with perhaps one small cannon, and which were deployed as temporary coastal gunboats.

These small open boats were jokingly known as "Spider Catchers" or "Spider Boats" because of their willingness to "entangle" (that is, to engage) an unarmed, slower, but much bigger ship in a fight.

These boats had a single mast with one sail but many sets of oars. Quickly and lightly built, they were crewed by as many as twenty privateersmen. These men were also described as "whaleboat privateers" because the sleek 30-foot-long boats they used were just the same size as the boats carried on the decks of whalers.

The best news for the embattled colonists was that they had easy access to many ports, especially in New England waters. These included Salem, which was the base of more than 158 privateers during the Revolutionary War (they took 445 prizes, that is, more than half of the prizes captured by the Americans during this war); Boston; New Haven; and Bridgeport.

As mentioned elsewhere in this book, most privateers set to sea with no other purpose but to inflict reprisals on enemy shipping. They carried no cargo except for a variety of cannons, plus a well-trained crew that was big enough and strong enough to man any prizes captured en route, and then to sail them to some port where they could legally be sold.

A privateer that sailed under a government commission, on the other hand, was known as a letter-of-marque ship. She carried a commercial cargo bound for a given port, but she was also fully armed and had the legal right to defend herself against any attackers and to seize any prizes that came her way.

Many sea-faring men in the Salem region were quite willing and, indeed, quite eager, to build fast topsail schooners that had "sharp-built hulls". These were relatively narrow hulls with greater deadrise (meaning that their hulls had a steeper angle of rise from the bottom of the keel).[148]

In short, they also had what were known in the maritime trade as "sharp fine lines", a term that refers to the shape of the hull beneath the waterline. A ship with "broad fine lines", on the other hand, would have a deep bow and a wide beam, thus creating a slow and more stable but much less manoeuvrable vessel. Broad fine lines would be appropriate for a ship that was transporting bulky supplies or carrying more heavy guns.[149]

The topsail schooners also had "raked masts": the masts of the boat sloped aft (to the rear). For reasons that even now are not fully understood, most boats seem to sail best with a bit of rake, and they are always certainly much more visually attractive than purely vertical masts.[150] Such schooners were also very fast and for this reason were ideal for privateering.

A topsail schooner had two or three masts with fore-and-aft rigging and with a square topsail on the foremast, to which was often added an extra upper sail known as a topgallant to give the ship more speed. Fore-and-aft rigging was more weatherly (it was better than square-rigging) because, with it, a ship could sail closer to the wind with little side-drift or leeway. This meant that it could go further and faster than a square-rigged ship could when tacking against the wind.

Topsail schooners were easy to convert into privateers simply by adding more guns and bigger crews. They were fast in the water because they also had, in addition to sharp bows, hulls with a great deal of "deadrise". Such hulls had a profile resembling the letter V and therefore cut through the water very well.[151]

To be effective in battle as a privateer ship, topsail schooners had to be able to "spread a lot of canvas" (to have many sails in the air at the same time) and to have enough well-trained men aboard to handle the sails, to man the guns, to board enemy ships and serve as prize crews on them, and, last but by no means least, to serve as sharpshooters when mounted in the rigging during an attack on a prize.

The official birthdate of the American navy was 13 October 1775: it was on that day that the Continental Congress first passed a resolution that officially sent American ships to sea as privateers.[152] The next spring, two American privateering vessels – *Chance* and *Congress* – which had previously served as pilot boats (small schooners used to deliver and to pick up ships' pilots from offshore vessels) in New York harbour, received commissions and gunpowder from the Continental Congress on 11 April 1776.

These boats and other closely related vessels were so valuable that in 1790 President John Adams wrote to the Secretary of the Navy that "we must have Bermuda Sloops, Virginia Pilot Boats or Marblehead Schooners" to use as light cruisers against America's enemies.[153] These ships were urgently needed because it would take a long time and would involve great expense for the American colonists to be able to develop a strong navy of their own.

The Continental Congress did commission about fifty lightly armed warships during the American Revolution, and almost all of them were quickly set to work as "commerce raiders" or "commerce destroyers". Their assignment was to locate and then sink or capture as many British cargo ships as possible – not to fight pitched battles against the very well-armed and well-manned British warships.

From a technical point of view, unlike privateers, which were always privately owned ships sailing under letters of marque, commerce raiders were government-owned ships with official orders to destroy enemy commerce, e.g., enemy cargo ships. Even though their legal status may have differed, however, in practice at sea, the activities of the privateers and of the commerce raiders were identical, meaning it was impossible to tell them apart.

Such cargo ships were of great importance in resupplying the British war effort. Moreover, from the Americans' point of view it was very much safer to attack enemy cargo ships rather than going up against the British men-of-war, which could be bristling with big crews and with ordnance ranging from heavy cannons and light swivel guns to the muskets, pistols, and boarding pikes that could be issued to the crew.

By modern standards, naval artillery aboard sailing ships was dangerous, inefficient, difficult and slow to load, and most accurate only at short ranges. During combat, "powder boys", typically boys only 10 to 14 years old, were assigned to carry powder from the magazine up to the gun decks of a ship, where strong and well-trained adults took over, loaded, fired, and maintained the cannons.

Perhaps even more important to the ultimate American victory, however, were the American privateers. During the war, as many as 792 letters of marque were issued by the American colonists to privateer captains. This implies a maritime force of some 792 privateer ships. Regardless of their exact number, they are estimated to have captured or destroyed more than 600 British merchant ships.[154]

Moreover, in this process American privateers are also thought to have captured at sea significant numbers of British seamen and to have confined them for varying periods of time, either afloat or ashore, until they were either exchanged for American seamen or they died of illness.

This total was quite significant because, in that era, the Royal Navy had neither enough able-bodied hands (trained seamen) nor enough fully equipped ships stationed in American waters to be able to blockade American ports effectively and thus close them off to unwanted ship arrivals or departures during wars.

Even small-scale losses in British naval manpower could mount up during the Revolutionary War. For example, the 240 Hessian (German) mercenaries captured at sea by the American privateer *Mars*, and the 100 British soldiers captured there by the American privateer *Warren*, were only very small leaks in the big bucket of British naval manpower, but they could, in time, add up to a significant drain. This statement must be understood in light of the fact that a full regiment of the British army during the Revolutionary War had only about 2,000 men in it.[155]

By the winter of 1775-1776, American privateers had become real threats to British ships in the waters near New England itself and adjacent to the mid-Atlantic coast. In roughly this period, thirty-one British or Loyalist (pro-

British) colonial ships were captured off Boston. These losses persuaded the British to leave Boston in the spring of 1776 and move to safer anchorages. At about the same time, however, the Royal Navy did capture a few American privateers and sent them to Boston as prizes, having first placed some British officers and sailors aboard them as prize crews.[156]

Between 1775 and 1777, at least 132 privateering licences were granted to thirteen American colonies, which then had access to a cumulative total of eighteen ports. There can be no doubt that privateering was both very popular and usually very profitable. For example, by 1782 about 323 privateering ships, many of them now converted and well-armed former merchant vessels, had been officially registered. It was indeed a rare vessel that could not be rebuilt by skilled shipwrights into a privately armed ship in a few weeks.

As the Revolutionary War continued, the American colonists became much better organized. Below is a summary of President John Hancock's authorization, issued on 3 April 1776, on behalf of the Continental Congress, giving privateers all the authority they needed to attack, destroy, or capture for later sale all British ships they might encounter.

Sonorously entitled "INSRUCTIONS to the COMMANDERS of Private Ships or Vessels of War, which shall have Commissions of Letters of Marque and Reprisal, authorizing them to make Captures of British Vessels and Cargoes", some of its main points of this lengthy document are as follows:

You may, by Force of Arms, attack, subdue, and take all Ships and other Vessels belonging to the inhabitants of Great Britain, on the high seas, or between high-water and low-water Marks, except Ships and Vessels bringing Persons who intend to settle and reside in the United Colonies, or bringing Arms, Ammunition or Warlike Stores to the said Colonies, for the Use of such Inhabitants thereof as are Friends to the American Cause, which you shall suffer [you shall permit] to pass unmolested, the Commanders thereof permitting a peaceable Search, and giving satisfactory Information on the Contents of the Ladings, and Destination of the Voyages.

You may, by Force of Arms, attack, subdue, and take all Ships and their Vessels [the smaller sailboats or tenders, that is, the rowboats, working with them] whatsoever carrying Soldiers, Arms, Gun-powder, Ammunition, Provisions, or any contraband Goods, to any of the British Armies or Ships of War employed against these Colonies.

You shall bring such Ships and Vessels you shall take, with their Guns, Rigging, Tackle, Apparel, Furniture and Landings to some convenient Port or Ports of the United Colonies, [in order] that Proceedings may thereupon be had in due Form before the Courts which are or shall be there appointed to hear and determine Causes civil and maritime.

You or one of your Chief Officers shall bring or send the master and Pilot and one or more principal Person or persons of the Company of every ship or vessel by you taken, as soon after the Capture as may be to the Judge or Judges of such Court aforesaid, to be examined upon Oath, and make Answer to the Interrogatories which may be examined upon Oath, and make Answer to the Interrogatories which may be propounded touching the Interest or property of the Ship or Vessel, and her Lading [her cargo]; at the same Time you shall deliver or cause to be delivered to the Judge or Judges, all Passes, Sea-Briefs, Charter-Parties, Bills of Lading, Dockets, Letters, and other Documents and Writings found on Board, proving the said Papers by the Affidavit of yourself, or some other Person present at the Capture, to be produced as they were received, without Fraud, Addition, Subduction or Embezzlement.

You shall keep and preserve every Ship or Vessel and Cargo by you taken, until they shall by sentence of a Couret properly authorized to be adjudged lawful Prize, not selling, spoiling, wasting or diminishing the same, or breaking the Bulk thereof [that means "you shall not remove anything from the cargo of a captured ship"].

If you or any of your Officers and Crew shall, in cold Blood, kill or maim, or by Torture or otherwise, cruelly, inhumanely, and contrary to common Usage and the Practice of civilized nations in War, treat any such person or persons surprised [encountered] in the Ship or Vessel you shall take, the Offender shall be severely punished.

You shall, by all convenient Opportunities, send to Congress written Accounts of the Captures you shall make, with the Number and names of the Captives. Copies of your Journal from Time to Time, and Intelligence of what may occur or be discovered concerning the Designs of the Enemy, and the Destination, Motions and Operations of their Fleets and Armies.

One Third, at the least, of your whole Company shall be land–Men. [This provision probably reflected the continuing shortage of sailors and the concomitant need to train landmen in nautical duties.][157]

Readers today should understand that, as a practical matter, the legal distinction between privateers, on the one hand, and pirates, on the other, was non–existent to the victims who were attacked by either of them on the high seas.

Both behaved in the same way by stopping, boarding, and capturing ships they encountered, using as much force as needed to accomplish their ends. The only real difference between them was that privateers held an official licence (the letter of marque) from their home government. This meant that, if captured, they would be treated as prisoners of war and jailed until they could be exchanged, rather than being executed as pirates.

What is perhaps most interesting to historians today, however, is that by ignoring the growing threat posed to British ships by the many American privateers until it was simply too late for the British to suppress them, the British had effectively sealed their own fate in the Revolutionary War.

This fatal end result was due to several interlocking factors:

- The intervention in the war in support of the Americans by some of the major European powers, notably France, Spain, and Holland.
- The successful maritime warfare being waged by American privateers against British shipping, and its concomitant result of appreciably strengthening the American desire for independence.

- The inability of the Royal Navy, chiefly due to its lack of enough ships and sailors and its urgent military involvements in other parts of the world, to blockade all the American ports at the same time and thus prevent the Americans from using them.[158]

This enabled the American colonists to continue to transport arms, ammunition, and military items to wherever they were most needed, and at the same time, to export desirable tropical products from the Caribbean islands to the American mainland.[159]

The wide range of American vessels had skilled men at their helms. These ships ranged in size from 20-foot to 30-foot-long whaleboats crewed by only a handful of men to much bigger and more heavily staffed vessels. Home ports for privateer ships included Portsmouth, New Hampshire; Boston, Salem, Beverly, Falmouth, and Newburyport in Massachusetts; Philadelphia, Pennsylvania; Baltimore, Maryland; New London, New Haven, Norwich, and Wethersfield, Connecticut; Providence, Rhode Island; and Richmond, Virginia.

In addition to fast single-masted Bermuda sloops, two-masted schooners and brigantines were also favoured because these were the ships most easily available to American seamen. The evasive capabilities of the Bermuda sloops made them ideal choices for pirates, smugglers, and privateers. A sloop rig on a boat gave it the availability to sail very close to the wind without the need to tack.

A Bermuda sloop could thus outrun most other ships simply by turning closer into the wind and leaving its pursuers far behind. Some naval historians have speculated about the likely impact of the large number of Bermuda sloops that were in action during the Revolutionary War. These fast little boats were built in Bermuda, outfitted as privateers, and then illegally sold to the Americans. There may have been more than 1,000 of them at sea in the Caribbean at any one time. If so, they must have played a notable if now-unsung role in helping the Americans to win their independence.

To conclude our discussion of the Revolutionary War as a whole, we can now return the work of Edgar Stanton Maclay, who made the following salient points:

- "The last three years of the war for American independence were marked by an almost complete suspension of maritime activity on the part of Continental [British] warships [due to their limited numbers at sea and to their losses to American warships], and a remarkable increase in the number and activity of our [own] privateers."[160]

- "It can readily be understood, therefore, that had it not been for our privateers, the Stars and Stripes [the American flag] would have been, for all practical purposes, completely swept from the seas. It was the astonishing development of this form of maritime warfare that enabled the struggling colonists to hold their own on the ocean..."

- "It is very much to be regretted that many of these cruises and actions have not been recorded. A number of battles were fought ... but as these vessels sailed merely in a private capacity, most of their logs were lost [or were simply destroyed] a few years after they returned to port, and what data have been preserved are, as a rule, [only] meagre and fragmentary. Enough, however, to show ... their [important] bearing on the results of the war."

Maclay also offers us two short but very informative tables, the first on the comparative numbers of British and American armed ships during the Revolutionary War, and the second on the numbers of guns carried by both British and American ships then.[161]

The first table shows that the number American privateers rose from a low point of seventy-three privateers in 1777, carrying 730 guns, to a high point of 449 privateers in 1781, carrying 6,735 guns. In the same era, however, the number of British warships fell from a high point of thirty-four in 1777 to a low of only seven in 1782, which was near the end of the war.

The second table shows that number of guns carried by American privateers rose from a low point of only 730 guns in 1777 to a high point of 4,845 guns in 1782. At the same time, though, the number of British guns fell from 680 guns in 1778 to a low of 164 guns in 1781.

The first privateers sailing from Massachusetts in 1776 were small craft taken from the working fleet of the merchant service and were not ideally suited to their new and more demanding work. Many were sloops, some were schooners, but the favourite rig was the brigantine because it was faster and more easily manoeuvred than a sloop or a schooner.

As a result, it was often chosen by privateers and pirates, for intelligence-gathering at sea, to protect bigger ships, and for supply or landing purposes during an invasion. Easily recognized because a brigantine carried a large spanker sail with a square-rigged topsail on the mainmast, rather than the usual gaff-topsail, it was usually armed with a light cannon, backed up by swivel guns, muskets, and even pikes.[162]

Summing up the role of American privateers in the early stages of the Revolutionary War, the historian Thomas Clark wrote this in 1814:

The success of American privateers during the year 1777, in the capture of English merchantmen, was extremely great. Their daring spirit and boldness were unparalleled. Their enterprise was no longer confined to the American seas. The coasts of Europe were now covered with them. The shores of Great Britain were insulted [that is, were attacked] by these privateers, in a manner their hardiest enemies had never dared to attempt. Even the coasting trade of Ireland was rendered insecure...

The British merchants were [therefore] forced to adopt the mortifying expedient of chartering foreign vessels, particularly French, to transport English goods to the continent of Europe. Thus was the immense naval force of Great Britain rendered incompetent fully to protect her own shipping, by the privateers of a country that possessed not a single sail of the line [that is, no large well-armed ship of the line], and that had only been a year in existence as a nation.[163]

Chapter 8

Famous Privateers of New England

Many of the American privateer ships came from New England and much of the information in this chapter comes from a short but remarkably useful and nicely illustrated survey on this subject, which was privately printed in Boston by the State Street Trust Company in 1928.[164]

This little book is not a scholarly study but nevertheless still contains a good deal of historically useful insights. It argues, for example, that it was chiefly the flourishing of American privateering that permitted the embattled American colonists, against all odds, to hold their own the high seas and to contribute to American victory.

To support this thesis, the following estimates were put forward regarding American privateers and their armament during the Revolutionary War years of 1777 to 1782. Each ship would probably have carried somewhere between ten and twenty-six guns. They can be listed as follows:

1777: 73 privateers with 730 guns
1778: 115 privateers with 1,150 guns
1779: 167 privateers with 2,505 guns
1780: 228 privateers with 3,420 guns
1781: 449 privateers with 6,725 guns

1782: 323 privateers with 4,845 guns. (This number is lower than the 1781 figure because of privateer losses due to captures by the British, shipwrecks, or being blockaded in American ports.)[165]

One of the best-known New England privateer seamen was Captain Nathaniel Silsbee of Salem, Massachusetts. The following account from his autobiography tells this good story:

- While on the ship *Benjamin*, which was then sailing to Boston, Captain Silsbee kept his eyes on an enemy schooner that had been following his ship and obviously wanted to attack it. As the enemy ship suddenly approached his ship, Captain Silsbee called his crew to quarters (that is, he ordered them to man their stations for the coming battle).

- One of his officers, however, reported to him that four or five of the seamen on his own ship had refused to get ready to fight, claiming that when signing onto his ship they did not expect to fight and were unwilling to do so now.

- Captain Silsbee thereupon ordered these men to climb up the shrouds to repair the ratlines[166] (that is, he ordered them to climb up the rigging of the ship to repair its uppermost parts, which where the most exposed to enemy gunfire). They could not possibly object in any way to this order because carrying it out was clearly one of their normal duties as privateersmen.

- When the rebellious sailors did climb the rigging, they found themselves isolated on the one part of the ship that was the most vulnerable to cannon fire from the enemy ship, which was drawing ever-closer. In short, they were now in much graver danger than their shipmates were below. Quickly realizing this, they asked Captain Silsbee "to allow them to participate in the defence of the ship" by joining their shipmates in the relative safety below.

- He quickly agreed, and as soon as they were at their places and manning the guns, he then ordered that all the six guns of his ship be fired at the enemy ship in one crushing broadside. As a result, the enemy ship quickly veered off, either because of the "unexpected resistance on our part, or by any damage caused by that resistance, we could not ascertain."[167]

Since being a privateersman could be very hard physical work during two eight-hour shifts each day, crewmen had to be well-fed in order to keep up their physical strength and their willingness to obey, unquestionably, any orders from the captain or from his officers. Even on a relatively short cruise, however, a big crew needed a great deal of food.

For example, when the New London-based privateer *American Revenue* set sail on a cruise of just over one month in the summer of 1776, she carried in her hold twenty-three barrels of salted beef, twenty-eight-and-a-half barrels of salted pork, 3,370 lbs of hardtack (rock-hard baked biscuits that first had to be soaked in water or coffee to make them palatable), and seven bushels of corn, each bushel weighing 65 lbs, and a sizeable amount of rum, too.[168]

Food on the privateer *America*, for example, was prepared by a ship's cook. The usual bill of fare ran along the following lines:

Monday:	beef, pork, and peas
Tuesday:	beef and potatoes
Wednesday:	lobscouse (a combination meat, fish, and ship's biscuit, served as a stew)
Thursday:	beef and pudding
Friday:	beef, pork, and beans
Saturday:	salt fish, pork, and potatoes
Sunday:	beef and molasses

In addition, each man received 1 lb of bread a day; ½ pint of spirit (probably watered rum); 1 pint of coffee, morning and night; and ½ pint of vinegar a week.[169]

An unusual bit of close and successful teamwork in New England between American land and sea forces during the Revolutionary War can be noted here.[170]

In 1783, the British privateer *Three Brothers* had been attacking American facilities along Long Island Sound. Under a prearranged plan, forty American soldiers boarded the fast sloop *Julius Caesar* as soon as the British privateer came into sight.

When the sloop got close to the privateer, "it received a broadside from the privateer for its trouble", followed by additional shots from swivel cannons and from muskets. However, the American soldiers who had been hidden from British sight until the privateer closed for boarding, that is, until it got so close that its men were ready to clamber aboard the American ship and conquer it.

The Americans then rose up and fired a single volley of heavy musket balls. Immediately afterwards, they swarmed aboard the British ship, armed with muskets and fixed bayonets, and captured it. In the process, it is said, the British captain and several of his crewmen "were snuffed out in this single volley". There were no American casualties.

Chapter 9

The Role of France in the Revolutionary War Era

From about 1521 to 1559, during a time of continuing warfare with Spain, the kings of France authorized their privateers to attack and plunder whenever possible both the Spanish galleons (treasure ships) and the Spanish colonial cities in the Caribbean. The privateers attacked both quite successfully with great gusto and for great profit.

Earlier, however, Spain's chief rival on the world stage had been the French king, Francis I. In addition to sponsoring French voyages of exploration and discovery to the New World, he had also encouraged French sea captains to siphon off a goodly share of Spanish silver, chiefly from the fabled Potosi silver mines in colonial Peru, which opened in 1546. In addition, by simple piracy, the French were also able to get their hands on a fair amount of gold mined in or stolen from other New World sources.[171]

By the seventeenth century, the French were showing even more interest in the trans-Atlantic world, especially in the vast region they now termed "New France".[172] They imagined that this vast and relatively unexplored area to be an unspoiled, freedom-loving, region which had never been shackled by before any rigorous confines of church or state. They also eagerly looked forward to exploiting all its boundless natural resources.

New France was huge, but despite its enormous size and its great potential wealth from fur-bearing animals, fisheries, and endless forests of fine and very tall trees ideal for ships' masts, it was peopled only very lightly by scattered tribes of pre-literate Native Americans and by tiny handfuls of hardy French explorers, beaver trappers, and missionaries. New France would remain under firm French control until it was finally lost to the British in 1763 as a result of the Seven Years' War.

The direct involvement of France as an ally of the rebellious American colonies began in 1775 when, very secretly, the French government began sending military supplies by sea to the Americans' Continental Army. Indeed, historians today agree it is very unlikely that the Americans could have conducted the war successfully and brought it to such a victorious conclusion without the influx of French money, weapons, ships, and troops.

Moreover – and last but certainly by no means least – France also gave official permission for American privateers to use French ports to repair and outfit their ships, to hire crewmen, to stage raids on enemy targets, and, finally, to sell at a goodly profit any of the prizes they seized at sea.

Considered as a whole, the active participation of France in the Revolutionary War era can best be summarized along the following lines:[173]

A good place to begin this story is with the Treaty of Paris in 1763, which ended the Seven Years' War of 1756 to 1763. France lost this war with Great Britain, in part because the French fleet was not able to deliver enough supplies and manpower to the front lines.

The net result of the war was that France was forced to surrender huge amounts of the territory it had occupied, e.g., Canada and the Ohio and Mississippi river basins, to the British. Moreover, the 1763 defeat also sparked a decline in the French economy, especially in its maritime trade.

To avoid any future setbacks, the next French king, Louis XV, therefore ordered the modernization of the French armed forces. He also kept a watchful eye on the proclamation of the independence of the thirteen American colonies in 1776.

The overriding goal of France was to weaken Britain's de facto control of the seas and to reduce its attacks on French merchant voyages in the Atlantic and elsewhere. Toward these ends, France would become the primary ally of the Americans, who as yet had no significant navy and who therefore had to rely chiefly on its numerous and very able privateers.

Until the Treaty of Amity and Commerce and the Treaty of Alliance was signed between France and the new American states in 1778, France had stopped short of direct military and naval intervention in the Revolutionary War. In April 1778, however, a French squadron left Toulon, the main French civilian and naval port from which French ships sailed between the Mediterranean and the French West Indies and America.

On 18 and 19 June 1778, a French ship, *La Belle Poule* (its name in French means "The Beautiful Hen"), which was en route back to France carrying the recently signed Treaty of Alliance between France and the United States, fought off a British frigate. This clash is said to have marked the official naval entry of France into the multi-sided Revolutionary War. On a more trivial fashion note, however, it also launched in about 1778 a large and very extravagant hairstyle among the rich, long-haired ladies of the French court. Sometimes referred to as *la Belle Poule*-style, this artistically arranged headpiece dramatically showed a ship under full sail in all its glory.[174]

It should not be forgotten that, at the beginning of the Revolutionary War, the thirteen American colonies had neither a trained well-equipped army (they had only militias) nor enough ships to constitute a viable navy. It was thus the American privateers, who had government permission to attack enemy shipping but who were funded by private investors, that became the precursors of the colonial navy.

The major turning point in overt French-American maritime cooperation did not come until 6 February 1778 when France and America formally signed two bilateral treaties, namely, a Treaty of Amity and Commerce, and a Treaty of Alliance.

The Treaty of Amity and Commerce gave "most-favoured-nation" trading privileges to the American colonies, which required that the trading partners treat each other equally. Even more important from a maritime point of view, however, these same treaties also made American privateers very welcome in French ports, where they could sell the ships that they had captured, repair their own ships, and recruit more crewmen.

In retrospect, the most important impacts of the entry of France into the turmoil of the Revolutionary War were two-fold:

- The first was the decisive role played by the French navy in the September 1781 Battle of the Chesapeake Bay. This two-hour fight resulted in a major French naval victory which had the decisively important result of preventing the British from reinforcing or evacuating the forces of Lord Cornwallis based at Yorktown, Virginia. This was the last major conflict in the Revolutionary War and, indeed, it was the one that directly cleared the way for American independence.

- The second impact was the subsequent Franco-American siege at Yorktown on 19 October 1781. This would prove to be the final nail in the coffin of British efforts to defeat their American colonists. The Revolutionary War was thus won by the Americans, who would formally seal their victory through the provisions of the Treaty of Paris in 1783.

Any account of the role of American privateers in the Revolutionary War must surely include mention of a brilliant young Philadelphian, William Bingham (1752-1804). He first made his mark in the Caribbean French colony of Martinique, which became a centre of American privateering.[175] Later in life, in 1780 he would be the richest person in the United States, thanks largely to his investments in privateers and to his trading skills.

Bingham entered the College (later the University) of Philadelphia in 1765 at the age of 13, graduating with honours three years later before investing in a number of successful shipping ventures. After going abroad for the customary Grand Tour of Europe, he was then given the plum assignment of being the secretary of the Continental Congress' Committee of Secret Correspondence (later renamed as the Committee of Foreign Affairs). Its goal was to develop close ties with potential allies, especially with France.

Soon, however, Bingham was reassigned to Martinique, ostensibly simply as an American businessman, but in reality, to arrange for munitions and supplies to be sent to the American colonies, and to learn to what extent France favoured their independence.

He was also instructed to extend American pioneering efforts by encouraging French privateers to attack British ships, and to get permission from the French to permit American privateers to use Martinique's port of Saint-Pierre to sell their prizes and to fit out for their next cruise.

This latter point was especially important because it would permit American privateers to operate in the Caribbean more easily: they would no longer have to sail all the way back to American ports to sell their prizes, and could buy in Saint-Pierre all the supplies and gear they needed for new voyages.

Bingham did extremely well in his assignment, handing out many blank commissions for privateers to fill in, helping American privateers to sell their prizes in Saint-Pierre, investing in privateering ships himself, and trying hard to involve France in the American war against Britain. He also took great care to make sure that while most of his crewmen were French, all his captains, plus a few token American sailors, were Americans, thus maintaining the fiction of American sponsorship for his privateering adventures.

Not surprisingly, however, Bingham's successes enraged the British. His actions threatened their lucrative sugar trade with their colonies in the Caribbean. These outposts generated by themselves an income of about £3 million, which was much more than the total amount earned by their imports from America.

The importance of the sugar island trade is evident because at a time when Britain and France were at war, King George complained to Lord Sandwich, one of his senior advisors, that "Our [Caribbean] islands must be defended, even at the risk of invasion of this island [the invasion of England itself]. If we lose our sugar islands, it will be impossible to raise money to continue [our war with France]."[176]

In addition, Britain's sugar colonies in the Caribbean employed many thousands of slaves, most of whom had been carried to the sugar islands by British ships. About 750,000 slaves were imported by Jamaica alone. The death rate of slaves was quite high due to overwork and lack of medical care, so continuing imports of new slaves were always necessary. The labour of these slaves generated huge profits. It was their life-long labour on the plantations, which were administered by white (usually British) overseers, that made these forced-labour enterprises so profitable.

American privateers were a very serious occupational hazard from the plantation owners' point of view. The British first tried to deal with this problem by having their sugar ships shepherded along by Royal Navy men-of-war, each of which could boast of up to 124 cannons and large, well-trained crews.

This is strategy worked well enough while the men-of-war were quite close to the sugar ships. However, as soon as the men-of-war left a convoy of sugar ships, then believing that all dangers were now well behind them, the very lightly armed sugar ships often came to grief.

In one case, for example, nine sugar ships were escorted for more than 500 miles by British men-of-war, but the men-of-war then peeled off as soon as they thought that any possible danger was now long past. However, as the London *Public Advertiser* reported, soon after the men-of-war departed, the American privateers *Revenge* and *Montgomery* appeared on the scene. They quickly captured seven of the nine sugar ships "with the greatest of ease", even though these two American raiders had a total of only twenty-two cannons between them.[177]

American privateers inflicted heavy losses on British convoys. Some examples of this are as follows:

- British losses to privateers were due in large part to the fact that the captains of Royal Navy ships, lacking both accurate charts and personal experience in these waters, could never estimate accurately just how many privateers were actually sailing out against them. This was because they basically sailed from all the secluded and, to the British, the largely unknown creeks and tiny bays of the scattered Caribbean islands.
- As a result, American privateers were virtually unchecked in their successful efforts to blockade colonial ports, seize merchant vessels, seriously threaten British colonial commerce, and even to raise real doubts about the continuing long-term security of these islands as British possessions.
- Privateers were thus always an important and low-cost way for nations to bolster their own sea power. When naval fleets could not guarantee security along the shipping lanes of the world, privateering would step in and would continue to play a major role in American colonial commerce.
- In 1777, London merchants complained to the British Admiralty that the capture of British vessels by American privateers and naval ships in the Caribbean Indies had already cost them £1.8 million.
- The next year, in 1778, statistics presented to the House of Lords showed that American privateers (both those commissioned by Bingham himself and others commissioned by the American states) had captured about 250 British ships trading in the Caribbean since the beginning of the Revolutionary War. As a result, the volume of British trade with the Caribbean had fallen no less than 66 per cent from its prewar levels.

- Losses of this magnitude not only ruined financially many British companies trading there, but also forced the British government to send out more Royal Navy ships as naval escorts for convoys of merchantmen. This simultaneously diverted these ships away from their more important naval duties, e.g., protecting convoys of British merchant ships; drove up insurance rates to reflect the ever-greater liabilities at sea; increased the prices of sugar, rum, and other Caribbean products ashore; and therefore made them much harder to consume and to export.[178]

In summary, then, the American privateers successfully continued to disrupt the Caribbean's plantation-based economy. Thanks to them, it became more and more dangerous for other traders to sail across the Atlantic and then to look for business among the many Caribbean islands.

American privateers seized about 25,000 hogsheads of sugar aboard ships sailing from the British Caribbean in 1776. Two captured ships from Barbados alone were estimated to have been worth £20,000. In short, by February 1777 American privateers had captured about 250 British West India merchant ships at sea. These successes contributed to the collapse of four major West India merchant companies in London and also involved the capture of some of their executives.[179]

The overall success of American privateers during the Revolutionary War, however, was due in no small part to one man: Benjamin Franklin (1706-1792), who was a polymath and variously excelled as an inventor, a printer, a philosopher, a publisher, a patriot, and perhaps most importantly for our purposes here, as an American diplomat.

He was also the only Founding Father of the United States to sign all four of the official documents that were critical in the creation of the United States. These were:

- The Declaration of Independence (1776)
- The Treaty of Alliance with France (1778)
- The Treaty of Paris (1783)
- The U.S. Constitution (1787)

Moreover, as if was not enough, in his diplomatic role in Paris it was Franklin who authorized American privateers to attack British ships. This was one of the most important steps in diplomacy ever taken by the Americans to bring the French into the Revolutionary War on the American side.

This he did by issuing letters of marque to both American ships and to foreign-owned vessels with foreign-manned crews – provided that the latter ships had some very tenuous American connection. For example, the captain of an American privateer was supposed to be an American, but Franklin sometimes ignored this stipulation entirely and allowed Irishmen to fill that position.[180]

The importance of France and of privateers to the United States did not, of course, end with the Revolutionary War. When Spain turned the Louisiana Territory over to an aggressive Napoleonic France in 1801, President Thomas Jefferson feared that France, then at war with Great Britain, would prevent American ships from using the Mississippi river.

As a precaution, Jefferson therefore sent Robert Livingston and James Monroe to France to arrange for the opening of a new port in New Orleans to encourage free trade for the United States. Unexpectedly, however, Napoleon then suddenly decided to sell the entire Louisiana Territory to the United States, the huge sale being finalized in 1803.

Jefferson also sent several American gunboats to New Orleans to maintain order there in the midst of what the American naval commander David Porter, who would later have a privateer named after him, described as "a very turbulent population".[181]

In 1810, this unruly population consisted of 24,552 people, the vast majority of whom were either French, Spanish or French-Spanish creoles, who were the descendants of African or of mixed heritage parents.[182] Only 3,200 of Louisiana's residents were ethnically Englishmen or Americans.

The majority of these residents strongly opposed the Americans because of their own support for the nascent Barataria Bay enterprise, which is defined below.

One of the Americans of the time complained that "The foreign Frenchmen residing among us take great interest in favour of their [own] countrymen, and the sympathies of the Creoles of the Country [the often multi-racial descendants of the French] seem also to be much excited."[183] Barataria Bay would become the linchpin of an illegal but very profitable privateering and smuggling business. It was located on the coast of Louisiana some 50 miles south of New Orleans.

It was accessible only to locals who knew the shallow local waterways very well, who were outlaws themselves, or who did good business with such disreputable local residents. Blank privateering commissions could easily be filled out to make visiting privateering ships appear to be fully law-abiding.

Chapter 10

Privateers in the War of 1812

The War of 1812, fought between the United States and Great Britain, was the last major act of American privateering, and one for which we have some fine historical sources, providing us with an excellent hands–on feel for combat operations afloat at that time. For all these reasons, a good deal of attention shall be devoted to them in this detailed chapter.

The War of 1812 drew to an end only because American privateers became unwilling to risk their own and their men's lives, and their own ships, by trying to break the strong Royal Navy blockade that had effectively closed off most of the American Atlantic ports to them.

In combat, no American privateer could, alone, hope to be a match for blockading British frigates or big British ships of the line.[184] Perhaps for this reason, the War of 1812 has never received anything like the amount of contemporary press coverage or later scholarly attention devoted to the Revolutionary War or to other American wars at sea.

The good news from our point of view, however, is that the modern reader has very easy access to one of the very best and most readable accounts of this struggle, namely, the 1899 *History of American Privateers* by Edgar Stanton Maclay. It has already been mentioned several times in this book, and much of the information in this chapter is drawn from his remarkably thorough study of the War of 1812.[185]

Maclay is also an excellent source on British opinions on the War of 1812. When this war was about to break out, he tells us that:

The English carried a vivid recollection of the damages our maritime forces [that is to say, the American privateers] had occasioned in first war [the Revolutionary War] and seemed to be more concerned with what American sea power might to in the impending war than what our land forces could do.

The *London Statesman* said:

> Everyone must recollect what they [the American privateers] did in the latter part of the American war. The [insurance] books at Lloyd's will recount it, and the rate of assurances at that time will clearly prove what their diminutive strength was able to effect in the face of our navy, and that nearly one hundred pennants [the flags of American privateers] were flying on our coast...

> In a predatory war of commerce [the War of 1812] Great Britain would have more to lose than to gain, because the Americans would retire within themselves, having everything they want for supplies, and what foreign commerce they might want to have would be carried on fast-sailing, armed vessels [that is to say, on privateers] which, as heretofore [in the Revolutionary War], would be able to fight or run, as best suited their force or inclination.[186]

Maclay noted that when the United States declared war against Great Britain on 18 June 1812, the American navy then consisted of only seventeen ships, armed with 442 guns and staffed by 5,000 men – a pitifully small force when compared to the might of Britain's Royal Navy. Indeed, during the first three months of the war, only eight of the American ships were in good enough shape to even to put to sea.

Nevertheless, the Americans responded very rapidly and effectively to the new war with Britain: "Every available pilot boat, merchant craft, coasting vessel, and fishing smack was quickly overhauled, mounted with a few guns, and sent out to sea with a [privateering] commission to 'burn, sink, and destroy' the enemy."

For its part of this concerted effort, between 1812 and 1815, Congress issued about 1,100 letters of marque. The American privateer ships that were so empowered managed to capture at least 1,200 British vessels – an impressive total when weighed against the only 250 such ships captured by the young U.S. Navy.

The Americans had only a few old frigates left over from the Revolutionary War, plus some weaker warships. In contrast, the Royal Navy had literally hundreds of ships and well-trained seamen, seasoned by fighting Napoleonic and European navies for more than twenty years. Although many of these British forces were already committed elsewhere, there were still enough frigates and other warships at hand to protect Britain's Caribbean possessions against the French, and to defend Canada against the Americans.[187]

An American newspaper on 1 July 1812, however, assured its readers that "The people of the Eastern States are laboring almost day and night to fit out privateers. Two have already sailed from Salem and ten others are getting ready for sea." By the middle of October 1812, New York alone had sent out twenty-six privateers, mounting some 300 guns and manned by more than 2,000 men.[188]

It was said during the War of 1812 that American privateersmen had an "audacious impudence" that stood them in good stead in combat operations. The case of the New York privateer ship *Paul Jones* can be cited here to make this point.

This vessel put to sea at the outbreak of the War of 1812 with a complement (a crew) of 120 men – but with only three guns in place, even though she had seventeen gun ports.

One of her first prizes was the heavily armed British merchantman *Hassan*, carrying fourteen guns but with a small crew of only twenty men. Her cargo, however, was worth $200,000 at the time. The captain of the *Paul Jones* is said to have hit on a clever plan to capture this lucrative prize.

He had his carpenters saw off some spare masts so that they were the same length as the barrels of his ship's guns; paint them black; mount them on empty buckets to serve as pretend-wheels; and then roll them into place at ship's empty gun ports.

At the same time, he also ordered all his men who could be spared for a few minutes to station themselves very visibly in his ship's rigging, so the enemy would be "overawed" by the apparently huge size of his crew. These deceptions worked so well that the *Hassan* quickly surrendered to the *Paul Jones* without a single shot being fired![189]

This same era heralded the end of large-scale international privateering, excluding a few low-level skirmishes in Central and South America. The gradual development of iron hulls, steam-powered ships, "torpedoes" (naval mines), rockets, and breech-loading cannons meant that privately owned merchant ships now had no chance of mastering the modern and very powerful naval vessels ready and willing to defend both themselves and their international trade routes whenever the need arose.

As already noted, because the War of 1812 war involved so many different players (even including Native Americans); was spread so far over the watery world; and was so inconclusive (it did not generate a single noteworthy historical result), this war has not received much scholarly attention in recent years. Nevertheless, it is now still useful to be able to say something here about the importance of privateering in it.

By the end of the War of 1812, there had been a great growth in American privateering. Ship owners and ship investors alike quickly exploited the opportunity to make money by building and launching literally hundreds of privateering vessels. From their own points of view, it was reasonably cheap to do so and might pay off very handsomely.

This process probably peaked during the second year of the war, when more than 500 American privateer ships were already at sea or were getting ready for action by supplying themselves in ports. They preyed so effectively on British commerce, in fact, that the British soon found it necessary to safeguard their own unarmed or only very lightly armed merchant convoys by having them escorted by Royal Navy warships.

The British countered this American privateering success by setting up such an effective naval blockade of the east coast of the United States that, by late 1814, most American privateers preferred to remain safely in port. When the war finally ended in 1815, the joint "butcher's bill" (a contemporary slang expression meaning "losses in combat") was that over 1,000 British ships had been sunk, captured, or destroyed, and the American economy itself had been badly hurt.

One of the best single summaries available makes the following points:

By 1812, privateering was acknowledged as an ideal way to harass the enemy at little or no cost to the government... Unlike the navy, privateers were essentially volunteer commerce raiders, determined to weaken the enemy economically rather than militarily.

So successful were they, that from July 1812 to February 1815, privateers from the United States, Britain, and the British provinces of New

Brunswick and Nova Scotia (as well as those sailing under the French and Spanish flags) all turned the shipping lanes from Newfoundland to the West Indies, Norway to West Africa, and even the South Pacific, into their hunting grounds.[190]

The American privateersman *David Porter* in the War of 1812

This ship was initially one of the best and fastest American pilot boats (nimble craft designed to pick up from or deliver a ship's pilot to a bigger ship located offshore) and she was later upgraded into being a privateer.

Captained by George Coggeshall, one of the ablest commanders in the privateer service, the *David Porter* carried one 18-pounder "long tom" amidships, and four 6-pounders elsewhere.[191] These guns gave her a respectable if not an enormous firepower.

The account used here, written by Edgar Stanton Maclay in 1899, is quite long but is so good and action-packed that it is included here more or less as printed, with only enough minor editing to explain some technical nautical terms.

The full dates of the events mentioned below are also given to make them seem more immediate. These events are, moreover, to use a traditional U.S. Marine Corps expression, "salty", meaning that they are very redolent of real-life experiences afloat at sea.

When this account opens, the privateer ship *David Porter* was lying at (moored at) Providence, Rhode Island, loading an assorted cargo destined for Charleson, South Carolina. As soon as he had finished loading, Captain Coggeshall sailed down the river to Newport, Rhode Island, where he moored and waited for a favourable opportunity to proceed to sea.

The major problem here was that the British feared entering into a fight with any well-armed American frigate, so whenever any large American ship was known to be in port, the British promptly stationed one of their own big ships of the line or their frigates near the same port for the express purpose of keeping the American ship bottled up there.

Captain Goggeshall, however, wanted to get out to sea at any risk, so he waited for a dark stormy night when he could rely both on his own thorough knowledge of the coast and on the cover of darkness to elude the British. Such an opportunity presented itself on 14 November 1813 when, toward evening, a big New England snowstorm rolled into the port from the northeast.

Captain Goggeshall correctly guessed that this storm would "cause the British officers to linger over their port and cheese after dinner longer than usual" and would discourage them from "keeping the deck" (taking up their supervisory positions on deck) in the snowstorm.

He also correctly guessed that the rank-and-file British sailors standing watch on deck would be "more anxiously seeking the protected lee side of a mast or a cabin" rather than actively looking for American frigates. For this reason, he boldly set sail and passed any hostile British ships that may have been nearby without being detected and challenged.

On her run to Charleston, the *David Porter* was chased several times by British cruisers, of which there were a good number along the American coast, but she managed to escape each time. On 26 November 1813, however, she experienced a chase that was too close to be pleasant.

At daybreak off the coast of Cape Romain, Captain Coggeshall saw a British brig of war just out of gunshot off his weather bow (the side of a sailing ship facing the wind), which promptly began to chase his own ship. The wind was off the land, and the British ship kept to windward, hoping to force the privateer leeward.

Just out of sight of the Charleston bar (a very shallow area where waves often break just outside the port), two more British brigs of war could be seen. Their job was to force the privateer into the trap that had been formed.

Knowing this, however, Captain Coggeshall resolved to risk sailing directly for the channel in the bar, where there would still be enough water to keep his ship from grounding. He therefore held steady on his course, while the two brigs did their best to get close enough to open fire on his ship.

After four hours of hard sailing, all the vessels being "bowed under the press of canvas" (their masts were bent by the force of the wind), the privateer reached the bar first and waited there for the leading brig to get within cannon-range. As soon as it did, the crew of the privateer opened fire with their "long tom", and with such accurate aim that its cannon ball hit the sea so close to one of the brigs that it threw spray onto its port quarter (the left side of the ship).

The brig did not have a "long tom", but only some short-range guns. This meant that she would have to "close quarters" (get much nearer to) the privateer in order to hit her with her guns.

This the commander of the brig quickly decided to do, but just at that moment two other American privateers (the *Decatur* and *Adeline*), sailed down from Charleston harbour to join the *David Porter* in the fight against the brigs.

The British ships, probably overestimating the power of all the American vessels, promptly squared their yards and ran to leeward (set their sails and headed downwind and away). Captain Coggeshall, for his part, safely unloaded his own cargo in Charleston, took on a new cargo of sea island cotton (the best-quality cotton) there, and then set sail for Bordeaux, France on 20 December 1813.

Reflecting the profits and the risk of privateering at this time, the value of the cotton that the *David Porter* took aboard in Charleston was $23,000. This cost seems quite high, given the fact that the cost of the cotton at the docks was then only 12 or 13 cents a pound. However, sailing a privateer with a big crew was not cheap: both marine insurance and seamen's wages were quite expensive, and prizes could be lost as well as gained.

A good example of a prize lost to the *David Porter* was that on 27 December 1813, during a strong gale out of the northwest, when she encountered a small English vessel (a brig) from Jamaica, bound for Nova Scotia, which she captured as a prize. Because the sea was too high to permit safe boarding, however, Captain Coggeshall ordered the master of the prize to follow the *David Porter* closely so that, when the weather improved, the captain could inspect her in more detail.

The English captain reluctantly obeyed, but when night fell, he had a disposition "to edge away" from the *David Porter*. Perceiving this, Captain Coggeshall called out to the British captain and told him "in pretty sharp language that if he continued to lag behind, or did not carry all the sail his brig would bear, he would soon feel the effects of *David Porter's* stern guns" (meaning that Captain Coggeshall would open fire on his ship).

This threat made the English captain do as he was told for a little while but later, at midnight, the weather suddenly became "very dark and squally", to the extent that Captain Coggeshall then "lost all trace of his first prize, nor did he [ever] see her again."

On 19 January 1814, Captain Coggeshall knew that several English warships were stationed off the Bordeaux Light (lighthouse) and so decided to run for the port of La Teste in the Arcachon Basin, west of Bordeaux. A powerful storm arose, however, and by the next day it blew with the force of a hurricane, raising a very dangerous cross sea. Such a sea-state of wind-generated ocean waves forms non-parallel wave systems, and has caused a large percentage of ship accidents because sailing into one set of waves necessitates sailing parallel to another set of waves. Vessels fare much better against large waves by sailing, whenever possible, directly perpendicular to the oncoming waves.

Captain Coggeshall prepared his ship for the storm as carefully as possible, heaving to (coming nearly to a full stop) under a double-reefed foresail, lowering his foreyard near the deck and making everything as tight (water-resistant) as possible.

At about noon, however, a tremendous wave struck his ship just behind the starboard fore shrouds, crushing in one of the stanchions, and split open the plank-sheer so that it was possible to see down into the hold (there was a grave danger that water could now run into the hold and sink the ship). The vessel was thrown on her beam ends, where for some time it was uncertain whether she would right herself or would continue to go over (there was now a grave danger of her turning entirely upside-down).

Fortunately, however, at this point the foresail split and the lee bulwark was torn away by the water. Being thus freed from such heavy pressure, the ship gradually righted herself, but the crew, fearing she would turn over, had already thrown overboard two of her heavy guns and some of her heavy water casks.

After nailing some tarred canvas and leather to keep water from running into the open plank-sheer, Captain Coggeshall got ready to make a sharp turn, fearing that the damage to his schooner might have affected the foremast.

To test whether this was indeed the case, he "jury-rigged" (made a temporary modification) to part of a small sail, attached a heavy rope and cable to it, and threw it overboard. "The effect was miraculous: [the drag of] this device broke the force of the waves and kept the schooner's head (bow) to the sea, so that she rode like a gull until the storm abated." It was not until the afternoon of the next day that the ship was finally able to set its sails again and make progress, and finally safely reached La Teste after a thirty-six-day voyage from Charleston.

At about this time, however, the British had captured Bordeaux. Captain Coggeshall feared that unless he could get his ship over the bar and out into the open sea, she would be seized by the British and made a prize.

The pilot of the port of La Teste, however, absolutely refused to take the ship over the bar at this time of war. He feared that, if he did so, he would then be forced to stay on the ship until it finally reached the United States – thus leaving his family impoverished in the meantime.

Captain Coggeshall offered the pilot triple his usual fee to cross the bar, and verbally also tried his level-best to persuade him to do so. Making no headway and fearing that his ship would be seized as a prize unless he acted very quickly, he then sized a loaded pistol, held it to the pilot's head, and declared that he would shoot him dead if he did not take the ship over the bar, and that he would do the same if the ship "took the ground" (if it hit the bar itself).

Now thoroughly frightened, the pilot navigated the ship safely over the bar in less than fifteen minutes. A few days later, he was reunited with his family, and the ship safely made her own way alone out into the open sea.

The next adventure was not long in coming. At daylight on 15 March 1814, the *David Porter* had a very narrow escape from being captured. Her lookout reported a large and well-armed frigate not far from her. This turned out to be an enemy ship and there seemed to be no way for the *David Porter* to avoid being attacked by her. However, Captain Coggeshall came up with a clever plan.

He gave orders that the large square sail on his own ship be hoisted so that he could use it to sail before the wind and thus outpace the frigate. This he did, and at first it worked well enough. The frigate, however, then raised some additional sails and thus increased its own speed.

Trying to sail as fast as possible, the captain now ordered that holes be bored into some of the four water casks, that the water from them be cast on the sails so that the canvas would hold the wind better, and that the heavy sand ballast of the ship be thrown overboard. All this was done and, thus lightened, the ship began to leave the frigate in her wake. By four in the afternoon, the frigate was only a speck on the far horizon.

Now having time to take stock of his situation, the captain discovered that, during the chaotic conditions of the ship's close escape from danger, the ship's carpenter had by mistake emptied two of the four big water casks, leaving only two casks still filled.

Moreover, as the wind began to pick up, Captain Coggeshall found that his ship, now with too few heavy items still aboard her, had hardly enough ballast "to stand upon her bottom" (that is, to stay upright in the wind). Moreover, as if all this were not enough, there were also only a few loaves of soft bread left aboard to feed thirty-five very hungry crewmen.

Salvation unexpectedly arrived the next day, however. As the sun came up, the *David Porter* soon found itself in the middle of a small fleet of British merchant vessels laden with food and other supplies for the British forces. They were part of a much bigger British fleet and were led by a British brig, but they had become separated from the fleet a few days before. They were now in the hands of the Americans.

After taking possession of brig and its little fleet as his prize, Captain Coggeshall entered into an agreement with the master of the brig: in return for giving the Americans the supplies they needed so urgently, the British ships would then be free to leave.

Captain Coggeshall described the remarkable episode:

The master's cabin was filled with bags of hard biscuit, the staff of life,[192] which we took first, then got a fine supply of butter, hams, cheese, potatoes, porter, etc., and last, but by no means least, six casks of fresh water.

After this was done, the master asked me if I would make him a present of the brig and the residue of the cargo for his own private account, to which I willingly agreed, in consideration of the assistance I had received from him and his men...

I then gave him a certificate stating that though the brig was a lawful prize, I voluntarily gave her to him as a present. This was, of course, only a piece of tomfoolery, but it pleased the master, and we parted good friends.[193]

The remaining ships in the British fleet could not get very far in the light wind prevailing at the time, so in a short time the *David Porter* also seized a ship and two brigs that had been a mile or two of her lee beam.

Their cargos were then loaded onto the *David Porter*, so she was now nearly filled with a varied but valuable assortment of provisions, officers' and soldiers' uniforms, cocked hats, epaulets, small arms, musical instrument, cloth, and general merchandise. There would have been a ready market for all these items ashore.

While this transfer was going on, a fresh breeze sprang up from the southwest. It was now almost dark, and rain began to fall, encouraging Captain Coggeshall to stop loading goods on his privateer. His lookout reported a sail to windward and, going aloft with a telescope, he recognized a British frigate that had chased his ship only a few days before.

For some reason, the other British ships anchored near him had not yet noticed the frigate, and when Captain Coggeshall sailed close to his prizes, he signalled them to hoist their own lanterns. This they did, but in doing so, in the darkness they inadvertently became targets for the frigate, which promptly opened fire on them.

Quickly extinguishing all the lights of his own ship, the captain later joked that "I heard the frigate firing at her unfortunate countrymen, while we were partaking of an excellent meal at their expense" – using the foodstuffs which he had captured from them! A few days later, Captain Coggeshall was chased by a British frigate and a brig of war, but escaped unharmed.

An interesting point here is that the chief of the "long tom" gunnery crew of his ship was a Black man. The "long tom" was the gun on which the captain relied most heavily: "My only dependence [the captain wrote] was on my 18-pounder, mounted amidships on a pivot [so that its direction of fire could easily be changed]." For this gun, the captain had selected ten of the largest and strongest men of his crew: Philip, the Black captain of the gun was a huge man, over 6 feet tall, and was a general favourite with the officers and the crew.

The *David Porter* was a successful privateer during the war, capturing fifteen prizes. These included earning $1,000 from the American government as a bounty for ten captured prisoners. All told, the ship earned her owners about $20,000, and she was finally sold in Boston for $10,000.

Her new owners sent her to sea under the command of Captain J. Fish and she continued to be a good earner, earning $20,000 for capturing hides and tallow, and outrunning a British frigate and two sloops of war that chased her for 940 miles until she reached safety in New York in September 1814.

She set off on her last cruise in January 1815, looking for prey in the West Indies, but had to return to New York after eighty days at sea after capturing only three ships, one of which, however, the "coppered" brig *Flying Fish*, had a cargo worth $200,000. Copper sheathing was a way to protect the hull of a wooden ship from attack by shipworm, barnacles, and other marine growth by using copper plates nailed to the hull below the waterline.

An unusual and noteworthy feature of the maritime aspect of the War of 1812 was the occasional direct conflict between American privateers, on the one hand, and their British counterparts, on the other. The story of "privateers versus privateers" is as follows:[194]

> One of the first engagements of this kind occurred on 4 August 1812, when the American privateer *Shadow*, commanded by Captain J. Taylor, fought the British letter of marque privateer named either *May* or *Nancy*, commanded by Captain Affleck. It will be referred to here as "the new ship".

On that day, the lookout on the masthead of the *Shadow* reported that another ship was nearby. Captain Taylor was so keen to overtake this new ship that he set more sail on his own ship than the masts could bear, and during the afternoon his square-sail mast was carried away (broke off). This damage was repaired quickly, but the new ship began firing from her stern guns, to which Captain Taylor replied with the guns of his own ship.

It was by now quite dark and the two ships had been firing at each other at longish range for half an hour, without doing any damage. The new ship then hoisted a light in her mizzen rigging (this was a signal that the new ship wished to contact the *Shadow*), and Captain Taylor responded with a light of his own, and called out to the new ship. It turned out that she was a British ship from Liverpool, so Captain Taylor ordered it to send a boat with an officer to his own ship, bringing the new ship's papers.

The officer arrived, but without the ship's papers. He instead brought a note to Captain Taylor saying that a significant political change had taken place in Britain. Captain Taylor wanted proof of this, which was not provided, so the outcome was that the two ships opened fire at each other and continued to do so from time to time during the night.

When the sun came up the next day, Captain Taylor sailed close to the stern of the new ship and opened fire on it. In its return fire, an enemy cannonball hit Captain Taylor's ship in her starboard bow, which shattered the wood, dislodged the plank-sheer, and smashed some of her heavy timbers.

Shortly thereafter, his ship was hit again, but this time on the port side. The cannonball knocked to pieces the carriage (the supporting mechanism) of the one of the rear guns; killed six men there; and wounded three other crewmen. It killed Captain Taylor instantly by a small cannister-ball in his left temple (such small balls were often part of a cannon-blast).

At almost the same time, a big cannonball hit the hull of his ship "between wind and water" and started a dangerous leak there. The surviving officers saw that there was already 3 feet of water in the hold, and so withdrew from the fight. Amazingly, they were able to patch up the ship and sail to Philadelphia, where she was refitted and soon afterward sailed out on another cruise.

Later in the War of 1812, the *Shadow* was captured by the British; refitted; renamed *Fanny*, and, carrying nine guns, was put into their service as a privateer. En route to London, however, she was recaptured by the Baltimore privateer *Lawrence* and was sent back to the United States with a prize crew aboard her.

In the process, she was sailed into a Cuban port in distress, due to bad weather, but when she went to sea again, she was then lost with all hands, probably due to another bad storm. Before that, she had been one of the most successful privateers of the war, capturing thirteen merchantmen and, on one occasion, even beating off a powerful British brig of war.

A tussle between an American privateer and a British privateer took place in the summer of 1812, involving the privateers *Globe* (commanded by Captain Grant) of Baltimore, and *Lloyd* of Liverpool.

Captain Grant had boarded several vessels to inspect them, but met no ship he could actually attack until 31 July 1812, when a sail was discovered and chased. When Captain Grant got within gunshot of her, she hoisted English colours and began firing at his ship with her "long tom".

Since it was stormy weather, Captain Grant was unable to bring his own broadside guns to bear, but he decided nonetheless to pursue the English ship. When at last he was in a good position to fire, he opened fire at short range with all his broadside guns, having first carefully loaded them with a double charge of round shot (firing two cannonballs from each gun at the same time, which made up in much greater striking power for what was lost in accuracy).

The English ship, which turned out to be the privateer *Boyd* en route to Liverpool with a valuable cargo of coffee, dyewoods, and cotton, returned broadside for broadside. As the two ships drew very close to each other (probably less than 50 yards), they also exchanged, volley for volley, shots from their muskets and pistols. In the end, Captain Grant won the battle and put a prize crew aboard the *Boyd*, with orders to sail her to the nearest American port.

In July 1813, the American privateer *Matilda* encountered a large ship that the Americans mistakenly thought to be a merchantman. However, she proved to be the privateer *Lion*, which had been built as a frigate but was later converted to private use. She was very heavily armed and well-staffed, however, carrying twenty-eight guns and 120 men.

The American captain did not discover what a powerful ship she was until he had boarded her with nearly all his officers. Had he been followed at once by his seamen, he would certainly have captured her because most of the British crew had run below for safety. A heavy sea, however, now carried the two ships apart, leaving the American officers unsupported by their own men.

The officers of the *Lion* thereupon quickly seized the initiative, rallied their men, and, overpowering the officers of the privateer, made sail for the *Matilda* and soon compelled her to surrender. In this action, the American captain and twenty to thirty of his men were killed. The survivors – now prisoners – were put into another ship, which eventually brought them to New York.

One of the last actions between privateers in this war took place on 31 January 1815. At noon on that day, the American sixteen-gun privateer brig *Macdonough*, with Captain O. Wilson in command, was sailing off Rhode Island when her lookout saw a large ship to leeward, some 6 miles away. As the American ship drew nearer, Captain Wilson noticed that she was making signals to his ship to lure it nearer and apparently had two rows of gunports along her hull.

As he drew closer, he saw that the lower row of gunports was false, which suggested a deceitful plan, namely, that the strange ship was trying to appear much better armed than she actually was. By 2:30 in the afternoon, this ship was also using only seven of her guns to fire a broadside, but at the same time she was also directing a tremendous amount of musket fire at the American ship.

This led Captain Wilson to conclude that she had a large number of soldiers aboard and was supposed to land them wherever they could best support British forces ashore. For this reason, he "passed close under the enemy's bow and raked with effect" (in other words, he sailed very close to its bow and fired a broadside into this ship at close range).

He could now see that the decks of this ship were swarming with enemy troops, all firing their muskets at his ship as quickly as possible. This went on for fifteen minutes until Captain Wilson saw that the sails and rigging of his ship were in tatters, and that many of his own men had been killed or wounded. Moreover, several enemy cannonballs had pierced his privateer's hull and started bad leaks.

The bottom line was that, seeing little chance of capturing the enemy ship, Captain Wilson now sheered off (turned away from fight); at the same time, the captain of the enemy ship, who had also had enough, sailed away towards Tenerife.

Numbers of the enemy's men were seen slung over the sides of their ship, sitting on rope seats, and plugging up the many shot holes near her waterline. This privateer eventually returned safely to Savannah on 7 March, having taken nine prizes during her career in this war.

A remarkable feature of the War of 1812 was that on several occasions, American privateers fought the Royal Navy's ships of war, which were invariably bigger and better armed than they were. It is worth recounting a few of these incidents here.[195]

On 8 September 1812, for example, the American privateer *Diligent* of Philadelphia encountered the British ten-gun cruiser *Laura*. This British ship had already captured three American merchantmen and was then in the act of seizing a fourth ship when, at 3 in the afternoon, the *Diligent* appeared on the scene carrying ten 18-pounder carronades (heavy short-range guns), two 9-pounders, and staffed by a crew of forty-one men. As soon as the British realized that *Diligent* was "a ship of force" (that she was very well-armed), the two ships opened fire on each other at pistol shot (very close range), sometimes even touching each other.

The fight continued for about an hour, but neither ship was able to overcome the other. The American ship, however, was at last able to take the wind out of *Laura*'s sails by sailing very close to her, before running her bowsprit up onto the rear deck of the English ship. With the two ships thus virtually locked together, the Americans then opened fire with their small arms (muskets), boarded the British ship, and carried the day (won the battle).

The "butcher's bill" was fifteen men killed or wounded on the British side, and nine men killed or ten wounded on the American side.

One of the last engagements between American privateers and Royal Navy ships occurred on 12 July 1814 in the English Channel.[196]

The seven-gun privateer schooner *Syren*, skippered by Captain J.D. Daniels of Baltimore, put to sea in the spring of 1814 and set her course for British waters. On 12 July, however, she encountered the British cutter *Landrail* (a cutter was a fast ship's boat that could be sailed or rowed), which carried four short-range 12-pounders and was crewed by up to thirty-three men. The *Syren* had about fifty men aboard her at this time.

Since the British ship was carrying important dispatches, its commander, Lieutenant Robert Daniel Lancaster, set all his sails to avoid a battle that might result the loss of these important documents.

The American privateer was faster than the British cutter, however, and gradually outran her. A running fight then ensured, lasting more than an hour. In the end, the British, with seven of their men wounded, had to surrender. The American losses were three killed and fifteen wounded.

Captain Daniels then placed a prize crew aboard the British ship with orders to sail her to an American port, but she was recaptured at sea by the British and was sent into Halifax, Nova Scotia.

As for the American ship *Syren*, she was returning to the United States and was off Delaware on 16 November 1814 when she was chased by the British ships blockading the coast. Not being able, alone, to fight off the British vessels, her captain decided instead to run her ashore, where her crew first destroyed the ship, probably by setting her on fire, and then escaped overland on foot. During her career afloat, however, she had taken six British prizes.

Much more could be said here about American and British ship actions during this war, which ground on until 1815, but it is clear that both the American and British governments used privateers in much the same way. To avoid repetition, however, perhaps it is now time to summarize some of what we know.

In one of the earliest American official statements on this war, the Library of Congress tells us, citing an 1845 source, that Congress formally declared the War of 1812 in words which focused on privateering:

[We are now in a state of war] and the same is hereby declared to exist between the United Kingdom of Great Britain and Ireland and the dependencies thereof, and the United States of America and their Territories; and that the President of the United States is hereby authorized to use the whole land and naval forces of the United States to carry the same into effect, and to issue to private armed vessels of the United States commissions of marque and general reprisal, in such forms as he shall think proper, and under the seal of the United States, against the vessels, goods, tells and effects of the Government of the said United Kingdom of Great Britain and Ireland, and the subjects thereof.

At least 606 American privateers and letters of marque ships were licensed in the war, but only 27 per cent of them made more than one cruise. This shows both the large number of lost or unsuccessful privateer ships, and the owners' high degree of caution and very low tolerance of risk.[197]

It also helps to explain why some of the contemporary maritime statistics mentioned in this book are little more than estimates. Thus, for whatever historical reasons, they should be treated as being merely illustrative, not as being definitive.

Granting this fact, American navy warships are held to have seized or destroyed fifteen British warships during the war, while American privateers accounted for three additional warships. American privateers are said to have captured as many as 2,500 British cargo ships.[198]

An interesting historical footnote here is that about 127 American commissioned privateers sailed out of the key port of Baltimore, Maryland alone, and are estimated to have captured about 550 British cargo ships.[199]

As a result of the declaration of war, President James Madison issued 500 letters of marque. During the war, about 200 American ships succeeded in taking many British prizes. It cost American investors about $40,000 to buy and fully equip a large privateer, but since each prize could possibly net as much as $100,000, this was not a bad investment.

In the end, it was only the very high economic and commercial costs of the war on merchants, tradespeople, and consumers alike that pushed the two warring sides into a peaceful settlement.[200]

These costs included a British blockade of American shipping; the urgent need, thanks to the swarms of American privateers, for the British to rely on expensive long-distance convoys to protect their own cargo ships; and, finally, the rising costs of marine insurance (chiefly due to American privateering), which forced down maritime trade and drove up consumer prices.

The War of 1812 did indeed witness a very sharp resurgence of privateering. For example, the three-masted twenty-gun privateer *America* was one of the very best privateers of this war, seizing a remarkable total of twenty-six prizes. This ship was owned by the well-known Crowninshield family of Salem, Massachusetts – a family which had made its fortune by canny investments in privateering.[201]

A good black-and-white illustration of her, reproduced from an old painting owned by the son of one of her captains, shows her to have been a handsome and fast privateer when under full sail. During the course of the War of 1812, she earned her owners $600,000. Ships never last forever, however, and in 1831 she was sold at auction and broken up for her metal parts and furnishings.[202]

The privateer *America* spread an enormous amount of canvas (meaning that she had huge sails) and needed a big crew to sail her fast, safely, and well. It consisted of from 142 to 168 men, among which twenty were assigned to provide security on the ship, day and night, and to serve as sharpshooters when posted aloft in the ship's rigging during combat.

It was remarked by local observers that "her deck and rigging swarmed like a wasp's nest" due to the always-active seamen and officers aboard her. Well-armed with guns consisting of "eighteen long 9-pounders and two 18-pound carronades" (short-range but very powerful cannons), she captured and brought safely to port twenty-six prizes worth about $1.1 million and probably did an even greater amount of damage to enemy ships at sea.[203]

A contemporary painting, showing her escaping from a British frigate on 23 January 1815, was the result of her crewmen pouring water on the sails. This was done only in calm nearly windless weather to take full advantage of any breeze that might suddenly spring up. The seawater closed the pores in the sails and therefore made them draw better (catch the wind better).[204]

By far the most successful American privateer of the war, however, was the well-armed Boston brig *Yankee*, which captured forty prizes with a total value of over $3 million. Other similar privateers inflicted a growing toll on British merchant shipping. Some of the most famous ships were the schooners *Prince of Neufchatel*, *Chasseur*, and *Lyon*.[205]

Hundreds of British, American, and Canadian privateers made a real dent in overall international maritime commerce during the war. During privateering's peak in the second year of the war, there were usually as many as 500 American privateers at sea, forcing the British to resort to expensive long-distance transatlantic convoys to safeguard their own ships.[206]

By the time peace was finally declared in 1815, the British ship owners had lost over 1,000 merchant ships, while the maritime sector of the American economy, for its part, lay in ruins. After the war, sea-going commerce revived again but now faced a new, if temporary, appearance of piracy.

This came about because some of the newly independent maritime nations in Latin America were not sufficiently strong or well-organized enough to be able to prevent their numerous privateers from quickly slipping into outright piracy. Thus the 1810s and the 1820s were not always safe times for trade in the Caribbean. Indeed, it was not until the 1830s that local navies had the power and the training needed to suppress this new pirate menace.[207]

In the meantime, however, the fall of Napoleon in 1814 had allowed the British to send many more troops to North America and permitted the Royal Navy to reinforce its strict wartime blockade of the American economy. Not surprisingly, however, American privateers turned out to be a more significant problem for the Royal Navy and for British traders than the small and feeble United States Navy had been.

From the American point of view, the stars of the show were the lovely Baltimore privateer schooners, which ranged from their home port of Baltimore far across the Atlantic. Estimates of total ship losses on both sides during the War of 1812 vary considerably, so here, in the interests of simplicity, only a few samples of this very mixed and often contradictory picture are offered below.[208]

(1) During the war about 515 American privateers, working in conjunction with about twenty-six other non-privateer vessels on the American side, sailed out against some 106 privateering vessels on the British side.

(2) The U.S. Merchant Marine itself predates both the U.S. Coast Guard (1790) and the U.S. Navy (1797). It began service in 1775, when American revolutionaries captured the British schooner HMS *Margaretta*. This event became a key factor in prompting the Continental Congress and various colonies to begin issuing letters of marque to their own privateers during the Revolutionary War.

(3) In the War of 1812, the insurance firm Lloyd's of London believed that 1,175 British ships were taken. Of these, 373 were recaptured, resulting in a net loss of 802 ships.

(4) Different estimates offered by the Canadian historian Carl Benn say that American privateers seized 1,345 British ships, of which 750 were recaptured by the British.

(5) After the War of 1812, the Baltimore journalist Hezekiah Niles estimated in 1815 that during this war, about 2,500 British prizes had been captured by American forces. Writing in Baltimore's *Weekly Resister*, he gave a very full-bodied defence of privateering.

In it, he so perfectly captured the rationale of this policy, as it was publicly proclaimed and was practiced by the Americans in both the Revolutionary War and again in the War of 1812, that it is useful to quote him at some length here. Niles made the following points:[209]

What is war? Mr. Jefferson [American President Thomas Jefferson] described it as a contest of trying [to find out] who can do the other [party] the most harm...

In the United States, every possible encouragement should be given to privateering in time of war with a commercial nation. We have tens of thousands of seamen that without it [privateering] would be destitute of the means of support, and useless to their country. Our national ships [the weak American navy] are too few in number to give employment to a twentieth part of them, or [to] retaliate against the acts of the enemy.

But by licensing private armed vessels [by turning them into privateers for the course of a war], the whole naval force of the nation is truly brought to bear on the foe, and while the contest lasts [in order that it may be over as soon as possible], let every individual contribute his mite [his tiny amount], in the best way he can, to distress and harass the enemy, and [thus] compel him [to] make peace.

(6) American forces captured about 2,500 British merchantmen (cargo ships). Of these, about 1,000 were destroyed, ransomed, or released at the point of capture; about 1,500 were sent with prize crews toward American ports to be sold there. Of these latter ships, however, about half of them were recaptured at sea by Royal Navy or British privateers before they got to their intended destinations.

Due to the great size and power of the Royal Navy, the British did not have to rely on privateers. Most of the American merchant ships captured in the war were taken by the Royal Navy, not by British privateers. That said, however, privateering was still a very popular calling in some British colonies in the Caribbean, especially in Bermuda.

It was there that the "handy" (very nimble) Bermuda sloops captured numerous American ships during the war. These sloops were so well-designed and so well-made that they became part of the evolutionary process of the ever-better sailing ship design and construction that would culminate in the world-famous, fast, and very beautiful clipper ships of the mid-nineteenth century.

It is worth mentioning here one of the most remarkable American officers of the War of 1812 era: Joshua Barney (1759-1818).

Barney served in the Continental Navy during the Revolutionary War; in the French Navy during the French Revolutionary War (1793-1802, Britain vs. France); in the United States Navy; as a privateer captain; and, finally, as a commodore in the United States Navy during the War of 1812.

After the United States declared war on Britain in 1812, Barney assumed command of the American clipper-privateer *Rossie* and set out against British shipping. His ship's record at sea was impressive.

In the earliest days of the War of 1812, the *Rossie* received the first letter of marque and sailed that same day for a three-month privateering cruise from Newfoundland to New England and then down to the West Indies, with a crew of about 100 men, armed with ten 12-pounder guns and one 9-pounder swivel gun. During a ninety-day period, the *Rossie* captured, sank, or burned eighteen British ships worth a total of $1.5 million.

In perhaps Barney's most creative achievement, however, he put forward a bold new plan to defend Chesapeake Bay during the War of 1812.

He used the following argument: "I am therefore of the opinion that the only defence [against the more numerous and more powerful British ships] we have in our power is a Kind of Barge or Row-galley, so constructed, as to draw [only] a small draft of water, to carry Oars, light sails, and One heavy long gun [one big cannon]."[210]

His plan was that a flotilla of such shallow-draft privateer barges – each only 100 feet long and 15 feet wide, equipped with light sails, a small cannon mounted in the bow, and crewed by well-armed sailors – could be used to attack and harass the British.

The flotilla could then retreat to the safety of the shoal waters that are so common in the Chesapeake Bay region and where the deep-draft British ships could never follow them. Probably thanks to this idea, Barney was commissioned as the commander of the United States Flotilla Service in 1814.

In this capacity, he had the following advertisement printed in the 1 March 1814 edition of the *American & Commercial Daily Advertiser*:

Chesapeake Flotilla

Where an honourable and comfortable situation offers to men out of employ during the [present wartime British] Embargo; where Seamen and Landsmen[211] will receive two months' pay advanced, and their wives to receive half-pay monthly, and single men can provide for aging parents, and widowers for helpless children, in the same manner; with the advantage of always being near their families, and not to be drafted into the militia, or turned over to any other service. Apply to the recruiting officers or to JOSHUA BARNEY, Com'dt of U.S. Flotilla.

During this period, many residents of Baltimore joined privateer crews in order to attack British merchantmen. Their attacks were so frequent that a London newspaper urged its Loyalist readers in Baltimore to follow a fierce retaliatory policy: "The American navy [the privateers] must be annihilated – [Baltimore's] arsenals and dockyards must be consumed, and the turbulent inhabitants of Baltimore must be beaten into submission." [212]

The role of privateers in this war has generated a good range of comments:[213]

- Commerce raiding, both by privateering and by commissioned ships, was a preferred form of naval warfare. It was very effective in destroying or disrupting the logistic abilities of an enemy on the open sea by attacking its merchant shipping rather than by waging war directly against its armed forces or by using a blockade against them.

- Regarding the War of 1812, given three factors – the implementation of Jefferson gunboat diplomacy, the historic American objection to a standing military force run by career officers, and the traditional American reliance on state-based militias, the only real choice the American government had during this war was to adopt the concept of privateers, much earlier than it actually did.

- The success of Irish privateers when attacking British ships in the Irish Sea drove up shipping rates three times higher than they had been during the earlier war with Napoleon. Whether this did more damage to British interests than one additional American frigate would have done is debatable, but what is clear is that, at the end of the war, the privateers (which were the handy Baltimore schooners) were still operable, whereas the Navy's frigates were not.

- Henry Adams, the great-grandson and grandson of the two Adams presidents and a famous historian in his own right, concluded that American privateer ships were the nation's greatest success in the war. They contributed, he believed, more than the American navy did to the eventual decision of British political leaders to seek a peaceful end to the war.

- The flexibility and resourcefulness of the American privateers during the war strengthened President Madison's hand in a way that his army and naval forces could not.

One of the most successful privateer ships of the times was the brig *Grand Turk*, the second privateer vessel of that name. Built in Wiscasset, Maine in 1812, she was bought by a consortium of thirty men, most of them from Salem, although the two owners were from Boston.[214]

Her first cruise lasted 100 days and resulted in her taking several prizes, but she was forced to end her voyage in Portland, Maine because of the presence of two British frigates in the area. On her second cruise, she made for the coast of Ireland and captured seven prizes there.

Other successful cruises followed, the most interesting of which involved the British ship *Active Jane* from Liverpool. The *Grand Turk* seized her off Pernambuco, Brazil and at first found nothing of any interest aboard her except for some kegs marked "Nails 1 ½", which seemed worthy of selling to a shipyard.

When one of these kegs was being transferred to the *Grand Turk*, however, it broke open, and a shower of Brazilian/Portuguese coins rolled out. It turned out that each of the fourteen kegs so marked contained about $17,000 at the current rate of exchange!

The War of 1812 was soon over, however, and the *Grand Turk* returned to Boston. There she was sold to a leading American shipowner, who in 1816 resold her to a Spaniard in Havanna, Cuba.

In the years after the War of 1812, many seamen lost their jobs afloat and, in the words of a nineteenth-century American naval historian, "for the rest of their lives ground out a humble existence as drudging clerks, longshoremen, or wage earners. Like the noble ships they once commanded, their occupation was gone, and they were laid up to rust and wear out the balance of their days in an inglorious existence..."[215]

A Baltimore armed schooner: the privateer *Patapso*[216]

This ship entered service as a letter-of-marque trader and in this capacity, made successful trading voyages to France, Italy, and the West Indies. She also served briefly in 1813 as a scout vessel on lower Chesapeake Bay during the latter part of the War of 1812 and then cruised the Atlantic as a privateer.

She performed very well; her owners profited from their investment; and she was finally sold to foreign buyers only because her limited cargo space made her uneconomic to operate after the war. The *Patapso* is important to us here chiefly because a full and unique record of her building and outfitting costs, as well as the cost of the cargo for first voyage, was found in old manuscripts now held by the Maryland Historical Society.

Thomas Kemp, the ship's builder, received $26 per ton for this 74-foot-long, copper-sheathed, vessel with a burden in tons of 259. She was narrower than some similar ships and had a deeper hold. One of her cargos consisted of about 100,000 pounds of sugar; 120,000 pounds of coffee; 13,000 pounds of cotton; and 3 tons of logs.

When full of cargo and armed with her heavy guns, the *Patapso*, rode low in the water and was quite tender (that is, she required delicate handling when underway at sea). This design made her a very fast ship in fair weather, but very dangerous to handle in a storm. The surviving logs of similar ships, for example, contain frequent entries of decks being awash and of men being swept overboard to their deaths.

Chapter 11

The 1856 Paris Declaration Respecting Maritime Law

This declaration was an international multilateral treaty devised by seven initial signatory countries or other entities involved in the Crimean War of 1853 to 1856. A chief goal of the two major signatories (France and Great Britain), as well as of most of the other countries attending this conference, was to end privateering.

The first major objection against privateering had come from Spain. In the seventeenth century, after Spain and King James I of England had made peace in their war, the English statesman, writer, and explorer Sir Walter Raleigh continued, on his own initiative – and notably without any specific approval from the English monarchy – to attack and capture Spanish ships. The Spanish Ambassador strongly protested to London, and even though he was a great favourite of the monarch, Raleigh was arrested and was later executed in 1618.

There were many other lesser protests against privateering, too. For example, when British insurance company loses mounted rapidly due to the depredations of what were termed England's "little fishermen-privateers" in 1758, the government responded by imposing a minimum size on privateering vessels and requiring them to post a considerable bond.[217]

The French government had, on its own, abolished officially approved privateering in 1814. At that time, the validity of all the letters of marque it had previously issued automatically expired; no more such letters were ever issued. France thus became the only country that took any legislative action to end privateering before the Paris Declaration was signed in 1856.

A total of fifty-five countries would eventually subscribe to this treaty,[218] with signatory countries agreeing that no port could receive privateers, thus making it impossible for any privateers to survive. Now lacking legal access to foreign ports, they would be forced to return to their home ports, which might well have been hundreds or even thousands of miles away, to sell any prizes they captured at sea.[219]

Signatories endorsed this policy because otherwise privateers from relatively weak countries could continue to force more powerful countries, which depended heavily on international trade, to use big warships in order to protect their merchant ships from privateers. This "protection racket" was expensive and time-consuming, but it was the only way for the strong countries to avoid potentially heavy losses due to privateers sent out by weaker countries.

The Paris Declaration defined new international policies and focused on both neutral and belligerent shipping on the high seas. These new rules addressed three major points:

1. "Free ships make free goods" (in other words, goods that are transported in neutral ships – and are not Contraband of War – are not legitimate targets for belligerent ships).
2. Blockades must, in order to be legally binding, be effective in maritime terms: that is to say, they must be strong enough in military terms to prevent any landing on an enemy coast.
3. Privateering by all the parties signatory to the Paris Declaration, now or later, and the issuing of any letters of marque by them, is strictly forbidden.

The United States, however, never signed this treaty for two reasons.

The first was that the Americans wanted it to protect non-contraband civilian cargo from seizure by enemy warships. Under the long-standing provisions of international law, better known then as "the law of nations", private property that was immune from seizure on land could still legally be seized at sea as a wartime prize.

An underlying problem, however, was that there was no single body of international law accepted by all nations, or even by all European nations. Moreover, both Great Britain and France strongly opposed changing this provision of international law, and would have vetoed any American effort to do so. Since any effort to change international law along these lines was so certain to fail, it was never made by the Americans.

The second and much more important reason for the American refusal to sign lay on another front. Since the United States did not have a navy of its own – unlike some other more powerful countries – it was quite eager to retain the legal right to use privateers if need be. With no American purpose-built privateers at hand, it was easy to reconfigure civilian cargo ships and turn them into armed privateers in short order.

Moreover, from the American point of view, prohibiting privateers would have tipped the balance-of-power scale too much in favour of the European powers, which already tended to have large navies and thus did not need to resort to privateering. At the same time, the ever-increasing cost of ships, coupled with the greater motive power of vessels with advanced firepower, made it most unlikely that any new private investments in privateers would make financial sense.

In any case, most privateering came to an end only after the Paris Declaration, which had the full support of Great Britain – by far the greatest commercial and naval power in the world. However, during the American Civil War, the United States said that, although it would still not sign the declaration, it would nevertheless continue to respect its principles and thus refrain from sending out its own privateers.

The United States had opposed the Paris Declaration in the following words:

The right to privateers is as clear as is the right to use public armed ships, and as uncontestable as any other right appertaining to belligerents.

The policy of that law has been occasionally questioned, not, however, by the best authorities; but the law itself has been universally admitted, and most nations have not hesitated to avail themselves of it; it is as well supported by practice and public opinion as any other found in the Maritime Code.[220]

It was the British point of view, however, that really carried the day. As the statesman Lord Palmerston argued in a letter to his queen:

With regard to the proposal for an engagement against privateering, it seems to the [British] Cabinet that as Great Britain is the Power which has the most extensive commerce by sea all over the world, which the Privateers might attack, and has on the other Hand the largest Royal Navy which would do that which Privateers would perform [by attacking enemy ships], Great Britain would find it for her Interest to join in an agreement to abolish Privateering.

In fact, during the last war with France, though the French Navy was cooped up in its Ports, British Commerce suffered very materially from French Privateers fitted out in Foreign Ports.[221]

The Confederacy, for its part, agreed with most of the provisions of the Declaration except for the right of privateering. As we shall see later, Confederate privateers would be ordered to attack Union merchant ships. Perhaps more successfully, they were also used to run the Union blockade, which had been set up to prevent any military and other supplies from reaching the Confederate troops and civilian populations.

The Paris Declaration was the most dramatic step ever taken to control privateering. Its long-term success, however, was also due in large part to the gradual development of modern state systems of governance, which centralized national military control and political accountability over the use of military force, whether by land or by sea. Few, if any, modern statesmen were willing to surrender their right to control their own use of military force if need be.

Moreover, with the coming of more powerful steam engines, better communications, and better hull designs, modern warships could easily outrun private ships. On balance, then, these slow but irreversible changes helped to prevent all private actors from experimenting with privateering for their own purposes.

Chapter 12

Privateers in the Civil War

During the Civil War, the Union and the Confederacy both used privateers and commissioned ships as commerce raiders, but each side approached the conflict from very different points of view.[222] Today, many historians believe that the Confederate commerce raiders had only a modest overall impact on the war, that is, beyond encouraging some merchants to ship their goods in foreign bottoms (that is, in foreign ships), and pulling some Union warships off their more important blockade duties.

The U.S. Navy itself was relatively small: in addition, some 10 per cent of its officers had even resigned their commissions to join the Confederate forces. That said, however, the North still had almost all the ship-building expertise, the industrial infrastructure, and the highly skilled labour force it would need to expand its fleet easily and quickly, and, in the end, to win the war.

The South, on other hand, was still mired in a cotton-based agricultural economy entirely reliant on unskilled slave labour motivated by only brute force and fear.

Moreover, in the South, at the peak of the socio-economic pyramid was a very small pseudo-aristocratic governing class that did not value educational achievements at all and devoted itself chiefly to economic, social, and leisure-time pursuits.

The South had no warships of its own and only very limited ship-building skills because, in peacetime, it had always relied on the North's flourishing industries and on the North's foreign trade. During the war, however, it hit upon a four-fold naval strategy:

- Defend key Southern ports and rivers with forts, gunboat flotillas, and (later) ironclad vessels.

- Send out both Confederate privateers and commissioned Confederate naval ships to attack Union commerce at sea.
- Arrange to have Confederate raiders secretly built in Britain, even though this was technically illegal because Britain was a neutral power.
- Make sure that Confederate raiding vessels like CSS [Confederate Steam Ship] *Alabama* had a full set of sails in addition to their steam engines so they could stay at sea longer without having to land frequently in order to take on more coal.[223]

Confederate President Jefferson Davis quickly tried to build up the South's naval power by using privateers. As a first step, he eagerly issued letters of marque to all ship captains who were willing to attack Northern ships, and to commission them into the Confederate Navy.

He announced that:

I, Jefferson Davis, President of the Confederate States of America, do issue this, my proclamation, inviting all those who may desire by service in armed private vessels on the high seas, to aid this government in resisting so wanton and wicked an aggression, to make applications for commissions or letters of marque and reprisal, to be issued under the seal of these Confederate States...

When it became known that the Confederacy was willing and eager to pay almost any price for badly needed military supplies, local entrepreneurs in the South began to design and build lightweight seagoing steamships. These were used by the South as blockade runners because they were fast enough to outrun the slower Union ships staffing the blockade patrols.

In reply, however, U.S. President Abraham Lincoln promised that anyone who attacked a Union vessel would be considered a pirate and, after being tried, would promptly be executed.

For his part, Jefferson Davis then responded that his own government would execute one high-ranking Union prisoner in retaliation for every Southerner executed for piracy. Fortunately, the courts intervened, and captured Confederate privateersmen were always treated simply as prisoners of war, eventually being exchanged for Union troops held by the South.

At first, Confederate privateers operated chiefly out of New Orleans, but their cruises soon focused on the Atlantic, where the Union Navy was expanding its own operations. Confederate privateers managed to sink several Union warships, but they were never numerous or strong enough to break the Northern blockade of Southern ports. As a result, and over time, the blockade had a very depressing effect on the Confederate economy.

When the war began, public support for the Confederacy was quite high in the South. Many ship owners there were initially eager to use privateers to further their cause that the spectre of Confederate privateers became a serious worry for the U.S. Navy. Although only a small portion of the many pro-privateer enthusiasts who applied for letters of marque actually set sail, numerous U.S. Navy ships had to be taken off their Union blockade duties and were reassigned to look for Confederate privateers.

The first Confederate raider, that is, a ship assigned to destroy Union commerce, came on duty in 1861. Before then, the Confederate government had acquired only a few insignificant vessels; Confederate privateering was not formally confirmed by the Confederate Congress until the spring of 1861.

After the former passenger steamer *Habana*, which had linked New Orleans and Cuba, was heavily modified, she reemerged as the Confederate commerce-raider CSS *Sumter*. Because she was now a formally commissioned ship of the Confederate Navy, she was no longer a privateer, but her story is still worth recounting for local colour here.[224]

This ship made eighteen captures and burned seven of them before she was laid up in Gibraltar for repairs in 1862 and was then sold to an English group to be used as a blockade-runner in the war.

She made her first capture when she overtook a ship from Maine known as the *Golden Rocket*. Raphael Semmes, the *Sumter*'s captain, has left us such vivid description of his burning of the *Golden Rocket* that a few excerpts are given below.

First, after *Sumter* had fired a warning shot across *Golden Rocket*'s bow to "bring her to", that is, to force her to stop, Semmes sent an officer with a boarding party, by a ship's boat, to interrogate the captain, to inspect the ship's papers, and to make sure that she was an American ship.

The crew of this now-doomed ship was then taken on board the *Sumter*, and the coal, the sailing gear, the chronometers, and any food or water needed by the *Sumter* were also removed. A burning torch was then applied to the ship.

To use Captain Semmes' own words:

The flame was not long in kindling, but leaped full-grown into the air in a very few minutes after its first faint glimmer had been seen...

[This] prize ship had been laid to [had come to rest] with her main topsail [her highest topsail] to the mast, and [because of the fire] all her light sails, though clewed up [tied up], were flying loose about the yards...

The mizzen-mast now went by the board [went overboard], then the foremast, and in a few minutes afterward, the great mainmast tottered, reeled, and fell over the ship's side into the sea, making a noise like that of the sturdy oak of the forests when it falls to the stroke of the axe man.

Not many Southern privateer vessels were captured, but two of them (*Savannah* and *Jefferson Davis*) were seized and did star in some important legal cases.

Of these two ships, the trial of the men of the privateer *Savannah* was the most important. The *Jefferson Davis* had run aground during a gale off St. Augustine, Florida in 1861 and could not get free. Her crew was saved but the ship herself was a total loss.

The United States government had initially maintained that the Civil War was simply an insurrection and that therefore, the Confederate letters of marque had no validity whatsoever. If this was indeed the case, however, it then followed that any Confederate seizure of a Union ship was simply an act of piracy, and one which deserved the death penalty.

Fortunately, in the trial of the crew of the *Savannah*, the government decided to treat them simply as prisoners of war, and they were later exchanged for other prisoners of war.

Nevertheless, Confederate privateer captains found it very difficult, due to the Union blockade, to get their prizes to a Confederate court to be adjudicated and sold there.

As a result, after the first heady year of the war, privateering was judged by the South to be a money-losing investment which was simply too risky for Confederate privateer investors, officers, and crews alike. Thereafter, as a practical matter, the Confederacy relied not on privateers but rather on the government-commissioned commerce raiders, such as *Alabama* and *Florida*.

The most beautiful ship to make Confederate history, however, was the finely built yacht *America*. She was not a privateer but had been owned by a self-styled English "Lord" who had bought her in Charleston at the beginning of the Civil War.

She first became a dispatch boat for the Confederate Navy; then carried Confederate officers to London to buy ships and guns there; and finally became a blockade-runner in 1861. Though she was mysteriously sunk in Florida (probably by Union supporters) in 1862, the U.S. Navy raised her for use as an armed schooner.

Long after the war ended, she remained moored in Annapolis, Maryland until a heavy snowfall crushed her old timbers in 1942. The high point of her long life, however, had come much earlier. This was when, as a private yacht, she had won the first International Cup Race in 1851, and had posed there, under full sail, for an impressive illustration.[225]

It is an interesting nautical footnote here that the most effective raiding vessels, for example, the *Alabama*, often had a full set of sails in addition to their steam engines. This backup let them stay at sea much longer because they did not have to stop at ports to take on more coal.

On a related naval front, President Lincoln had established a strong blockade of the South, which required a large number of Union ships to patrol the 2,500-mile-long Southern coast stretching from Virginia to Texas. This blockade by the U.S. Navy was very effective, and cut trade by the South to only 5 per cent of its peacetime levels.

At the same time, the navy's control of the inland waterways and of the coastal navigation of the South forced the Confederates to rely entirely on its very limited number of railroads, which soon became overloaded to the point of failure.

The efforts of Southern ships to run the blockade and thus bring essential military and other supplies to the hard-pressed South did become the stuff of legends, novels, and films. For example, Rhett Butler, one of the main characters in the 1936 novel *Gone with the Wind*, was a very successful blockade runner.

Despite Rhett's fictional achievements, however, more than two thirds of the 300 ships that tried to run the blockade were eventually captured or destroyed. The end results of such heavy losses were that the cost of imports rose, the income of the Southern government fell, and it became very much harder for the South to pay for the essential military items that had to be imported from abroad.[226]

The Confederate Navy's ships consisted of nine commerce raiders, five of which were built in Great Britain. Taken collectively, they destroyed or captured more than 250 Union merchantmen. These commerce raiders were not privateers under private ownership but were instead the official state-commissioned ships of the Confederate States Navy.

Aside from a few incidents of Confederate privateering, the South accomplished nothing of substance in this field because of the Union's vigilance in maintaining its blockade of the South. Most of the Confederate privateers were captured, sunk, or burned at sea. As a result, the Confederacy more or less had to abandon privateering – to the extent that, after 1861, it issued very few letters of marque.[227] Instead, Confederate seamen focused on blockade running to take out Southern products and bring in munitions of war.[228]

When the Civil War was finally over, however, the United States claimed that Great Britain had violated British neutrality by building commerce raiders, which had inflicted a great deal of damage on American ships.

After protracted legal proceedings known as the *Alabama* Claims, the Treaty of Washington (1871) at last awarded to the United States the sum of $15.5 million. This payment was for the damage inflicted on American vessels by the then-commissioned Confederate ship (and former privateer) *Alabama* during the war. The ship had destroyed or captured more than 250 American merchant vessels during the conflict.

There was also one major and unexpected result of this legal decision. The U.S. Merchant Marine soon lost fully one-half of its fleet of cargo ships: about 700 of them decided to re-register under foreign flags to avoid the legal liability of remaining under American registry.

Chapter 13

Privateers in Charleston, South Carolina

Charleston provided a great many privateers over the years because it was so conveniently located in terms of shipping. It also had both a skilled and an unskilled multi-racial labour force right at hand – ready, willing, and able to build and to maintain these and other vessels.

The net result was that, during the Revolutionary War and the War of 1812, approximately seventy-nine sail-powered privateers (mainly sloops) were built there. Later, a much larger number of steam-powered blockade runners either entered or left Charleston during the American Civil War.[229]

Charleston's maritime history is extremely interesting and is unusually well-documented. It had two early periods – namely, 1600-1700 and 1716-1720 – in which privateering-piracy flourished. These two activities were so intertwined that we can safely lump them together in the early parts of this chapter. Later, moreover, Charleston was also actively involved in privateering during the American Civil War. Its story, in brief, is as follows:

First settled by Europeans in 1670, Charleston soon became the principal port of the province of Carolina. It was a strategic point in a region important to the Spanish, the English, and the French alike during their frequent wars, which highlighted the region.

The English proprietary government was very weak and was often run by corrupt officials. Most of the traders and businessmen in Charleston had begun by dealing with legal commerce-raiding wartime privateers: the uncertain and violence-prone settings of the city suited all parties very well.

Moreover, the increasing trade of Charleston also lured in many foreign privateers who, understandably, were seen by the local citizens simply as pirates. Indeed, many had started their own careers as legal wartime privateers. Later, when there was so little law and order in the Charleston region, they thrived in this turbulent and uncertain setting: one could almost say that rule by cutlass replaced rule by law.

Like the merchants in most of the other colonies, Charleston's commercial figures were accustomed to working with smugglers, and therefore continued to welcome the cheap goods and currencies always on offer. Customs officers could not resist all the handsome bribes that helped trade to flow so smoothly, so "consorting with pirates" thus became one of the accusations flung by Charleston politicians at their rivals.

When word of the colony's deplorable reputation eventually drifted up to the Privy Council in England in 1684, the provincial government in Charleston was encouraged to pass a law suppressing "piracy". If this was ever done, however, it had no noticeable effect. Instead, the commercial dealings that Charleston men continued to have with the "pirates" eventually led to the expulsion of one provincial official in 1686 and of two provincial governors in the 1690s.

Throughout the colonial period, however, Spanish and French privateers did pose a real threat to Charleston during Queen Anne's War of 1701-1713.

In August 1706, for example, a Dutch privateer sloop from New York anchored in Charleston's harbour. Its captain and crew reported to the English defenders that a few days earlier they had fallen in with a French ship that was planning to attack Charleston.[230]

The captain of the Dutch sloop had hardly finished making his report when six columns of smoke arose from nearby Sullivan's Island – the signal that many ships were then waiting off the bar of the island. These ships turned out to be a French squadron from Martinique that had assembled at Havana but had been dispersed up the coast by a storm. It later attacked Charleston. Some accounts say that these ships were all privateers with commissions from Paris, but others speculated that they were French warships.

In any case, a nice story soon made the rounds about how clever the British defenders had been during this incident.

When the French raised a flag of truce, the English expressed their willingness to let a French officer meet with their governor to see if a truce could be negotiated by both sides. The English sent over a shallow-draft galley powered by sails or by oars to pick up the French officer – but only on the condition that he agreed to be blindfolded during the crossing.

This done, the officer (his eyes now uncovered) met with the governor and was quite amazed, during a very slow and formally escorted walk through the local town, by how many armed colonial militiamen he could see on the town's streets – and even stationed between the buildings. Indeed, there were four times more militiamen than he had ever expected to see in such a small town.

What the French officer did not realize, however, was that he was actually looking at the same militia units again and again. As soon as he walked very slowly by one site, these same men darted behind the buildings, only to reappear a short time later as a "new" military unit further down the street!

The end result of all the above was that a combined low-level attack by a joint expedition of French and Spanish privateers and naval ships raided targets near Charleston. They were beaten off, however, by a colonial flotilla led by Colonel William Rhett, a local English military officer.

That said, it should be noted that by the end of Queen Anne's War many thousands of unemployed privateers made their way to the Bahamas, where, desperately needing work, some of them flocked to New Providence Island because it was an up-and-coming centre for piracy.

This was particularly unfortunate, because what was now South Carolina itself had just emerged from a bloody war with the local Indians. This struggle left the colony weakened and singularly unprepared to repel all the pirates now flourishing along the South Carolina coast in 1717 and 1718.

Blackbeard, who we met in earlier pages of this book, was by far the most famous of them. With his death and the subsequent mass executions of other pirates, however, piracy in the province slowly died out in the 1720s.

Charleston evolved into being an important port in the British Empire when it became a major crossroads of maritime trade, chiefly between the 1730s and 1820s. Two famous prints of the city in 1739 and 1774 depict Charleston's harbour at the time as being crammed full of sailing vessels.

During the cool winter months from November to March, there were often about 100 ships riding at anchor in this port, waiting to load or unload their cargo. The large number of privateers that prowled the waters off Charleston resulted in an increased Royal Navy presence. This in turn increased the need for more extensive ship repair facilities there.[231]

Throughout the year, between 200 and 300 ships would leave Charleston habour. These were vessels of all shapes and sizes. As the South Carolina historian George C. Rodgers, Jr. wrote in 1969:

Vessels of all kinds – ships, brigantines, snows, schooners, and sloops – came after the hurricane season in order to transport the crops to market. Captured xebecs (ships similar to old-fashioned galleys), guarda-costas (coast guard ships), two-masted shallow-draft sailboats, large American Indian canoes, and plantation flats (flat-bottomed plantation boats) – all these were part of the very busy ship traffic.

Charleston's golden age coincided with the last century of the age of sailing vessels. As long as the age of sail lasted, Charleston remained on the main Atlantic route, which circumnavigated the Bermuda High (a major feature of the regional weather system).

To do so, vessels leaving England, or leaving any European port for North America, generally sailed south to the Azores to catch the trade winds there, and then made full sail for the West Indies. They next made their way through these islands to the Gulf Stream. From the Florida Keys to Cape Hatteras they hugged the American coast before veering off to England and northern Europe. It was a great circle course and Charleston was on its western edge: sailing vessels brought men from all parts of the Atlantic world to Charleston.[232]

Historically, commissioning a fleet of privateers was the easiest and fastest way for a country to begin building up an armed naval force from scratch. This was especially true for an English colony such as South Carolina, which already had a great deal of civilian maritime expertise right at hand, but no standing navy that was funded by and responsible to local authorities.

The earliest account of privateers at Charleston (then known as Charles Town) dates from 1682, when an Englishman named Thomas Newe wrote home to friends in England that among the local ships in Charles Town, he also saw a number of privateer ships, which he said were then "tolerated, if not encouraged". He also saw a French privateer of four guns and thirty men bringing in a Spanish prize of sixteen guns and 100 men.[233]

In 1739, a privateering commission was granted in Charles Town to the merchant George Austin and the shipmaster James Whitefield. They had to post a bond of £2,000 and had to swear "to obey all orders from the governor who empowered them to take and destroy the ships, vessels, and goods of the King of Spain and his subjects, and to bring any captured prizes into English ports for adjudication in the Vice Admiralty Courts."[234]

In the runup to the Revolutionary War, South Carolina wanted to strengthen its feeble colonial navy. In so doing, it sometimes acted before thinking very carefully. A good example here is William Henry Drayton, a Revolutionary War patriot who was quite intelligent and socially well-connected, but far too much of a self-promoter and who knew absolutely nothing about warships.

Drayton wanted, among other things, to be the senior caption of South Carolina's navy. Toward that end, he asked for and received colonial permission and funding to have a small heavily armed schooner built. Named *Prosper*, she was designed to attack and sink British warships off Charleston. When war did break out, however, South Carlina's naval experts decided that this ship, now outfitted with more than twenty heavy guns, would be "cranky and unseaworthy" and therefore lacked the stability necessary for combat.

The upshot was that this ship was stripped of her crew, armament, and gear and was auctioned off. She was bought by a local businessman, who in 1777 sent her out from Charleston, bound for Bordeaux, France, with a cargo of rice and tobacco.

She was captured en route by a British privateer, however, and her only lasting achievement was to be the subject of a satirical British poem about "Admiral Drayton, who never smell'd powder, nor handled a rope".[235]

French privateers at Charleston after the American Revolutionary War

From the outset of revolutionary France's war with Great Britain in 1793, Charleston, due to its important position on the flank of the Gulf Stream and on the main trade route to Europe from the Caribbean, was a priority base for French privateers.

That same year, an important French official, "Citizen" Edmond Charles Gênet, arrived in Charleston on a French warship en route to Philadelphia, where he was to take up his duties as the French Ambassador to the United States.

Believed to be acting under authority of the French government, Gênet quickly issued about 250 privateer commissions to various privateering syndicates in Charleston. Within ten days of his arrival, five of these privateer ships had set sail, and one of them had already captured a British brig, which it proudly brought into Charleston's harbour. This British ship, named *Little Sarah*, was promptly given a new French name (*La Petite Democrat*, that is, "The Little Democrat") and was immediately sent out to sea as a privateer.

By September 1793, the French privateers commissioned in American ports had moved elsewhere. No national authority would now allow them to keep their prizes, which they had previously been able to retain, after simply first sending them to American courts for legal condemnation.

However, privateers commissioned in France and in her colonies were permitted to keep their prizes after condemnation. The bad news from the privateers' point of view was that northern harbours in the United States were not so favourably inclined. Nevertheless, through the first half of 1793, French privateers still continued to operate out of Charleston and to bring their prizes there for disposal.

Popular support for France grew in Charleston in the wake of France's victories in Europe. Indeed, Charleston soon became filled with the privateers and other soldiers of fortune – to the extent that their raucous behavior and drunken brawls gave rise to the first stirrings of anti-French sentiments there.

The upshot was that while the French government replaced Gênet with a less controversial ambassador, new privateers quickly appeared in Charleston, many of them converted from captured prizes. Moreover, thanks in no small part to the decisions of Judge Thomas Bee of the U.S. District Court (who will be discussed later), privateering peaked in Charleston in the first half of 1795.

It fell off thereafter, however, due to the 1795 Jay Treaty with Great Britain, which the American public saw as an American sell-out to British arrogance. It would spell the end of French privateering in American ports because it prevented French ships from arming, selling prizes, or provisioning beyond whatever was necessary for them to reach the nearest French port.[236]

Long afterwards, Charleston became a very active if short-lived centre of privateering activity during the War of 1812 and the Civil War. While its colonial ship-building industry was not as extensive or as impressive as that of its more-developed counterpart in the northern American colonies, some of the privateer and other ships built there were famous for their quality and their durability. This was due to two interlocking factors.[237]

First, the Charleston region had an abundance of excellent timber for shipbuilding. Live oak timbers, when properly cured, were one of the very best and most long-lasting ship-building materials in the whole world.

These trees flourished in the coastal areas of the southeastern region from North Carolina to Texas. The great durability of live oak ship's timbers was a result of their growing best along the banks of the saltwater creeks and inlets. As the wood ages, it increases in toughness, to the extent that it was also impossible to cut it with the hand tools of the time, so naturally curved pieces of the wood were much preferred. For this reason, live oak was best suited to making the curved frames of a ship.

Second, Charleston itself already had a dynamic trade-oriented economy and an outstanding natural harbour, both of which encouraged coastal, regional, and international trade.

The downsides, however, were that Carolina businessmen could make much more money as planters than as shipbuilders; there was very stiff competition from better-equipped northern builders; and the presence of large numbers of slaves discouraged to both white and Black workers from developing their own skills and abilities to the maximum extent.

During the War of 1812, the Charleston privateer *Saucy Jack* took the following prizes: six ships, six brigs, nine schooners, and two sloops. As part of this booty, she seized the "large and elegant ship *Pelham*" in 1814, whose cargo consisted of 194 packages containing the dry goods, hardware, and the wide range of other items listed verbatim below, all of which could be sold for a goodly profit:

India checks and stripes, gurrahs, romals, seersuckers, bedticks, ginghams, calicoes, shawls, Madras and Malabar handkerchiefs, Irish linens, lawn, shirtings, brown linen, duck, sheetings, osnaburgs, baggins, shoes, boots, saddlery, etc. 300 packages of sundries, consisting of hardware, glassware, mustard pickles, sauces, preserves, porter, ale, Madeira and sherry lines, white lead, paints, gunpowder, linseed oil, glue, ochre, twines, seines, hats, etc.; one organ and one pianoforte.[238]

During the Civil War, Charleston sailors were not at all eager to serve in the Carolina State Navy: the level of pay was much too low and the level of danger much too high. Instead, these men lined up to join the crews of privateer ships.

Because most privateers were financed by Charleston merchants more interested in prize money than in naval glory, and who could afford to pay much more than the Carolina State Navy, their crews were well paid, chiefly when (but only if) lucrative prizes were actually taken at sea.

Another attraction of privateer service, however, was that standards of discipline aboard privateers were much more relaxed than on Carolina State Navy ships. Privateers usually attacked only unarmed or very lightly armed ships which would surrender quickly, so no spit-and-polish naval discipline was ever needed to capture them.

Earlier, the Continental Congress had based some of its own privateers at Charleston because of its favourable waterway location and the shipbuilding and ship-repair facilities so readily available there. To provide a flavour of these challenging times, a few selected examples of early privateer activities in the Charleston area can be cited.[239]

In August 1776, for example, the sloop *Swift*, under Captain Francis Morgan, became the first vessel commissioned in Charleston as a privateer. Captain Morgan was soon followed by Captain Andrew Groundwater, who together with the twelve-gun sloop *Vixen*,[240] under Captain Downham Newton, "came across" (encountered while under sail) the ten-gun schooner *Comet* at the harbour of Nassau.

To avoid the dangers of combat, the *Comet* retreated until she was under the protection of the cannons of the harbour's fort, and the *Swift* therefore left the scene. Shortly after this, however, the *Swift* was grounded on a reef during a gale and broke up. Her captain and crew were saved by being taken aboard the *Vixen*.

With shipwrecked Captain Groundwater as a passenger, the *Vixen* continued her cruising and her hunt for prizes. She captured the British sloop

Polly from Mississippi, which was bound for Dublin, Ireland with a cargo of barrel staves. This prize was sent to a South Carolina port to be sold.

The *Vixen* then teamed up with another Charleston privateer, the sloop *General Washington*, under Captain Hezekiah Anthony, and they jointly seized a rum-laden sloop, *Sally*, and sailed her to a safe port for sale. They next managed to capture the *Nancy*, a ship bound for London carrying 250 hogsheads of sugar, fifty hogsheads of rum, and eighty pipes of wine – a considerable amount of wine.

All told, however, privateering out of Charleston was neither a very easy nor a very safe business. For example, after his other adventures at sea, in March 1779 Captain Groundwater was charged with having had treasonable dealings with the British. He was convicted and hanged for this offence.

Contemporary records of Charleston's later privateers are, alas, quite incomplete. They suggest, however, that in the era of the War of 1812, numerous American privateers operated out of Charleston and that about seven Tory (pro-British) privateers did, too, but of course not at the same time.

The best summary of Charleston's privateers can be found in P.C. Coker's highly technical and brilliantly illustrated 1987 book, *Charleston's Maritime Heritage*. It makes some of the following historical points:

After word of the declaration of the War of 1812 finally reached Charleston (this process took six days), Congress passed legislation allowing American privateers to be commissioned to attack British ships. Local syndicates of patriotic investors quickly found three schooners that would meet this need and gave them letters of marque to prove that they were not pirates.

The crews for these and for later privateers were chiefly French citizens who had already had long histories of serving in privateers, both off the American coast and in the West Indies. The French ports they used were subject to attacks by the British during any war, however, so sailing out of American ports gave these men some degree of security while they were refitting their ships for further privateering activities against the British. It is believed that about thirty privateers used Charleston as a home port at one time or another.

The first privateer to set sail there at that time was named *Nonpareil* (French for "Matchless"). Four days after leaving Charleston, she captured and sent into port, as her prize, the 66-ton schooner *Leita Ann*, which was then bought by the U.S. Navy in Charleston and was recommissioned into the American fleet. The *Nonpareil* was later captured by the British brig *Decouverte* (French for "Discovery"), but her crewmen were exchanged and were returned to Charleston.

The American privateer schooner *Rapid* fought, boarded, and then burned a British privateer in the Bahamas. After that, she captured the schooner *Comet* and sent her into Savannah as a prize. Finally, however, off the coast of Louisiana, when *Rapid* was being chased by a British ship, she set far too much sail and thus capsized during her frantic efforts to escape. Her crew, however, was saved by the British ship.

Another contemporary Charleston privateer was named *Poor Sailor*. We do not know the reason for her name, but she did have a run of very bad luck. First, she twice suffered serious damage to her rudder, which required her to dock for repairs.

Later, during a fight with the British warship *Garland*, the *Poor Sailor* was left entirely helpless by a flat calm, during which time the British sailors, rowing toward her in *Garland*'s oar-powered longboats, boarded her and captured her. These boats were not little rowboats but were instead the bigger and much more formidable ship's boats, up to 33-feet long and capable of carrying a crew of ten well-armed men under the command of an officer.

Charleston's very modest contributions to the War of 1812 consisted mainly of using both its own privateers and the emerging public "battle fatigue" to help erode British resolve to continue the fight. This result forecasted the later failure of Confederate privateers to have any major impact during the Civil War as its privateers fell victim to far-reaching political and maritime changes.

For example, the decentralization of decision-making power that was so fundamental to privateering, coupled with rapid improvements in steamships and in naval cannon fire, meant that it was only the regularly commissioned Confederate raiders, and not the Confederate privateers, who would have any chance against Union and foreign merchantmen.

The Revolutionary War had ended in 1783, but, ironically, privateering peaked at Charleston more than ten years later, in 1794, due in no small part to Judge Thomas Bee of the U.S. District Court. His rulings laid the foundation for American maritime law, as explained in Melvin H. Jackson's 1969 book, *Privateers in Charleston, 1793-1796*.[241]

Judge Bee was a wealthy gentleman of the Charleston establishment and shared his colleagues' distaste for the excesses of the French Revolution. He therefore threw one barrier after another into the efforts of U.S. officials to enforce the officially neutral position of the American government in this uprising. He denied, for example, any American jurisdiction over the activities of French privateers near Charleston and also ruled that the Franco-American treaties were far more sweeping than those with other nations.

The net result of Judge Bee's legal decisions was a great proliferation of privateers in the West Indies, many of them financed by groups of American businessmen in Charleston and elsewhere. These ships were often staffed by American sailors who paid little or no attention to the difference between legal privateering, on the one hand, and downright piracy, on the other.

Not until after the Jay Treaty of 1794 between the United States and Britain did French privateering using American ports finally come to an end.[242] The main purpose of this agreement was to ease the tensions between the two nations that had lingered on in the wake of the American Revolution, and the new stresses created by the French Revolution.

Chapter 14

Privateers in the Caribbean

It was only after about fifty years of privateering raids and contraband trade in the Caribbean that the British finally decided to set up permanent settlements on the islands of the Lesser Antilles in the 1620s and 1630s. Slightly earlier, however, between 1604 and 1619, semi-permanent privateering bases had been located there and in Guiana.

These locations were close enough to shipping routes to permit occasional attacks on Spanish treasure ships, but were also very unstable and violent places, marked by fights with the local Indians and raids by Spanish, Portuguese, and occasionally Dutch ships.[243] Thus by 1624 it had become clear to investors that British colonies based on Caribbean agriculture held out much more hope of profit than remote British outposts based only on occasional privateering.

By the end of the seventeenth century, the European nationals of the West Indies had devised a unique zone of foodstuff production that required the large-scale movement of capital and labour to and from their colonies. This was, alas, never a peaceful era, suffering as it often did from the depredations of privateers and buccaneers on the seaborne commerce that formed the economic backbone of the region.

In July 1712, for example, the French corsair Jacques Cassard overran Montserrat and Antigua and carried off to Martinique 1,500 slaves and other valuables. Under the terms of the 1713 Peace of Utrecht, the French had to cede half of the island of St Kitts to Britain, after the British sent twenty ships filled with troops. From 1700 to 1722, scarcely a year passed without some conflict between white settlers and Black rebel slaves in Jamaica.[244]

English colonists occupied sparsely settled islands in the Caribbean. There they developed an unusual and highly-successful agricultural combination, protected by the ships of the Royal Navy, which featured African slave labour;

European technology, finance, and management; Asiatic and American plants; European farming skills; and Caribbean soils and climates.[245]

Sugar plantations, in particular, became a great economic success for white settlers and, especially for the British, a great social success as well. Before the nineteenth century, the sugar plantation islands of the Caribbean were Imperial Britain's most valued possessions overseas.

Indeed, many British colonists in the Caribbean believed that their interests would best be served by taking over the French islands there, too. Prior experience had shown them to be a serious threat in wartime because they could so easily be turned into anti–British privateering bases.[246]

In 1776, there were a total of twenty-six British colonies in America – not just thirteen, which was the number of colonies in what would become the United States. Of these twenty-six colonies, the six in the Caribbean (Jamaica, Barbados, the Leeward Islands, Grenada and Tobago, St Vincent, and Dominica) were among the wealthiest, and were all closely linked to the mainland by social ties and by trade.

During the American Revolution, however, the great majority of the white residents of the islands refused to side with their revolutionary compatriots on the American mainland and instead remained loyal to Great Britain.

An interesting cultural fact is that, at the outset of the American Revolutionary War, a French visitor remarked on the sharp difference between the island colonies and the mainland colonies of British America.

"Far from settling in the islands", he wrote, the white colonists regarded them only as "a land of exile, never as a place where they plan to live, prosper, and die." In contrast, he added, the American colonists of the mainland were "permanently born in the country and attached to it; they have no motherland save the one they live in."[247]

Nevertheless, all outsiders were quite keen to profit from the islands. One dramatic result of this profound interest was that, by May 1776, at least 100 New England privateer ships of various shapes and sizes, and with various degrees of armament, were already in action in the Caribbean.

They were provided by and manned by a wide range of American merchants, whalers, fishermen, and sailors, all of whom were patriotic citizens but who also hoped to make some money from their great adventure. During their

Caribbean voyages, they managed to capture hundreds of West Indian ships carrying rum, molasses, sugar, indigo, and many other tropical products.[248]

The activities of American privateers strongly contributed to the rise in prices in the Caribbean and to the concomitant shortages of important supplies. The privateers disrupted established patterns of trade, increased insurance costs, drove up freight rates, delayed the sailing of convoys, and inflicted heavy financial losses on many local businessmen.

For example, American privateers seized two to three ships each day off the Windward Islands in 1777; intercepted most of the supplies sent from Britain to Tobago in 1777-1778; and intercepted the most valuable ships in the Jamaican fleet in 1777. As early as 1777, these privateers did about £1.8 million of damage to the trade of the British West Indies.[249]

It was the 1803 Napoleonic revolution in Haiti (under its former name of San Domingue) that began the heyday of privateering in those waters.

Napoleon's agents quickly commissioned as privateers all those who applied from the French colonies of Guadeloupe and Martinique. Many of these new privateers prevented American ships from trading with the now-independent Haitians. For example, Captain Dominique of the armed privateer *La Superbe* captured three American ships that had been condemned in the prize court in Guadeloupe and sold them in Cuba.[250]

After 1803, British and French privateers frequently seized ships of the weak and neutral United States, simply ignoring its maritime rights. Indeed, one expert had warned American Secretary of State James Madison that if the Napoleonic War in Europe continued much longer, "I am fearful that the Gulph will be crowded with Privateers and that much Spoilation of our Commerce will be committed."

This prediction came true in late 1805 and early 1806, when several ships out of New Orleans were taken by Spanish and English privateers.[251]

The role of the Caribbean as a whole

We have touched on this subject in earlier pages of this book, but it is now time to ask the broader question, namely, what role did the Caribbean as a whole play in the American Revolutionary War?

The very short answer is that it became the essential base for rival European powers to use when they wanted to play more active roles in the conflict. The longer and much better answer, however, will require us to go back to 1492, when Christopher Columbus became the first outsider known to have sailed into the Caribbean.[252]

Ever since the time of Columbus, the sugar-rich islands and fine sailing weather of the Caribbean had attracted no end of hardy European adventurers, mariners, and settlers, especially the Spanish, British, French, and Dutch.

The Revolutionary War especially appealed to Europe's non-British powers as a unique opportunity to humiliate the British, who by 1776 already held Jamaica, Barbados, the Leeward Islands, Grenada and Tobago, St Vincent, and Dominica. For example, a British subject living in Grenada complained in 1778, "From London, we hear of nothing but stoppages, bankruptcies, want of money, universal diffidence in the commercial world, West India produce daily falling, and in a word, a picture of horror for all of us interested in these islands."[253]

A good example of the type of ship-to-ship fighting that went on in these waters was chronicled by the South Carolina naval historian P.C. Coker.

In December 1777, about twenty miles north of St. Eustatius and commanded by Captain Francis Morgan, the American ship *Experiment* met a British ten-gun privateer sloop out of Antigua, commanded by Captain Phillips.

When hailed, Morgan replied that he was from Charlestown [*sic*]; Phillips responded with a broadside, and Morgan returned fire. The engagement went on for over an hour. *Experiment* badly damaged her adversary and killed four men and wounded seven.

The sloop ceased fire for almost ten minutes; then, suddenly and without any explanation, *Experiment* blew up and sank [probably because the gunpowder magazine exploded]. Captain Phillips did not pick up the eighteen survivors. Five of them either swam to the enemy sloop or made it to shore. All of the others perished.[254]

We mentioned earlier the two American privateers *Chance* and *Commerce*, which began their careers as pilot boats in New York.[255] Both were small sloops, each armed with four to six guns and with from forty to fifty crewmen. Because they sailed in tandem to the Caribbean to see what prizes they could seize there, it is useful to say something about this region now.

The privateers' choice of the Caribbean, then known as the West Indies, was a very sound one. Historically, the term "West Indies" was first used by the European colonists who came to the region after the arrival of Christopher Columbus in 1492. It then referred to all the island nations and the dependencies of the area. The more recent term "Caribbean", however, now encompasses a much wider geographical and cultural context that includes both the islands and the mainland coastal regions.

In the sixteenth and seventeenth centuries, the use of privateers there was really nothing more than legal, state-sponsored, piracy. Because the cost of creating and maintaining large fleets was well beyond the abilities of the national governments, privateers were commissioned to form a de facto "navy". When equipped with letters of marque, these privateers received a large share of the proceeds of the sale of any prizes they captured, the remainder going to their rulers.

One of the most successful and best-known privateer captains was Miguel Enríquez, a shoemaker from Puerto Rico who went to work on a privateer in the Spanish colonies and eventually became one of the richest men in the New World. In addition, Amaro Pargo, a Spaniard, frequently traded in the Caribbean while looting enemy ships on behalf of the Spanish Crown and retired in great luxury to the island of Cuba.

By the seventeenth century, however, both piracy and privateering in the Caribbean had become much less attractive ways of life as governments began to hunt down the pirates themselves and to replace the corrupt officials who supported them. Indeed, by 1730, governments' anti-pirate campaigns had largely suppressed organized piracy in the Atlantic.

Nevertheless, during the eighteenth century, the Caribbean still lured many unemployed maritime adventurers because of the islands' great prosperity, which was ultimately based on the large-scale sugarcane cultivation made possible only by a flourishing slave trade. Good weather probably attracted these roving seamen, too.

This trade generated a great flood of ship-borne commerce between the Caribbean and Great Britain, which was precisely what brought *Chance* and *Congress* to these waters. The two ships began, easily, to pick off British cargo ships from Jamaica that were bound for London.[256]

For example, they soon captured four British merchantmen and found that they held 1,000 hogsheads of sugar; 25 tons of cocoa; nearly 22,000 gallons of rum; 22,420 Spanish dollars; and 200 gold Spanish coins, which had a value of about 1,600 Spanish silver dollars.

It is said that the two owners of the privateer ships, plus a few other major investors, each pocketed £5,000, which would be the equivalent of about $650,000 today. Each sailor in the crew struck it very rich, too, receiving at least £500.

News of these payments quickly spread far and wide. For example, James Warren, president of the Massachusetts Provincial Congress, wrote that "The spirit of privateering prevails here [in New England] greatly. The success of those that have before engaged in that business has been sufficient to make the whole country privateering-mad."[257] Many New England ships, large or small, were fitted out and were sent out to sea as privateers. These included even the jokingly named "Spider Catchers" mentioned earlier.

Moreover, the Caribbean also gave the Americans and the other anti-British Europeans a comfortable base from which they could secretly and indirectly transfer money, cannons, and gunpowder to the embattled American revolutionaries. Indeed, this continuing transfer was seen as such a potential threat by the British, for whom these sugar-producing islands were extremely important in both economic and strategic terms, that the British even considered pulling back from other theatres of the war in North America to make sure they did not lose these invaluable sugar-islands.[258] The most important islands for the Americans' war effort, meanwhile, were Martinique and Saint-Domingue, the latter of which is now known as Haiti.

Because the British refused to sell cannons and gunpowder to their American colonies after 1774, the Continental Army urgently needed to find sources for gunpowder, money, military supplies, and even clothing for its troops.

Before its own entry into the Revolutionary War in 1778, however, France had arranged for secret financing and for other supplies to be sent to American ports via merchantmen from Martinique and Saint-Domingue. As has been described earlier in this book, William Bingham, who often used Martinique as a base for his operations, played an essential role by developing very close French-American relations and by supporting American privateering against British ships.

The Continental Congress had commissioned more than 2,000 privateer ships, many of them with orders to look for and to attack any British ships carrying cargo from the Caribbean islands back to Britain. This strategy forced the cargo ships to be convoyed by British warships. It thus prevented the warships from being able, while thus employed, to participate in any other and more aggressive anti-American naval operations in the Caribbean.

In this same era, the tiny Dutch island of St Eustatius, which is only about 12 square miles in size, played a surprisingly big role. In the early 1770s, about 2,000 American ships had come to this island every year to trade for sugar. This changed radically in 1779, however, because more than 3,500 American ships, many of which had been commissioned by the Committee of Secret Correspondence, now sailed to St Eustatius to bring in arms and gunpowder diverted from routes to Africa.

This illicit smuggling trade not only generated huge profits for Dutch merchants but also helped keep the American infantry well-supplied with gunpowder and weapons. The famous British Admiral George Rodney was later moved to complain that St Eustatius "had done England more harm than all the arms of her most potent enemies and alone supported the infamous American rebellion."[259] At last, however, when they had finally collected enough evidence on this trade, the British officially declared war on the Dutch Republic and eventually seized St Eustatius itself.

After the siege of Tobago in 1781, French Admiral de Grasse, now fully equipped with 3,000 fresh troops and lots of ready cash, sailed north from Saint-Domingue to Chesapeake Bay. His victory over the British there blocked the delivery of the British soldiers desperately needed by Lord Charles Cornwallis and his army at Yorktown.

The end result was that Cornwallis was forced to surrender to General George Washington on 17 October 1783. This was the last and major battle of the Revolutionary War and was the essential final step in guaranteeing American independence. British shipping losses due to American privateers were a significant part of the reason why Britain surrendered to its rebellious colonists.

One of the best modern accounts on the role of privateers in the Caribbean, in terms of giving the reader a good sense of their activities, comes from Andrew Jackson O'Shaughnessy's 2000 book on the American Revolution and the British Caribbean.

> Large American privateers such as *Oliver Cromwell*, *Rattle Snake*, *Pilgrim*, *Manley*, *Hampden*, *Bunker Hill*, *General Washington*, *Black Prince*, *Revenge*, *Retaliation*, and *Reprisal* cruised among the British islands, where their names became infamous. They were armed and refitted in North American ports and in the French West Indies.
>
> A [typical] privateer like *Governor Trumbull* was crewed by 150 men with 24 guns. Such ships hovered off the popular sailing routes near Martinique, northern Cuba, and the southern coast of Florida, and they even awaited the West India trade in the English Channel.
>
> Some American privateers were bold enough to launch raids on the outer ports of the British islands, where they cut merchant vessels and fishing boats from their moorings "in sight of the inhabitants" and where they mounted landing parties. They briefly invaded Nassau in the Bahamas and twice tried to capture Tobago in 1777.
>
> It was even more galling for the British planters that the American privateers found sanctuary in the islands of rival European colonies in the Caribbean.[260]

To all this, it may be added that the raids of American privateers also forced prices to increase and new supplies not to be forthcoming. The expenses of running the sugar plantations rose sharply, while the market prices went in the opposite direction.

Moreover, planters found it very difficult and expensive to obtain credit to cover their losses because some key London merchant houses either failed due to the war or decided to cut back on their own lending. By 1788, to use only one of many possible examples, the once-vast plantation empire of the Price family in Jamaica was entirely ruined by the war and by soaring interest rates.[261]

Chapter 15

Privateer Ships and Weapons

Both ship captains and shore-side investors modified many different kinds of vessels and armed them for their new duties as privateers.

Such ships, which included both former warships and converted merchantmen, were given more guns and the much bigger crews needed, both to man any captured prize vessels, and to guard any prisoners, namely, men captured from prize ships. Privateer ships themselves included two-masted schooners, brigs, brigantines, obsolete warships, and refitted cargo ships. Faster ships were usually preferred to slower ones in this business: this was often essential when trying to overtake a lumbering but potentially lucrative prize.

Although privateers often cruised alone, they could also join forces with other privateers or could cooperate with official naval forces. However, they tried very hard to avoid fights with warships of any country when out at sea on their own. Such ships not only would be much better-armed than they were, and, unlike a captured civilian cargo ship, they could not be sold at a neutral port and thus had little monetary value to privateers.

The United States had relied on mixed squadrons of privateers and frigates during the Revolutionary War. In the wake of the French Revolution of 1789 to 1799, however, French privateers now became a real threat to American and British shipping, chiefly in the western Atlantic and in the Caribbean.

These hostilities resulted in what is now called the Quasi-War. This was a very short and undeclared naval conflict from 1798 to 1800 between France and the United States, fought chiefly at sea in the Caribbean and off the east coast of the United States.

This mini war is of interest chiefly because of its reliance on privateers and because it has also formed the legal basis for some modern controversial undeclared wars (e.g., American participation in the Vietnam War, and in the 1991 Gulf War). It will therefore be discussed at greater length in Appendix 4.

In terms of privateer life, guns were just as important as sails. Only sails could bring a privateer ship within firing range of its intended target, e.g., an enemy ship, but only guns could, by their threat or actual use of great physical force, compel an enemy ship to surrender and thus become a prize, or risk instead being sunk by naval gunfire.

By the seventeenth century, European ships were already carrying up to 100 primitive guns of various sizes on as many as three separate decks. Special shot (special artillery rounds) had been perfected for naval use and included both bar-shot and chain-shot. Each consisted of two cannonballs linked together, either by an iron bar or by a chain, which whirled around furiously in flight to slice up an enemy ship's sails and rigging.

Antipersonnel shot included bundle shot, canister shot, and grape shot, all designed to break up in flight and to kill or wound as many enemy sailors as possible every time a gun was fired. In addition, land-based artillery batteries could use red-hot shells with molten metal interiors to set an enemy's wooden hull on fire. Explosive shells were used at sea, too.

As if all this was not enough, by the beginning of the eighteenth century warships had improved a great deal. Cast iron muzzle-loaders ranged from small 6-pounders, which fired a ball weighing about 6 pounds, to 32-pounders firing a heavier ball of about that weight.

Great accuracy was neither necessary nor possible, given ceaseless rolling of the ship; the dense smoke from the gunpowder propelling the cannonballs; and the fact that dueling ships were often very close together when they fired, sometimes less than 50 yards apart.

In a Royal Navy ship of the late eighteenth century, a typical broadside (the virtually simultaneous firing of all the cannons on one side of the ship) could be accomplished two to three times in roughly five minutes, depending on the training and on the strength of the crew.

Privateer crews tried to use this same tactic, trying to force an enemy ship to surrender by pouring repeated broadsides into it. At the same time, sharpshooters stationed near the privateer's masts or in its lower rigging would use their muskets to kill as many enemy officers and key crewmen as possible.

Finally, amid the roar of the guns, the bellowed command of "Borders away!" when the ships were alongside each other, sent teams of privateers, each man armed with a cutlass or a pistol, over the rails of their own ship and onto the deck of the enemy ship in order to subdue it.

A ship's cannon might have a maximum theoretical range of about 2,000 yards. It could be aimed – and only in a very rough sense – by using a wooden wedge known as a quoin to raise or lower the elevation of the barrel. Most naval battles were fought at well under 1,000 yards, but some nearly at point-blank pistol range, that is to say, only 25 yards.

Ship cannons, despite their great weight (a 24-pounder could weigh up to 4,000 pounds) wore out quickly and had to be replaced after only 500 to 1,000 shots. Strong ropes were used to control the cannon's fearsome recoil.

In terms of personal armament, sailors routinely carried sheath knives aboard ship for cutting lines and rigging, and because at mealtimes they had to cut up food with their own knives. When boarding an enemy ship, however, they would have relied chiefly on the short but trusty seaman's cutlasses issued to them when combat was expected. Officers were probably armed with pistols, in addition to their uniform (dress) swords, which were more a mark of rank rather than their primary weapon.

In addition, the crew could also use boarding axes, boarding pikes, and blunderbusses. These latter weapons were handy short-barreled flintlock shotguns with big flaring muzzles. Although much less accurate than flintlock rifles or even flintlock muskets, they were much easier to handle in close quarters and easier and faster to reload. Great accuracy was never needed aboard a ship.

The *Liverpool Packet*,[262] the name of a small privateer of 1812, carried a crew of forty men who were well-armed when going into combat with a total of forty cutlasses, backed up by twenty-five muskets (muzzleloading shoulder arms which were probably issued given to the best shots).

British and American gunsmiths also offered for sale to privateers and any other seamen some clever and very lethal boarding pistols. There were big-calibre single-shot flintlock pistols that might also be equipped with a small "switchblade" bayonet underneath the barrel, for really last-ditch emergency use in the final throes of any belly-to-belly fighting.[263]

Chapter 16

Noted Privateering Figures

Short biographical sketches of some of these men (no women are ever known to have become privateers) are listed below in alphabetical order. They can give us good insights into their lives and times, both ashore and at sea.

John Adams

It was mentioned earlier that, in 1790, in an era when the United States still could not afford to build a navy of its own, President John Adams told the Secretary of the Navy that the United States urgently needed to have some "light cruisers" to use against Ameria's enemies.

What the Americans needed were ships about the same size and function as privateers. Technically speaking, such "light cruisers" were not privateers because, unlike true privateers, they had in fact received official governmental approval. In practice and in casual conversation, however, both then and later on they would often be lumped together with the many privateers already in the stocks (under construction) or then on duty at sea.

To this we may add that Adams strongly believed that "Foreign powers can not be expected to acknowledge us, till we have acknowledged ourselves and taken our station among them as a sovereign power [that is, until we can prove this by having an adequate number of ships], as an independent nation."[264]

Congress certainly agreed: by 1776 at least 100 New England privateers would become active in the Caribbean, having first been approved by Congress on 23 March 1776. Adams was very much in favour of this programme, writing that "Thousands of schemes for privateering are afloat in American imaginations."[265] Moreover, it was Adams himself who drafted the first set of rules and regulations for an American navy.

This fact would, indeed, remain a point of pride for him for the rest of his life.[266] Knowing nothing about armed ships to begin with, he soon made himself an expert on this subject and, in the future, would look back on his work on the naval committee as the pleasantest part of his labours for the fledgling United States.

Nevertheless, Adams had to field questions from his supporters about why it was taking so long for the colonists to cut their ties to the mother country and to declare independence.

He, too, felt the frustration of forced inaction, but called a supporter's attention to what had already been accomplished, writing to him with a touch of anger: "Have you seen the privateering resolves [legal proposals which approved the use of American privateers]? Are these not independence enough for my beloved constituents? Have you seen the resolves opening of our ports to all nations? What more will you have?"[267]

Despite all his energy and abilities, sometimes Adams failed on the privateering front. He gave his full attention, for example, to the difficult question of what to do about the American prisoners of war being held by the British. Adams and his colleagues had hoped to get some negotiations started on this issue, but they were halted by the British insistence that captive Americans were only traitors, not legitimate prisoners of war.[268]

Joshua Barney

This man was a captain of privateer ships, as well as of Continental Navy and Pennsylvania state navy ships, during the Revolutionary War.[269]

In his capacity as privateer captain of the ship *Hyder Ally*, Joshua Barney won a dramatic fight against the British sloop of war *General Monk* and the British privateer *Fair American*. This occurred when Captain Barney took his own ship down the Delaware river in 1782 as the armed escort ship for a group of merchantmen.

Because *General Monk* was a fast ship, she was able to move ahead swiftly, with the goal of overtaking *Hyder Ally* and then boarding and capturing her. Captain Barney, however, had a bolder plan in mind.

Still being slightly ahead of the enemy ship, suddenly Captain Barney unexpectedly swerved very sharply, directly into *General Monk's* path.

As a result of this planned collision, the bowsprit of his own ship became thoroughly entangled in the rigging of the enemy ship.

The British were unable to board his ship because of the entanglement and because, earlier, Captain Barney had prudently rigged anti-boarding nets along the deck of his ship. He now fired a broadside into the enemy ship with his starboard guns.

At the same time, his own sharpshooters, armed with muskets and stationed in the rigging of his ship, shot down any enemy sailors who tried to return fire by using their ship's swivel guns. Soon Captain Barney and his men were completely victorious in this engagement and had captured the enemy ship.

John Carnes

A privateering captain from Salem, Massachusetts during the American Revolution, John Carnes came from a family of prominent shipowners that was part of what historians have called "the privateering gentry", which did very well financially during the Revolution.[270]

In 1772, he served as captain of the privateer *Porus* and during that assignment led an expedition of four privateer ships against the British-held Caribbean island of Tortola. His plan to surprise this island leaked out, however, and, after some salvos of cannon fire with defending ships, his own force had to withdraw when a well-armed British squadron heard about his idea.

Later, in a more successful adventure, John Carnes brought back the first shipload of pepper from the Dutch Spice Islands (the Moluccas), opened that trade to the Americans, and in the process made a fortune for himself and his family.

The Derby family

Thanks to its privateering expertise and international commercial skills, this highly successful business family was responsible for what is now the Salem Maritime National Historic Site, located in Salem, Massachusetts.[271]

The site was established in 1938 by order of the Secretary of the Interior to preserve a group of buildings and wharves which, for the greater part of a century after 1760, comprised one of the most important centres of American maritime activity. A guidebook to the site, written in 1940, is still in use today.

The first town in the Colony of Massachusetts Bay and founded in 1628, before the settlement of Boston, it was Salem that became the main point of debarkation for the great Pilgrim migration from England, led by Governor John Winthrop in 1630. Because the land was so rocky and farming prospects there were so poor due to thin soil and the harsh climate, the early settlers of Salem turned instead to fishing, shipping, and forestry to make their living.

The British Grenville and Townshend Acts of 1764-1768 created new customs duties (financial charges) to raise revenue and to control colonial trade. Merchants such as Richard Derby suffered financial hardships from these higher costs, and Salem's booming trade with the West Indies was seriously depressed. When the British imposed such punitive measures, their political relations with its American colonies were greatly strained, and resistance to British rule increased.

On 26 February 1775 (two months before the beginning of the Revolutionary War), a regiment of British soldiers was ordered to seize a large amount of ammunition and nineteen cannons being held by the American colonists.

The senior American merchant on the spot was Richard Derby, who owned eight of these cannons and who had no desire to give them up. He shouted to the British officer charged with confiscating the cannons: "Find them if you can! Take them if you can! They will never be surrendered!"

This British officer, now facing a very hostile crowd that was probably armed because its members were also members of the colonial militia, prudently withdrew his own troops. There was no bloodshed, but, unfortunately, that would come soon enough.

The role of the Salem Maritime National Historic Site is to explain to us the international trade of the American colonial era in cotton, rum, sugar, and slaves; the actions of the many Derby-funded and other privateers during the American Revolution; and the far-reaching Salem-based maritime trade with East Asia, chiefly China, after American independence.

Derby House and Derby Wharf, both located in Salem, reflect the achievements of Captain Richard Derby and especially of his second son, Elias Hasket Derby. Derby House, built in 1762, is still a fine example of Georgian architecture. The nearly half-mile-long Derby Wharf, built that same year and extended in 1806, was once lined with warehouses stacked high with goods from all corners of the world.

This site thus reflects the fact that, during the Revolutionary War, privateering based in Salem and in other ports contributed a great deal to the ultimate American victory through the capture and destruction of British cargo ships.

Indeed, the port of Salem alone provided the greatest number of American privateers. From 1776 to 1783, for example, more than fifty privateers were based there and were usually out at sea hunting for more British ships to attack.

One of the very best of these privateers was a new and remarkably fast ship named *Mount Vernon*. Owned by Elias Hasket Derby, Jr. (see below), she was only 100 feet long with a 28-foot beam, but was well-armed with twenty 6-pounder and 9-pounder guns, and a strong crew of thirty-four men. She turned out to be admirably suited for running urgently needed commodities into some of the ports of war-torn Europe.

Elias Hasket Derby himself (jokingly known, but never to his face, as "King Deby") either owned or was part-owner of at least 158 privateers, that is, one half of all the privateers that hailed from Salem. He was probably therefore the best-known shipping man in Salem when the port was one of the very busiest in all of North America.

The privateer ship *Grand Turk*, for example, was built for Derby in Hanover, Massachusetts in 1781. It was Salem's biggest privateer ship and became the most successful, capturing seventeen prizes between 1781 and 1782 during the last years of the Revolutionary War.

Four notable facts about Derby's life are that:[272]

- Although he was an extremely successful merchant, he never went to sea for any length of time himself, instead sending his ships to trading posts all around the world – in the Philippines, Russia, India, Africa, China, and the Caribbean.
- At a time when most newly built vessels were paid for in cash, he paid for his own ship only in goods: that is, probably in rum and butter – the rum coming from his privateer trade with the Caribbean and the butter coming from his Massachusetts cows.

- He was very quick to try bold new ideas, such as using a "supercargo" (a senior seagoing business agent who always sailed aboard one of Derby's ships) to take full charge of all commercial aspects of a voyage, thus leaving the captain of the ship entirely free to focus only on nautical matters.

- From the Revolutionary War until his death in 1799, Derby's fleet made more than 330 voyages. He employed 100 captains; treated his sailors much better than average, e.g., by providing fresh vegetables for them on voyages; sent forth more than half of the 158 privateers that sailed out of Salem; never trafficked in the slave trade; and managed to make a vast fortune as the sole owner of his privateering operations: virtually all of their income, after expenses, came to him alone, and not to any consortium of investors.

The privateer ship *Grand Turk* did very well during the Revolutionary War. She ended her career as a privateer in 1783, after only her fourth cruise. In the short time of one year and ten months, she managed to capture seventeen enemy vessels, and brought all of them safely to port to be sold there at auction.

She then became a peaceful merchantman and, in 1786, was the first vessel from New England (and the third from America) to trade with China.

One lasting result of this memorable voyage was "the Grand Turk Punch Bowl": a large China bowl decorated with a fine painting of the ship under full sail. It was a gift from Pinqua, one of the most famous Hong merchants of China.

Under Chinese law, all ships' business with Chinese businessmen and craftsmen had to be conducted by the Hong merchants, not by any ships' officers or Chinese interpreters.

Known as the Canton trade system, this unique business model lasted from 1767 to 1842. Its purpose was to centralize, to simplify, and to maximize the Chinese government's profits from, and its political control over, China's foreign trade.

The end of the *Grand Turk*'s story is that she sailed from Salem in 1787, bound for Paris. She was sold there the next year to a French merchant and thus passed forever out of the early annals of American shipping.

Jonathan Haraden

Appointed in 1776 as first lieutenant aboard the privateer schooner *Tyrannicide*, Johanthan Haraden gradually earned a reputation for very effective bluff and deception at sea, while building up his own fortune in prize money.[273]

After successfully capturing a Royal Navy cutter, a packet schooner (a boat that followed a published travel schedule), and numerous merchantmen, Captain Haraden had to burn his own schooner to prevent her from falling into British hands when captured. In the spring of 1780, he then took command of the new Salem privateer *General Pickering*, which was armed with fourteen 6-pound cannons and a crew of forty-five men.

He had planned to use the Spanish port of Bilbao as his base, and headed there with a cargo of West Indies sugar to help pay for his expenses in Europe. During this voyage, however, he first had to fight off a British cutter, but he later also encountered the British privateer brig *Golden Eagle* during the night.

This meeting surprised both ships, whose crews could hardly see each other because of the darkness. Captain Haraden, however, had such presence of mind that he immediately shouted out to British captain to surrender, falsely claiming that his own ship was a "United States frigate of the heaviest class: strike [surrender] or I will sink you with a broadside!"

The darkness prevented the British captain from being able to judge the size of Captain Haraden's clearly, so he fell for the bluff and promptly surrendered, only to discover that Captain Haraden's vessel was in fact no more powerful than his own!

Later, as he was drawing near Bilbao with his British prize, Captain Haraden was attacked by the large forty-gun British privateer *Achilles*. The British managed to recapture the prize, and the two privateers then fired at each other for nearly three hours, watched avidly by many spectators on the shore, until *Achilles* finally had enough of the fight and broke off the engagement.

It is said that when Captain Haraden ran short of cannonballs during this fight, he loaded his guns with crowbars. These flew toward the enemy ship like "huge iron arrows" and drove the gunners off their decks.[274]

Captain Haraden then returned to Salem and captured other British ships off the New York coast.

Hugh Hill

A famous privateer during the Revolutionary War, Hugh Hill left his poverty-stricken home in Ireland at the age of 15 to join the Royal Navy as a cabin boy. Although he had no formal schooling, being very bright and very upward-mobile, he managed to get an elementary-level education with the help of some literate sailors. He was also physically huge and strong. Indeed, it is said that he was 6'6" tall and weighed over 25 stones.[275]

In 1775, he was appointed captain of the privateering vessel *Pilgrim*, which was owned by the very prosperous Cabot brothers of Beverly, Massachusetts and was sent out to attack British shipping in the Atlantic. In his first major success, he captured the British ship *Industry* and delivered it to George Washington.

During the Revolutionary War, Captain Hill seized many British merchantmen and was given command of one of them. His captures of prizes off the coasts of Britain and Ireland earned him the fierce reputation among British captains there as being the "Scourge of the British coast".

The following story was told of him because of his great size, great strength, and very quick temper.

On one occasion in a bar in France, a French officer believed that Hill had somehow insulted him. The Frenchman said to Hill: "I will send my seconds to you in the morning" (which meant that he was formally challenging Hill to a duel).

Hill replied, while drawing two loaded pistols from his belt and offering one of them to the Frenchman, "What is the matter with here and now?"

There was no duel: the Frenchman immediately decided not to pursue the matter any further![276]

Due to his successful efforts during the Revolutionary War, Captain Hill is now remembered for the launching of the ship *Hannah* at a local wharf. This was the first official ship of the Continental Navy and made the town of Beverly famous. In honour of him and other privateers, the Beverly Historical Society now operates a summer "Privateer Train Walking Tour", which passes through the part of where Hill owned his home and operated a business.

Captain Hill's major achievement over the long run, however, was his capture of the British merchantman *Duke of Gloucester* in 1781. The greatest treasure-trove aboard this ship was not gold or silver, but was instead the library of the Irish geologist and chemist Richard Kirwan.

This library was later donated to the newly formed Salem Philosophical Society, which evolved into the celebrated Salem Athenaeum. The world-famous mathematician Nathaniel Bowditch, who in 1802 produced a definitive book on navigation, credited this institution for giving him his love knowledge of mathematics.[277]

Esek Hopkins

This man was variously an American naval officer, a merchant captain, and a privateer. He was also a fine sailor, a skillful merchant, and the only Commander-in-Chief of the Continental Navy during the Revolutionary War.

He is remembered today, on the plus side, for his successful raid on the British port on Providence in the Bahamas and for capturing large amounts of British military supplies there. Nevertheless, his memory is seriously marred by his taking command of the ill-fated slave ship *Sally*.

In September 1764, Hopkins, then a privateer and a merchant, took the helm of this slave ship, which was owned by Nicholas Brown and Company, even though Hopkins himself had no earlier experience in this appalling trade. The net result was an unmitigated disaster.

When, after a fifteen-month voyage, the *Sally* finally docked at her destination in the West Indies late in 1765, 109 of the 196 slaves aboard her had died and had been thrown overboard. Moreover, the very few surviving African captives were in such bad health that they could only be sold for a pittance. Not surprisingly, Hopkins' disastrous command of the ship contributed to Brown and Company's decision to leave the Atlantic slave trade.

Although Hopkins himself does not appear to have been punished for his slave trade debacle, he was censured by Congress in 1776 for not being able to find full crews for all the American navy ships then under his command.

This was chiefly due to the fact that American seamen much preferred to serve in the higher-paying and less dangerous privateer ships than in the poorly paid and more dangerous U.S. Navy ships., whose vessels were more dangerous because while privateers tried hard to avoid combat at sea, fighting at sea was always the stock-in-trade of the navy ships.

Hopkins' naval commission was formally terminated by Congress in 1778. There were several reasons for this, of which the chief appears to have been the legal fallout from two whistle-blowers' reports that he had tortured British prisoners of war.

In any case, Hopkins was not otherwise punished for these alleged crimes, and in fact continued to serve in the Rhode Island General Assembly through 1786 until he finally retired to his farm, where he died in 1802. His home, the Esek Hopkins House, is now listed in the National Register of Historic Places.

Jean and Pierre Lafitte

These two brothers were at the same time privateers and pirates: the dividing line between these callings was, as always, only a very narrow one.[278] The Lafitte brothers were active both in Louisiana from 1803 to 1820, and in the Gulf of Mexico and the Caribbean from 1803 to 1823.

Jean Lafitte, the younger brother, always insisted that he was simply a privateer – but never a pirate! – and that he was only an innocent land-based entrepreneur rather than a sea-going businessman.

Their life stories are so remarkable, however, that, over the years, they have readily lent themselves to presentations in print and on the screen. Of these two men, Jean Lafitte (c.1780–c.1823) is historically the most important and thus will be discussed first in this book. He was variously a soldier, sailor, diplomat, and merchant, being very friendly, intelligent, resourceful, and enjoying drinking, gambling, and women.

Jean was born either in the French Basque Country or in the French colony of Saint-Domingue in the Caribbean. By 1805, he was already in charge of a warehouse in New Orleans where contraband goods smuggled by his brother Pierre were being stored and then sold.

Because the American government passed a law in 1807 prohibiting trade with Great Britain, however, the Lafittes moved their business to a very remote port in Barataria Bay in Louisiana. Most of the Lafittes' many working-level employees probably believed that their employers did in fact hold valid privateering commissions, although there must have been a great deal of uncertainty over which countries had allegedly issued them.

In any case, by 1810 their new port enterprise had become a clear financial success, both in terms of the smuggling business and of outright piracy. When the United States and Great Britain went to war in 1812, however, the Lafittes at first lost most of their ships to an American naval force.

Nevertheless, Jean Lafitte had soon pulled together a new fleet and, in return for a legal pardon from the Americans, helped General Jackson defend the city during the Battle of New Orleans. In official dispatches, General Jackson paid a warm tribute to the Lafitte brothers and to their fellow privateers for all their help.

The Lafittes then became spies for the Spanish during the Mexican War of Independence. For his next adventure, Jean founded a new colony on Galveston Island, named "Campeche", where 100 to 200 colonists and privateers were rumoured to have made millions of dollars each year, thanks to stolen or smuggled coins and goods.

There Jean also forged and sold false letters of marque from an imaginary nation, which he claimed gave their recipients the only permission they needed to attack the ships of any nation.

Later, he and his men entered into a conflict with the local Indians on the island, killing most of the men of the tribe by cannonfire. Subsequently, a hurricane flooded much of the colony, destroying four ships and most of the buildings. Finally, in 1823 Jean was badly wounded in a battle with two Spanish heavily armed privateers, and is believed to have died at sea shortly thereafter.

His fame lived on, however. In 1909, a man was given a six-year prison sentence for fraud, after swindling thousands of dollars from people by falsely claiming that he knew where the rumored "Lafitte treasure" was buried. He took their money by first promising to find it, but then gave them nothing at all in return.

Pierre Lafitte, for his part, was a privateer, a New Orleans blacksmith, and a spy. Much less well known than his brother Jean, Pierre was hailed for his wit, charm, and his skill in selling smuggled goods – mainly slaves. He was, in effect, the public relations man for the Lafitte enterprises, openly living with his large family in New Orleans.

Pierre was also very good with words. For example, when asking for a pardon from territorial governor Wiliam Clairborne, he wrote to him that:

"I am the stray sheep, wishing to return to the sheepfold. If you were thoroughly acquainted with my offenses, I should appear to you much less guilty."[279] Stricken with fever after other adventures, however, Pierre finally died in 1821 in Mexico's Yucatan Peninsula.

In 1978, Congress created the Jean Lafitte National Historical Park and Preserve. Later, the Acadian Cultural Center, the Prairie Acadian Cultural Center, and the Wetlands Acadian Cultural Center were all added to the park.

Andrew Sherburne

Some American colonists had had a great deal of experience working as privateers for the British forces that had been sent out to fight in the eighteenth-century wars against Spain, France, and the Netherlands. A few of these men now began to use their nautical skills against the British forces in North America during the American Revolution.

Writing in 1828 about his experiences as a 13-year-old American sailor in 1779, Andrew Sherburne had been quite eager to participate as soon as possible in the exciting Revolutionary War against the British.[280]

Because his father disapproved of privateers, however, Sherburne agreed to serve at sea, not on a privateer ship, as he himself had very strongly desired, but instead as a common seaman aboard the conventional and respectable Continental Congress' commissioned ship of war, *Ranger*.

Sherburne's "dreams of glory" are useful because they give us a unique "I was there" insight into privateering in New England – in this case, in Portsmouth, New Hampshire. It is very likely that many other young American men had similar hopes and fears before they finally came face-to-face with war at sea.

This is what he tells us:

- An abundance of new objects was [in Portsmouth] presented to my view. Ships were building, prizes taken from enemy unloading, privateers fitting out, standards [flags] waved on the forts and batteries, the exercising of soldiers, the roar of cannon, the sound of martial music, and the call for volunteers so infatuated me that I was filled with anxiety to become an actor in the scenes of war.

- The continental ship of war, *Ranger* of eighteen guns, was at this time shipping a crew in Portsmouth. This ship had been ordered to join the *Boston* and *Providence*, both frigates, and the *Queen of France* of twenty guns, upon an expedition directed by Congress. My father having consented that I should go to sea, [he] preferring the service of Congress to privateering.

- Accompanied by my father I visited the rendezvous of the *Ranger* and shipped as one of her crew. There were probably thirty boys on board this ship. As most of our principal officers belonged to the town [Portsmouth], parents preferred this ship as a station for their sons who were about to enter the naval service. Hence most of the boys were from Portsmouth.

- As privateering was the order of the day, vessels of every description were employed in the business. Men were not wanting who would hazard themselves in [small privateering] vessels of twenty tons or less, manned by [as few as] ten or fifteen hands.

- We proceeded to sea sometime in June 1779. A considerable part of the crew of the *Ranger* being raw hands and the sea rough, especially in the Gulf Stream, many were exceedingly sick, and myself among the rest. We afforded an object of constant ridicule to the old sailors.

- [Finally, after on a short cruise during which they successfully captured several prizes and took some prisoners from them], we then shaped our course for Boston, where we arrived some time in the last of July or the beginning of August 1779.

Robert Surcouf

First going to sea at the age of 13, Surcouf rose rapidly to become a privateer captain, a slave trader, and a shipowner. He attacked both British merchant and naval ships, not only on the seas of Europe but also in the Indian Ocean, where he earned the nickname of being the "Tiger of the seas".

Attacking British shipping off the coast of India between 1795 and 1809, he was a totally fearless warrior who charged into every fray himself, brandishing his pair of heavy, custom-made, flintlock pistols, making a fortune in the process. Finally, at the age of only 36, he retired from the sea and became a rich and respected French financier.

Surcouf won many French honours and become one of the richest and most powerful owners in Saint-Malo, Normandy in western France, as well as becoming a big landowner there.

Perhaps his most-remembered exploit, however, was his victorious battle, as commander of the small French privateer ship *Confiance*, with the much bigger East India ship *Kent* in October 1800. This fight was immortalized in a stirring painting by Ambroise Louis Garneray.

The turning point of this battle came when the two ships were firmly locked together by grappling hooks. At that point, some of the crewmen of the *Confiance* climbed high up the rigging of their own ship and, from there, dropped grenades directly down onto the *Kent*'s crowded decks.

Another action-at-sea painting, now in the Mariners' Museum in Newport News, Virginia, shows the French privateer *Emile*, commanded by Surcouf, successfully attacking the much bigger English merchant vessel *Hope* in the Indian Ocean in about 1798. His men, stationed high in the rigging of his own ship, successfully dropped grenades down onto the decks on the English ship and forced it to surrender.

Surcouf was so skillful and such a newsworthy privateer that many tall tales sprang up around him. The best of these asserted that, in 1816, he got into a duel with twelve armed Prussian officers at the same time. These men were part of a foreign force occupying France, and one of them had angered Surcouf by jostling him, on purpose, when passing him in a local bar.

The punchline of the story is that, in the combat that followed this incident, Surcouf is said to have killed or wounded all of the Prussians, sparing only the very last man, who he allowed to escape unharmed so that this remaining Prussian could carry out Surcouf's order: "Go tell in your own country how a former soldier of Napoleon fights!"

Dramatic as it is, however, this story was, alas, nothing more than a creative fabrication. What is true, however, is that Surcouf continued his successes at sea after the French Revolution and was finally made a baron by Napoleon Bonaparte.

Silas Talbot

There were two main prisons in Great Britain where captured American privateersmen were held during the Revolutionary War. Living conditions in both prisons were shockingly bad. They contained a total of 2,500 to 3,000 prisoners during the course of the war, but they had neither the facilities, the funds, nor the reasons to take good care of them.

For example, Silas Talbot, a famous captain of the American privateer *General Washington*, was captured by a British ship in autumn 1780 and was sent to the Mill Prison ship. Among the points he made after being released were the following:[281]

- There were about 1,100 prisoners on board this prison-ship. There were no berths or seats to lie down on, not a bench to sit on. Many were almost without clothes. The dysentery, fever, frenzy and despair prevailed among them, and filled the place with filth, disgust and horror.
- It was now the middle of October, the weather cool and clear, with frosty nights, so that the number of deaths per day was reduced to an average of ten, and this number was considered by the survivors a small one, when compared to the terrible mortality that had prevailed three months before.
- The human bones and skulls, yet bleaching on the shore of Long Island, and daily exposed, by the falling down of the high bank on which the prisoners were buried, is a shocking sight, and manifestly demonstrates that this prison-ship had been as destructive as a field of battle.

On a more positive note, Captain Talbot may have been the only privateersman ever to have been the subject of a ballad. In 1782, for example, a "Ballads of Rhode Island" publication tells us this about him, in a sing-along ballad format:

Talk about your clipper ships, clipper ships, clipper ships,
Talk about your barquentines [another type of sailing ship], with all their spars so fancy;
I'll just take a sloop-o-war with Talbot, with Talbot (Si Talbot),

And whip 'em into all 'er chip [maybe "hardship?"], and just to suit
my fancy.
So heave away for Talbot, for Talbot, for Talbot,
So heave away for Talbot, an let th' Capting [the Captain] steer;
For he's the boy to smack them, to crack them, to whack them,
For he's the boy to ship with, if you want to privateer.[282]

After the Revolutionary War, Captain Talbot was assigned to the U.S. Navy
and was given command of the famous American frigate *Constitution* in 1799.
Many years later, in the 1920s, a U.S. Navy torpedo boat was named after him
thanks to his many successes as a privateersman.

John Ward

Born in southeast England in about 1553, John Ward (also better known as
Jack Ward) was an English privateer and pirate who also became a corsair for
the Ottoman Empire, operating out of Tunis during the early seventeenth
century. His life story was the inspiration for the fictional character Jack
Sparrow, from the film franchise *Pirates of the Caribbean*.

In about 1605, in the wake of the failed invasion of England by the Spanish
Armada in 1588, Ward, who had previously been a simple fisherman, soon
found a new and much better calling – plundering Spanish ships under the
terms of a privateering licence issued by Queen Elizabeth I of England.

This was possible because when James I of England ended the war with
Spain when he came to power in 1603, many privateers had refused to give
up their very lucrative line of work and simply began to plunder the local
ships as pirates.

Ward had been pressed (forced to serve against his will on an English ship)
and was assigned to the Channel fleet in around 1604. The next year, however,
he and some fellow seamen deserted and became pirates.

According to a contemporary report, Ward had first encouraged his thirty
followers at a shoreside bar in Plymouth, England along the following lines:

My mates [he said], what shall we do now? This is a scurvy world, and
we live in it scurvily. We live here upon the sea, feeding on the King's

salt beef, but without even a penny to our own name to buy ourselves a bushel of grain when we go ashore.

But right now, have a very good time, eat well, be merry, and pay for all this out of your own pocket! For this very night, while the Captain and the officers of our ship are asleep and think that all we are doing here is trying to drink the bar dry, if you will follow me, we will soon be diving arm-deep into the baggage of the ships' passengers!

Thus motivated, Ward and his men soon stole a small 25-ton barque from Portsmouth harbour. His comrades quickly elected him to be their captain, a move said to have been one of the earliest cases of pirates choosing their own leader – a policy later widely followed in pirate circles. He was so successful in his new incarnation as a pirate that it is worth summarizing some of his achievements here.

He and his crew first sailed to the Isle of Wight and seized a ship said to be carrying the treasures of Roman Catholic refugees. This turned out to be only a rumour, but he used his new ship to capture a much bigger French ship, which he then sailed to the Mediterranean and there seized a powerful thirty-two-gun Dutch vessel. This he took first to Algiers and then on to Morocco.

In 1606, Ward captured a dhow (a lateen-rigged ship with one or two masts, used chiefly in Arabian waters) which was said to be carrying Catholic slaves. He made a deal with a local ruler, Uthman Bey in Tunis, that, in return for letting Ward and his men live and work under his protection, Uthman Bey would have the right of first refusal of all the goods taken at sea by Ward and his crew – up to 10 per cent of the total value of all the goods captured.

Ward and his men then seized an English merchantman, which he playfully renamed *Little John* after the powerful English folk hero of that same name. With this vessel, Ward was easily able to capture many more ships from several European countries.

One victory led to another, and a high point for Ward was the capture in 1607 of the big Venetian ship *Reniera e Soderina*, after a three-hour gun battle. This ship had tried to repel a boarding party from Ward's ship, but a volley of chain shot from Ward's men tore two of the defenders into pieces. This bloody result quickly led the rest of the crew to surrender. Her cargo, variously estimated to have been worth between £500,000 to £2 million, was seized by Ward and his men.

Ward later asked James I for a royal pardon but was refused because he had previously attacked many Venetian ships, and Venice threatened to go to war with England if the pardon was granted. As a result, Ward had return to Tunis, where, in order to stay on the good side of Uthman Bey, he nominally converted to Islam, along with his entire crew. Ward continued to raid Mediterranean shipping and eventually ended commanding an entire fleet of corsairs.

After 1612, however, when he was already an old man by contemporary standards, he voluntarily ended his career in piracy and began to teach younger corsairs the arts of gunnery and navigation. Ward had profited greatly financially from his many years as a pirate and was thus able to live in great comfort in Tunis until his death at the age of about 70, possibly due to plague.

Chapter 17

Fine Examples of the Prize Game

In Britain, privateers' commissions, namely, letters of marque and reprisal, were issued by the Admiralty on behalf of the ruling king or queen. In the United States, they were issued both by state governments and by Congress during the American Revolution.

Once the Constitution was adopted, however, the right to commission privateers was then vested solely in Congress, which delegated it to the officials of the State Department or to the Customs officials of the U.S. Treasury. Thanks to the labours of prize judges over many years, however, scholars today can readily find a great deal of information in law libraries about the legal details of prize practice.

The best modern summary of this long and historically complicated process is probably Donald A. Petrie's book, *The Prize Game*. It is the source of much of the information used in the present chapter, especially on the ships *Eliza Swan*; *Scourge*; *Rattle Snake*; and *Siren*.[283]

Ransoming the whaler (whaleship) *Eliza Swan*

During the War of 1812, on 24 July 1813 the British whaleship *Eliza Swan* was heading south from the Greenland whaling grounds back to her home port of Montrose, Scotland.

She was intercepted en route, however, by the American warship USS *President*, one of the U.S. Navy's new forty-four-gun frigates. It was clear to the captains of both ships that since Britain and the United States were at war, the *Eliza Swan* and her valuable cargo of whale oil was now a valid prize of the Americans and that the American crewmen were now prisoners of war.

All that being understood, however, it still seemed that there might be room for a legitimate and mutually advantageous deal. The Americans were under instructions from their navy to stay at sea as long as possible, but they had now been afloat for almost four months. Their crew of more than 400 men now needed more provisions, especially food, and taking aboard forty-eight whalemen from the *Eliza Swan* would have made this issue even more pressing. For this reason, the following agreement was reached.

The American captain agreed to "ransom" [to sell], his prize to the British owners of the *Eliza Swan*. He did this while at the same time releasing the whaleship's crew, and the whaleship itself, in return for an initial token payment, namely, a ship's boat and some minor items of ships' tackle that the Americans needed.

The agreed price for this deal was £5,000, which included the estimated value of the whale oil aboard the *Eliza Swan*. Since British captains did not carry large sums of money on their ships, however, this transaction had to be arranged entirely on credit.

The bottom line here is that the British captain gave the American captain his bills of exchange for £5,000. In the nineteenth century, such bills were used much like modern cheques, but they were drawn on commercial companies rather than on banks. These companies were legally obliged to pay them when they were presented. In this case, the bills were also backed up by a bond, so full payment was guaranteed.

The law of nations in the late eighteenth and early nineteenth centuries took care to spell out in detail the necessary four steps involved in ransoming a vessel. They were as follows:[284]

1. Several copies of a bill of exchange were drawn up and were signed by both parties to the agreement. Each party kept one copy.
2. The bill of exchange was, in essence, an order from the former owner to the masters of the prize to pay to the captor, in cash, the ransom amount stated in the bill as soon as the bill was presented to the owners.
3. In addition, the bill of exchange also served as a licence of safe conduct for the prize. It was issued by the captor's government and it authorized the ship to sail to a stated port over a given route within a specified limit of time. While following these instructions, the prize could not legally be captured again by the warships or privateers of the captor's government or by its allies.

4. Another document, namely, a bond, also signed by the former master of the prize, guaranteed payment of the bill as soon as it was presented. If payment was refused, however, if it was "dishonored" when presented (as the saying had it), the captain then had to pay the ransom out of his own pocket. Moreover, the captain himself could also be held hostage to ensure the payment of ransom. The threat of being held hostage sometimes led to protracted negotiations.

Rattle Snake: gaining access to the prize courts in other countries

Some American ships played significant roles in the War of 1812 and are well-documented in *The Prize Game*. This book contains, for example, a copy of the official privateering commission issued to the American privateer *Rattle Snake* by President James Madison.

This ship is of historical interest because she was one of the largest privateering vessels ever built during the American Revolutionary War and, after she was captured at sea by the British in 1781, she became part of the Royal Navy.

At that time, "her lines were taken off", in other words, accurate nautical drawings of her hull shape were made. She was a fast boat, and the Admiralty wanted to be able to duplicate her design easily if need be. She thus became one of the few eighteenth-century privateers whose specifications have survived intact to the present day.[285]

For our purposes in this chapter, however, the most important point to note here is that the Danish/Norwegian prize courts established the validity of voluntary agreements between maritime nations which, although not formally allied themselves, were in fact co-belligerents in war. These prize courts ruled that such nations could legally use each other's prize courts, and it upheld the validity of the titles of ships which had been purchased through such proceedings.[286]

Blockade and the spoils of war: the seizure of *Siren*

At an early point in the American Civil War, President Abraham Lincoln established a blockade of Confederate ports. Under the provisions of the law of nations as widely understood in 1861, a belligerent power had the right to blockade the ports of its adversary.

Such a blockade also permitted the belligerent to seize any neutral ships and cargo that were captured while trying to run the blockade. When this happened, these ships and cargo could be legally be sold and the proceeds given to the blockading sovereign and to the officers and crews of the capturing vessels.

If a blockade runner could not complete its assignment – if, for example, as in this case, the port where it was due to land was in flames thanks to a civil war – its captain could then order his officers and crew to scuttle (to sink) the ship and to escape ashore as best they could.

The *Siren* was a fast British-built schooner-rigged "sidewheel steamer" (she could proceed under both steam or under sail), which had already run the Union blockade thirty-three times – a record for Confederate blockade runners.

Approaching Charleston in 1865 via the River Ashley, however, her captain saw that the port was now in flames. Not having any alterative, he therefore ordered the crew to set fire to the ship and to open the seacocks in order to sink her near the shore. After paying off his men, who escaped on their own, he and his officers made their way to one of the railways serving Charleston and melted into the crowds there.

Remarkably, thanks chiefly to some longshoremen near the sinking *Siren* and to some Union engineers who happened to be on the scene from another ship, the *Siren* was soon repaired and was seaworthy once more. She was now considered to be a Union prize, however, and was ordered to be delivered to the District Court of the United States for Massachusetts.

There Richard Henry Dana, the U.S. attorney for the district and the author of the world-famous book entitled *Two Years Before the Mast*, filed a libel asking the District Court to condemn the *Siren* and her cargo as a lawful prize of the United States. Accordingly, on 7 April 1865 the judge found the *Siren* to be such a prize and ordered the ship and cargo to be sold.

However, en route to Massachusetts, the *Siren* was involved in a collision with another ship, and the prize court was thus faced with the thorny problem of what was technically known as "multiple captors".

To make a complicated story very short, however, we will conclude here simply by saying that the Massachusetts District Court was charged with assessing the damage this collision had caused and how much should therefore be paid to the various claimants.

Chapter 18

Racial Minorities and Women Associated with Privateering

Many Black men were privateersmen. Although there are a few records of female pirates, there are no records at all of any female privateers. It is clear, however, that some women did cooperate willingly with the activities of some seamen. Let us look at each issue in turn.

Black men as privateers

There were no colour bars on privateers and there was always a shortage of men ready, willing, and able to go to sea. Thus, while Black workers may have found it hard to get a good job ashore, for the most part they could usually find a job on a ship, either as a privateer or perhaps simply as a fisherman.[287]

There was a long-standing shortage of sailors in the nineteenth-century United States. Indeed, Blacks flocked to seafaring jobs, which, unlike most other blue-collar jobs open to them at that time, paid reliably and relatively well. Before the War of 1812, for example, seamen's wages were often higher than or equal to the wages paid to labourers ashore. Probably because of the higher pay and the lack of any discrimination there, during that war about 20 per cent of the American privateer crews were African Americans, compared to only about 16 per cent of all naval personnel.

To quote from a contemporary petition entitled "To Feel Like a Man", which argued against slavery and which was written by a Black abolitionist in 1788, jobs afloat offered Blacks "a hanceum livehud" ["a handsome livelihood"] for themselves and their families".[288]

The National Park Service has a good article on George Roberts (1766-1861), a Black American seaman who in 1812, at the age of 46, signed on in Baltimore to serve aboard Captain Richard Moon's privateer *Sarah Ann*.[289]

This privateer captured a British merchantman bringing coffee and sugar from the Caribbean to Canada, but it soon ran to big trouble. The privateer had encountered a British frigate, whose captain decided that Roberts and five of his shipmates were British subjects and therefore impressed them (put them on a ship to work against their will). They were taken to Jamaica in irons, with the plan to deliver them to the British fleet.

Captain Moon, however, vouched for Roberts, knowing him to be a free American citizen who had papers to prove it and a family back home in Baltimore. As a result, Roberts and the other prisoners were set free.

Roberts then crewed in several other privateer ships over the next two years before making his way back to Baltimore. There, in 1814, he signed on as a gunner on the famous privateer, *Pride of Baltimore*, under Captain Thomas Boyle, who we have met in earlier pages of this book.

Roberts and his colleagues remained on this ship for the next ten months, capturing and sinking British cargo ships, before finally returning to Baltimore in 1815. As a result, they were hailed in the city as war heroes and would participate each year in the events there at Fort McHenry commemorating the Battle of Baltimore in 1814.

Black men also served on many other privateers. Some of these individuals were free men who had signed up out of their own volition. Others fled from their slave owners in hopes of starting a new and freer life at sea. Still others were rented out to make money for their owners.

A good example of the latter is an ad appearing in the *New Hampshire Gazette* in 1776:

To be SOLD for a CERTAIN TIME, or let by the month, a genteel sprightly NEGRO FELLOW, in fine health, about eighteen years of age, he can be recommended for many good qualities, has served at sea and land, waits on company well, and is extremely desirous of belonging to a captain of a privateer, or going in one, as may be agreed.[290]

Women at sea

It is clear from historical records that there were often some women at sea, whether as wives, girlfriends, prostitutes, or women simply dressed as and passing as seamen.[291]

Females were sometimes seen jumping from sinking ships, and female corpses were found in the wreckage of ships. One shipbuilder reported that in one naval ship there were "Divers men drowned, and some women". Sometimes a captain's wife would accompany her husband at sea, or sometimes the wife of a petty officer would join her husband afloat to serve as a nurse for the crew. Such ladies, however, would never appear officially on crew lists.

Commissioned officers could often have a girlfriend aboard if they so wished, but this liberty could lead to excesses. In a letter to a senior British shipping official, for example, one naval officer pleads for the redress of such abuses "in order that the king's ships may not be made Bawdy houses, nor the Captains publiquely carry and entertain their whores on board..."

There were some more legitimate women seafarers working as part of a family on small family run coastal vessels, and a handful of women who served at sea disguised as men. None of the above, however, would be on crew lists.

Probably the closest approximation to other women of the sea would be the stay-at-home women of privateer-pirates. Two good candidates for such a role are Marie and Catherine Villard, the mistresses of the New Orleans-based brothers Pierre and Jean Lafitte.[292]

Pierre had at least seven children by Marie, and his relationship with her proved to be invaluable in protecting his family's property from creditors.

Marie, born in New Orleans in about 1784, was a free mulatto (in legal terms, a person of one-quarter African and three-quarters European ancestry). Her younger sister Catherine was also born in New Orleans in about 1793. The Villard family had been in Louisiana since the 1730s and may originally have come from Saint-Domingue, near what is now Haiti.

Pierre Lafitte and Marie Villard began their relationship between 1803 and 1805, which may – or may not – have been a formal "placement" (*plaçage* in French). Under this arrangement, white men entered into a form of common-law marriage with women of African, Native American, or mixed-race descent. The women were not legally recognized as wives but were known as *placées* ("placements"). The man was expected to provide a house and financial support for the woman and their children, even if he also had a white family of his own at the same time. The house became the property of the woman, and she could pass it on to her heirs.

There are no descriptions or portraits of the Villard sisters themselves, so no one knows what they looked like. However, we can learn what the British writer Harriet Martineau, who spent ten days in New Orleans in 1835, had to say about the quadroon (one-quarter Black) girls she saw there:

> The Quadroon girls of New Orleans are brought up by their mothers to be what they have been: the mistresses of white gentlemen... The girls are highly educated, externally, and are, probably, as beautiful and accomplished a set of women as can be found.

> Every young man early selects one, and establishes her in one of those pretty and peculiar houses, whole rows of which may be seen in the Remparts. The connection now and then lasts for life: usually for several years...

> Some men continue the connexion [*sic*] after marriage. Every Quadroon woman believes that her partner will prove the exception to the rule of desertion. Every white lady believes that her husband has been the exception to the rule of seduction.[293]

Chapter 19

Conclusions – Private Trade with the East Indies and other Matters

In this book a good deal has been said about classical privateering, but it is now time to understand how the world-famous English East India Company, which was in commercial shipping business from 1600 to 1874, handled both its official and its extensive private trade.[294]

This trade involved selling and buying goods not only from China but also from the region then known as the East Indies. A sweepingly broad term, it encompassed the Indian subcontinent, the Malay Peninsula, Sumatra, Java, and the many islands dotting the South China Sea.

The carefully selected captains of this company's many ships, which were collectively known as the "East Indiamen", were some of the very few British officers afloat who ever had the legal right to execute or to imprison members of their crews. This power may never have been exercised, but it was still a cherished privilege available for use if ever needed to keep mutinous men in line.

The East India Company differed from classical privateering in that it was a highly centralized enterprise very closely associated with the policies of successive British governments. It had a legal monopoly on British goods shipped between Asia and Great Britain and worked hard to defend that monopoly.

In contrast, classical privateers can best be likened to the totally independent "hired guns" of the nineteenth-century American West. They were self-starters who came and went as just as they pleased, but always with an eye open for a lucrative assignment that was exciting but not suicidally dangerous.

There were probably not too many dramatic occasions when ships of the East India Company were, outside of the ports, directly in contact with American ships, but one such event became the subject of an unsigned painting in the style of the maritime artist Francis Holman (1729-1784).

It shows the large and well-armed East India Company ship *Bridgewater* successfully beating off an attack by the much smaller American privateer *Hampden* on 8 March 1779 while the East Indiaman was en route from St Helena to England.[295]

The master of a merchantman had the legal authority to "correct or chastise" any member of his crew, and his boatswain likewise had the "power to beat any under his command on a just cause, this being the custom of the sea".

One master of an East Indiaman, however, even flogged his men on an unproven charge of mutiny. He described them as "this intolerable scum of rascals, whom the land hath ejected forth for their wicked lives and ungodly behaviour". He may have been going a bit too far, however, because this case ended up in an Admiralty court.[296] We do not know its outcome.

Powerful and far-reaching as the East India Company was in its heyday, however, nothing in this world lasts forever. The Company's continued abuses of its great economic and political power, coupled with its severe financial problems, eventually forced the British government to seek direct control over it. Thus, in 1858, after a long winding-down process, the Company's rule in India was finally ended, and by 1874, as a hollow shell of its former glory, the Company was officially dissolved.[297]

Between 1600 and 1833, ships sailing under East India Company colours had made about 4,600 trading voyages from London to Asia. This was England's, and later Britain's, biggest single commercial venture and one of its most profitable. According to Captain Robert Eastwick, a Company commander in its later days, "no finer fleet [ever] sailed the seas than that directed from Leadenhall Street", which was the location of the Company's bustling headquarters in the City of London.[298]

This firm can best be described here as being a quasi-privateering commercial enterprise. Some of its most complicated relationships lay in the lightly defined "middle ground" between the theoretical monopoly on trade held by the Company, on the one hand, and on the extensive and nearly unrestricted de facto free trade (the private trade) enjoyed by Company employees, on the other.

The private trade of the English in the East came in many different forms, all of which lay outside the normal channels for privateering. The East India Company, for example, severely frowned upon private traders, which it denounced as "smugglers".

It defined these men as people who were not affiliated with the Company in any way whatsoever but who were merely citizens of the British Crown actively trading in the East Indies or bringing goods into Europe by way of the Cape of Good Hope. The Company believed that these undisciplined private traders not only cut into the Company's profits but also besmirched its good name by their – from the Company's point of view – illegal activities.

For this reason, passengers who were not officially part of the Company were often searched onboard for smuggled goods. In one such case, a search of the ship *Maclesfield* in 1732 discovered 126 ounces of gold tucked away in the padded pockets of a certain Mr Flower, a passenger aboard the vessel.[299]

From a nautical point of view, a modern account of a typical 800-ton British East Indiaman of 1775 will explain to us that such a ship was in fact "a beauty with much less than met the eye".[300]

When moored in port, such a ship would have greatly impressed any casual stroller along the waterfront. He or she would certainly have considered the vessel to be "a floating palace", with a wooden heraldic shield and floral ornaments carved along on her highly varnished taffrail (the handrail around the open deck near the stern of the ship), accentuated by a lavish use of gold leaf.

The massive, rounded lines of the ship's hull would also have called attention to her enormous size: 140 feet long and 35 feet wide – twice the size of an ordinary eighteenth-century merchantman. Moreover, even the smallest Indiaman carried sixteen 12-pound carronades, which were short-range but very powerful guns able to keep both privateers and Malay pirates at bay. Any experienced ship's officer, however, would quickly have spotted some of this great ship's inherent weaknesses.

Without going into too many details here, he would have noticed that the hull of the ship was much too long for its breadth. This fact arose because the English tonnage laws after 1773 calculated tax assessments and harbour fees based chiefly on a ship's beam (her width), paying little or no attention to her length or to her depth.

Thus, in order to stow the maximum amount of cargo at the lowest possible fees, the East India Company built its ships to be long, narrow, and very deep. The results of this design, however, were both good and bad.

The positive news was that an 800-ton East Indiaman such as the one described here could stow nearly 1,000 tons of tea, the most important commodity of the time. The negative news was two-fold: first, thanks to her very bluff bow and her rounded hull, she was a very poor sailor, being only able, under very good conditions, to plow through the sea at just 3 or 4 knots (about the speed of a fast walk). This was only about half the speed of a contemporary English warship.

Moreover, she could never sail very close to the wind. When she tried to do so, she made almost as much leeway (sideways movement) as headway (forward movement): her high superstructure (high sides) in effect acting as a sail and pushing her sideways.

As if all this was not enough, however, even in a calm sea and when laden with heavy ballast to help her maintain a straight course, she was always very "cranky", wallowing from side to side in a heavy roll that could soon make all but the most experienced sailors quite seasick.

This whole complex process was described in large part by Emily Erikson's excellent 2014 book on the East India Company, which covers the years between 1600 and 1757.[301] It can be used here to paint a good picture of this unique enterprise. It will cover the private trade of English ships with the East Indies; the expansion of the East India Company's trading privileges; contemporary and East India Company views on private trade; and, finally, the end of extensive private trade by Company employees.

The key fact here was that, initially, and begun simply as an effort to cut down the East India Company's soaring commercial expenses, its Court of Directors gave to their employees the right to buy and sell some goods in Asia "on their own account", and thus increase the employees' personal financial profits in so doing. This meant they were officially permitted to trade for their own benefit, while at the same time still working as full-time employees of the East India Company.

Moreover, these employees could also legally make full use of the Company's invaluable and far-flung trading and interpersonal social networks. Both they and the Company were thus usually able to respond quickly to ever-changing commercial situations in the East Indies and to earn good profits by doing so.

Employees of the Company could engage in both legal and illegal private trade, the latter being better known today simply as smuggling. Because the Company was able to negotiate official diplomatic agreements with foreign powers, it had excellent and unofficial sources in, and excellent access to, many different British and foreign officials, ports, and markets. This made smuggling easy to do.

Indeed, the Company's influence was so great that it was long able to send back to Europe the private fortunes earned by its employees in the East Indies; to offer these employees protection from any aggressive competitors overseas; and, in the process, to make high profits from any goods they wanted to smuggle back to Britain. Such private trading was, in effect, firmly protected by the Company's overall monopoly on East Indies trade, and thus was not simply a new or a criminal version of free trade.[302]

Modern readers will perhaps be surprised by the frequency of the illicit private smuggling trade among Company employees. This can best be understood by casting our minds back to workings of the patrimonial monarchies of the day, for example, that of Stuart England of 1603 to 1714, which in modern times has been termed as "proto-corruption". In our time, however, it has some Mafia-like overtones.

The modern scholar James Scott has offered us insights into the premodern patrimonial mind-set of those days. He wrote:

...Seventeenth-century English politics fostered a proliferation of practices we would now consider corrupt. Seeking offices for one's clients regardless of their qualifications was an integral part of the patron-client loyalties of the period. The purchase of sales and offices, the exchange of favourable government decisions for cash or kind, the enrichment of family and friends from the Crown's coffers, and the abuse of less powerful or less well-connected citizens was typical of English government in this phase of its development.[303]

Judged by their own standards, however, the senior members of the Company were not in fact remarkably corrupt. In fact, the Company's records show that these private trade allowances were considered by the Company to be its intelligent responses to two of the most intractable problems the Company faced.

The first of these was simply the inability of senior members to control the private smuggling trade of their employees by simple administrative means. In one notable case, for example, on a single trip, an English captain carrying a cargo of cotton and other produce from India to China managed to make a personal profit of at least £30,000.[304] There was no feasible way to stop such a lucrative trade.

The second problem was the Company's inability to pay its employees high enough wages so that it would not be worthwhile for them to engage in any private trade. Needless to say, paying them much more would have cut much too heavily into the Company's profits.

By the 1760s and 1770s, however, the Company had decided to try to reform its operations to make them more efficient and thus more profitable. It therefore issued new orders to its ship captains, which reduced their traditional patterns of patronage and venality. These orders successfully undermined to some extent the captains' abilities to engage in and to direct their own private trade.

That said, however, illicit free trade still seems to have continued to flow on by other means, at lower but not alarming levels. In any case, by about 1833 – that is, towards the end of the Company's own lifespan in 1874, when it was officially dissolved – private trade appears to have seamlessly melted into the general growth of free trade arising from the many new trade sources springing up outside the Company itself.

Backtracking now at this point to finish up on privateering per se, in retrospect and in summary it can safely be said that the last great era of privateering and of seizing prizes at sea began with the Seven Years' War of 1756-1763 and ended with the American Civil War of 1861-1865.

This period embraced the last century of "fighting sail" before the coming of steam engines; the Napoleonic Wars; the American Revolution; and the War of 1812. Many of the points made so far in this book offer a rather positive interpretation of privateering, but there is, of course, another side to the story that needs to be told as well.

One of its most articulate spokesmen, for example, was Solomon Drowne (1753-1834), who shipped on a privateering cruise as a surgeon aboard the Providence, Rhode Island privateer *Hope*, probably in 1781. Another notable spokesman was Benjamin Franklin himself.[305]

Drowne made these points:

If virtue is the doing good to others, privateering cannot be justified upon the principles of virtue; though I know it is not repugnant to the Law of Nations [that is, it is not illegal], but rather deemed policy among warring powers thus to distress each other, regardless of the suffering individual. But however agreeable to, and supportable by the rights of war; yet, when individuals come thus to despoil individuals of their property, 'tis hard: the cruelty then appears, however, political.

Franklin, for his part, had been a very vocal advocate of privateering during the Revolutionary War because the Americans had no navy of their own, but after the United States had won the war, he changed his mind very significantly.

In early 1783, for example, he wrote to the British peace commissioner, expressing the hope that an anti-privateering clause could be included in the peace treaty being drafted between the United States and Great Britain.

Franklin made these points:

[If privateering was abolished] one of the encouragements to war is [thereby] taken away, and peace [is] therefore more likely to continue and be lasting...

[The evils of privateering include] the national loss of labor of so many men during the time they have been employed in robbing; who besides spend what they get in riot, drunkenness, and debauchery, lose their habits of industry, are rarely fit for any sober business after a peace, and serve only to increase the number of highwaymen and housebreakers.

Even the undertakers, who have been fortunate, and by sudden wealth led into expensive living, the habit of which continues when the means of supporting it ceases, and finally ruins them.

Journal of the Newport Privateer Sloop *Revenge*

The early journals and correspondence of privateer owners and captains are now, alas, quite rare. Scholars are thus forced to rely on American newspaper accounts from Boston to Charleston involving privateers.

Although Britain's King George II had ordered all privateer commanders to maintain an accurate log of their activities, it now appears that only the journal of *Revenge* has survived and is therefore accessible to modern naval historians.[306]

Unfortunately, it is very incomplete, covering only the five-month period from 5 April to 5 September 1741. Although it ends before the end of the ship's cruise, it is still enough to provide a feel for the challenges of this line of nautical work.

The excerpts cited in this chapter all come from Carl E. Swanson's excellent 1991 book, *Predators and Prizes, American Privateering and Imperial Warfare, 1739-1748*. The spelling and punctuation quoted here are as in the original text.

Revenge set sail from Newport in June 1741 on a privateering voyage against the Spanish. Since the ship needed more men, she first called at Manhattan "to Gett more hands" to add to the forty sailors already aboard.

The journal of *Revenge* highlights the problems that all ship captains faced during the wars of 1739 to 1748. Basically, sailors preferred the higher pay, the less ferocious discipline, and the greater safety of serving on privateers rather than on official navy ships.

That said, however, privateer captains also had to compete with each other in order to hire enough crewmen. The underlying problem, then, was the relative shortage of crewmen needed to staff all the naval, merchant, and privateer ships afloat at the same time. For example, the journal of the *Revenge* mentions that Captain Norton had to ask the lieutenant governor of New York for permission "to beat about for hands", but was turned down.

In any case, on 5 July 1741, the *Revenge* received the very welcome news that two coast guard vessels had just returned from chasing Spanish privateers and that their men were quite willing to serve on *Revenge*.

Nine days later, the *Revenge* was therefore at last fully manned with sixty-one officers and men. She embarked "with the wind att SWW with a fresh Gale and by Gods leave and Under his protection" for the West Indies on a "Cruize against the proud Dons the Spaniards". To celebrate their departure, the captain of the *Revenge* "ordered [for] the people [for his crew] a pale of punch to drink to a Good Voyage".

The privateer's journal entries explain the great difficulties involved in overtaking and trying to capture a potential prize: "Saw a top Sail Vessell and a Sloop. Bore down upon her but it is Coming Calm could not Speak with her [our ship was catching up with the sloop, but then the wind died and we could not get close enough to her to learn who she was]."

Poor weather continued on 29 July 1741:

Saw a Sloop. Gave Chase but the Weather being Calm was forced to Gett out Our Oars. Fired our Bow Chase [bow cannon] to bring her too [make her stop], but [we fired our bow cannon] taking about and the people in Confusion, Night coming on, it being very Foggy, Could not Speak to her. [We had to tack, that is, to change direction; our crew was disorganized; it was very foggy; and we thus we could not communicate with the sloop.]

On the morning of 3 August 1741, the *Revenge* chased a schooner, but again with no success:

Att 5 PM. Gave her a Gun in hopes to bring her too, to know who she was, but did not mind it neither hoisting any Colours, she bore down upon Us, then takt [tacked] and bore away. We fired 10 shot but all did not signify for she hugged her Wind and it Growing dark and having a Good pair of heels we lost Sight of her. [At 5 PM we saw a ship and fired a cannon to make her stop so we could identify her, but she paid no attention to us; did not hoist any identity flag; and sailed away from us. We fired 10 shots at her without any results and, since it was getting dark and she sailed faster than we did, we soon lost sight of her.]

Naval Gunnery in the Age of Sail

S ince cannons played such an important part of life on a privateer, it is worthwhile saying something about them now, albeit only briefly.

Naval gunnery in the age of sail dates from about 1571 to about 1862. In this era, what were traditionally called "the old wooden walls", namely, the large, sail-powered, wooden warships and cargo vessels that ruled the high seas, carried a wide range of muzzle-loading cannons as their chief armament for both aggressive and defensive actions.

In principle, these weapons were extremely simple, but it took a great deal of muscle power and experience to be able to use them safely and effectively. They were so very heavy, however, (some of them weighing nearly 3 tons), that ship captains might order them to be heaved overboard if the ship ever encountered a storm so severe that getting rid of them was the only to help her stay afloat.

Indeed, their chief qualities were their enormous weight, their very slow rate of fire, the great difficulty in loading them and aiming them accurately when mounted on a moving ship, and the imperative need to keep the gunpowder, which had to be stored in a special compartment below deck to keep it dry and stop it from igniting before it was safely tamped down into the barrel of a cannon.

A cannon itself consisted of only three major parts: the barrel with one or more cannonballs in it; the gunpowder; and the touch hole at the very rear of the barrel, into which some kind of ignition device was inserted to set the gunpowder itself alight.

The sequence of firing one of these weapons ran along the following lines:

- "Powder monkeys" (the 10-year-old boys of the crew) must first hoist the powder and shot up to the main deck from the shot locker, using the main hatch.

- Adult crewmen remove the tampion from the muzzle of the gun.
- They raise the gun port so that the barrel of the gun will protrude from it.
- They push a wet swab into the barrel to kill any embers from the last shot that might otherwise ignite the next shot prematurely.
- Gunpowder is then pushed into the barrel, either loose in granular form or packaged into a parchment cartridge, and then rammed home together with a cloth wad.
- The cannonball is rammed in, followed by another cloth wad to prevent the cannonball from rolling out if the muzzle is depressed.
- The cannon on its heavy carriage is then "run out" by rope tackles and by sheer muscle power until the barrel protrudes from the bulwark (the side of the ship). This was no easy matter because a large cannon on its carriage could weigh over 2 tons, and at the same time the ship itself was probably rolling in the waves.
- The touch hole is filled with very fine gunpowder (priming powder) which burns extremely rapidly with a very hot flame. It is ignited by a gunlock (a flintlock mechanism) fitted to the cannon.
- This sets off the main charge of gunpowder, which violently propels the cannonball down the barrel.
- When the cannon is fired, its fierce recoil backwards is halted by strong ropes.

A well-trained crew could fire a broadside two or three times in about five minutes. Bigger ships could carry more cannons and of larger calibres. Standard sizes of cannons ranged from 42-pounders, which fired a 42-pound iron ball 7 inches in diameter, to 6-pounders firing a 3.5 inch ball weighing 6 pounds.

The longest cannons, called "long toms" or "long nines", were 8 or 9 feet in length and were designed to fire at distant ships. During the War of 1812, for example, the 18-pounder long guns could penetrate the wooden hull of an enemy ship about 500 yards away. The maximum effective range of a 12-pounder, however, was estimated at being only 280 yards.

Experts were always trying to improve naval gunnery. One early success was the Paixhans gun of 1822-1823, the first naval gun to use explosive shells to set wooden ships on fire. It heralded the end of the wooden warship and ushered in a new era of ironclad vessels.

That said, however, even before its advent, no American privateer was bold or foolish enough to risk tackling, by itself, one of the very powerful British frigates or ships-of-the line that formed part of the Royal Navy blockade sealing off the American Atlantic ports during the War of 1812.

British, Spanish, and French Privateers in the Mid-Eighteenth Century

Much of the modern writing in English on privateers often focuses chiefly on the American colonists during and after their Revolutionary War, which began in 1775. As indicated in earlier pages of this book, however, the story of privateering in Europe predates this by a number of years.

The most important introductory point in our story here is that shipping by sea during the eighteenth century handled a wide range of cargos in the waters of the Americas.[307] Not surprisingly, the huge variety and volume of this maritime trade generated many opportunities for sizeable profits for privateers and pirates alike. These cargos can be summarized along the following lines:

- Cane sugar, raw cotton, finished linens, American spices, and American tobacco all moved east to Europe.
- The slave trade carried large numbers of Africans from Africa to the Americas.
- Young European women headed toward the colonial American marriage market. Once settled there, they wanted the latest Paris fashions and more delicate teas.
- Rum flowed in both directions, but the American colonists always wanted gin and wine from Europe.
- Other much-desired imports from Europe included manufactured goods, tools, firearms, and edged weapons.

A second key point in this appendix, drawn both from Carl Swanson's 1991 study *Predators and Prizes: American Privateering and Imperial Warfare,*

1739-1748, and from Coker's *Charleston's Maritime Heritage*, is to note how many of the British, Spanish, and French privateers fought during two mid-eighteenth century wars, namely, the War of Jenkins' Ear, and King George's War.

British colonial privateers

The contemporary press gave thorough coverage of the importance of privateering to colonial merchants and to colonial officials. Merchants in leading American seaports, for example, built and outfitted scores of ships and staffed them with thousands of men in their efforts to capture Spanish and French cargo ships.

Charleston's lucrative rice trade with Spain was lost as a result of King George's War of 1739 to 1748. In addition, over many years, many privateers operating out of Charleston had raided outlying plantations, looted them, and made off with their slaves for sale elsewhere.

The war also carried the additional threat of a Spanish invasion fleet gathering in Havana for this purpose (it never set sail). The Spanish did, however, encourage Indian raids into what is now South Carolina, to which the English replied by encouraging retaliatory Indian raids against Spanish towns. The Spanish also promised to free all the British-owned slaves who managed to escape across the border.

Newport and New York were the major privateering ports of what is now the United States, and merchants there found it quite worthwhile to invest in the kinds of ships needed by local seamen to take prizes.

Interestingly, however, Quaker businessmen in Philadelphia avoided investing in privateers because of their strong pacifist inclinations, so it did not play any significant role at that time. In addition, shortages of ships and crews in Charleston kept it on the privateering sidelines, too. Because the richest prizes were located in the Caribbean, most American privateers turned their attentions toward those balmy southern and lucrative waters.

Charleston's overall trade had suffered greatly from the attacks of privateers operating in the area, and by their raids of outlying plantation to loot them and to steal their slaves for sale elsewhere. War also brought the new threat of an invasion by a Spanish fleet, but this never materialized.

Spanish and French privateers

By 1642 the government of France was empowering French privateers to prey on English shipping off India, even while at the same time endorsing peaceable trade with England across the Channel. Remarkably, in a single year – 1692 – England authorized at least fifty privateers, giving them a free hand and state-supplied weapons to attack the merchant shipping of any of England's trading rivals.[308]

Much later, the most important Caribbean cruising grounds for Spanish and French privateers became Bermuda; the Bahamas; Jamaica and the Windward Passage; the Gulf of Honduras; Curaçao and the South American coast; the Windward and Leeward Islands; and Cuba, Hispaniola (known as Santo Domingo after 1697), and Puerto Rico.[309]

Merchants in Havana, St Augustine, Cap François, Jamaica, and Martinique, together with their fellow businessmen in Newport, New York, Jamaica, and New Providence, all dispatched literally hundreds of privateers and thousands of sailors in efforts to turn enemy merchantmen into prizes.

Because of all this activity, the gentry of the times, for example, educated Philadelphians, Bostonians, Connecticut Yankees, Carolina plantation owners, Chesapeake tobacco "factors" (growers), and West Indian sugar producers all stayed in close touch with privateering news.

A good example of this level of interest was Dr Alexander Hamilton, a travelling Maryland physician, who wrote that a fellow traveler "a younge gentleman ... gave me a whole paquet of news about prizes and privateers, which is now the whole subject of discourse."[310]

The demise of privateering and rebirth after the War of 1812

Aside from some inconclusive attacks by Confederate raiders during the Civil War, after it most European and North American privateering came to a de facto end following the War of 1812.

Latin American privateering, however, continued unabated and even flourished by targeting non-Spanish shipping. The net result was that, as two British naval historians have put it, "a new wave of sea-going terror washed over the Caribbean and the Gulf of Mexico."[311]

The Quasi-War with France, 1798-1800

This little and brief war arose from a dispute between the United States and France over the repayment of French loans to the United States incurred during the American Revolutionary War.

The disagreement was acerbated by conflicting interpretations of the 1778 treaties of Alliance and Commerce between these two countries. France, which was then fighting a war with Great Britain, believed that one treaty (namely, the Jay Treaty of 1794) was incompatible with the 1778 treaties and therefore retaliated by seizing some of the American ships that were trading with the British.

The failure of diplomatic efforts to solve these problems encouraged the French privateers. In October 1796, they began attacking merchantmen sailing in American waters, no matter their nationality.

However, the drawdown of American naval forces after the independence of the United States now made it impossible for the Americans to respond militarily. The result was that by October 1797 more than 316 American ships had been captured. Congress therefore reconstituted the U.S. Navy in March 1798, and in July that year approved the use of military force against France.

Losses of American ships in this conflict, however, were appreciably reduced by informal cooperation with the Royal Navy. Under this bilateral agreement, ships from both nations were entitled to join each other's convoys, thus providing more safety in more numbers. Diplomatic negotiations between the United States and France continued, however, and led to the Convention of 1800, which ended the war and which was held to have been an American victory.

While it was going on, the Americans deployed a number of ships; 5,700 sailors and Marines; and 365 privateers. Casualties and losses included, for the Americans, about eighty-two men killed, about eighty-four wounded, and twenty-two privateers (which are said to have captured up to 2,000 enemy merchant ships). French losses were about twenty men killed, forty-two wounded, and 517 captured; eighteen French privateers were sunk or were captured.[312] The only good news from this quasi-war was that the Convention of 1800 ensured the United States would remain neutral during the forthcoming Napoleonic Wars.

Privateering Songs

On a privateer ship or, indeed, on any other form of wind-powered vessel, "chanties" (pronounced "shanties") were widely used to make hard physical work quicker, easier, and safer (safer because the simple instructions for the crew were embedded in the song itself). Here are some parts of such songs.[313]

Single-pull chanties

These called for the crew to perform a single hauling-on-a-rope effort, followed by a short catch-your-breath pause before the next pull. This process was repeated until the work was done. A sailor with lots of energy and a strong voice was the solo singer, backed up by a chorus provided by the crew:

> Solo: We'll haul the bowline so early in the morning.
> Chorus: We'll haul the bowline, the bowline. HAUL!

Double-pull chanties

In these, all hands pulled twice on each chorus.

> Solo: A Yankee ship came down the river,
> Chorus: BLOW, boys, BLOW.
> Solo: And all her sails they shone silver,
> Chorus: BLOW, my bully boys, BLOW.

One double-pull chanty was extremely popular. Entitled "Blow the Man Down", this song probably first meant a physical blow delivered by the mate to a lazy sailor to make him work faster. Some of these anonymous verses, taken from a website called "The Wayback Machine", were as follows:

I'll sing you a good song of the sea
With a way, hey, hey, blow the man down
And trust that you'll join in the chorus with me
Give me some time to blow the man down.

There was an old skipper I don't know his name
With a way, hey, blow the man down
Although he once played a remarkable game
Give me some time to blow the man down.

His ship lay becalmed in the tropical sea
With a way, hey, blow the man down
He whistled all day but in vain for a breeze
Give me some time to blow the man down.

Windlass or capstan chanties

Hoisting up the anchor or working the pumps of the ship needed a longer chantey with two choruses.

Solo: Old Stormy he was a bully old man,
Chorus: To me way [that is, "show me the way"] you storm along.
Solo: Old Stormy he was a bully old man,
Chorus: Fi-i-i, [maybe a contraction of "faithful"], massa ["Master",
             the title a sailor might give to an officer], storm along.

Excerpts from the Preface by Naval Historian Edgar Stanton Maclay in his *History of American Privateers* (1899)

At twenty-eight pages in length, this Preface is much too long to reproduce fully here, but we can profitably note the selected summarized points mentioned below.

Parts of them may have already been touched on in earlier pages of this book. Given the vagaries of reporting during the Revolutionary War and the War of 1812, however, some of the statistics cited below may be more illustrative than definitive. In any case, this is what we learn from Maclay:

- American privateers played a most important, if not the predominant, role in both of the two wars with England – the Revolutionary War and the War of 1812.

- In the Revolutionary War, there were sixty-four American war vessels of all descriptions, armed with a total of 1,242 cannons. This force captured 196 British ships.

- There were also 792 American privateers, armed with more than 13,000 cannons. These privateers captured or destroyed about 600 British vessels.

- During the War of 1812, the regular navy of the United States numbered only twenty-three vessels, armed with 556 cannons. This force captured 254 British ships.

- In this second war, the Americans had 517 privateers, which took at least 1,300 prizes (British ships).

- From a financial point of view, the monetary value of the British prizes taken by American government cruisers and privateers during the Revolutionary War totaled $18,000 (all figures used here are in contemporary American dollars).

- During the War of 1812, the monetary value of prizes taken by American government ships was $6,600,000, while that taken by American privateers was $39 million.

- Considering the entire maritime forces of the United States – both navy and privateers – about 800 ships were captured from the British during the Revolutionary War, valued at over $23.8 million and that about 16,000 British prisoners of war were taken. In the War of 1812, the value of prizes was $45.6 million and about 30,000 prisoners of war were taken.

- A letter from an Englishman, written in Jamaica in 1777, is quoted by Maclay to this effect, "to show what havoc was created in British commerce by American privateers". The letter says that "Within one week, fourteen sail of our ships have been carried into Martinque by American privateers".

- Another Englishman, writing from Grenada in the same year says: "Everything continues to be exceedingly dear, and we are happy if we can get anything for money, by reason of the quantity of vessels taken by the Americans." He continued: "God knows, if this American war continues much longer we shall all die of hunger. There was a ship from Africa with 450 Negroes, some thousand-weight of gold dust, and a great many elephant teeth – the whole cargo being computed to be worth £20,000 – also taken by an American privateer, a brig mounting fourteen cannon."

- Maclay tells us that "So loud were the protests of the British mercantile classes against carrying on the American war that every pressure was brought to bear on Parliament for its discontinuance."

- Towards the close of the War of 1812, English newspapers were full of articles recounting the vast amount of damage that had been inflicted on British commerce by American privateers. The master of one English vessel, who had been captured three times by American privateers, reported that he had seen no fewer than ten Yankee privateers on his voyage.

- As far as the British were concerned, Maclay believes that it was the American maritime forces, e.g., American privateers, and not the American armies, that played the dominant part in both the Revolutionary War and in the War of 1812.

Appendix 7

An Historical View from the Coast of the English Channel

The English maritime historian James W. Wilson, born in 1886, was a leading authority on English maritime history and expansion, who had sailed and had walked along the Channel coast many times. Many of the comments below are drawn from his instructive 1959 book, *The English Channel: A History*, pp. 281-283.[314]

The Channel is the arm of the Atlantic Ocean that separates southern England from northern France. It is linked to southern part of the North Sea by the Strait of Dover at its northeastern end and has long been one of the busiest maritime areas in the whole world.

Looking back on the eighteenth century, the naval wars between Britain and France, and often against Spain as well, grew more intense between 1739 and 1815. During this seventy-six-year period, there was war between one or both of these rival powers for forty-two years. In Britain's final struggle with the French Revolution and with Napoleon, there was non-stop war for twenty-one years, being broken only by the Peace of Amiens from 1802 to 1803.

The *guerre de course* (that is, privateering, or the war of commerce destruction) was how France compensated for its inferiority in battle fleets when compared to the Royal Navy. France's fast frigates combed the oceans, capturing merchant ships at sea and then sending them, under prize crews, to the many French or Spanish colonial ports willing to receive them and to facilitate their sale.

When Holland eventually became a satellite state of the French, her far-flung colonial possessions in the Far East were of great assistance to the war on British merchantmen. Moreover, in addition to the heavy cruisers of France, a river of privateers looking for prizes flowed out of the European ports of France and Spain and from their colonies all over the world.

Since official French trade on a vast scale was often blockaded during war years, the many unemployed private French seamen were ready and eager to take jobs on privateer ships. The insecurity that was an inherent part of multi-ocean maritime trade encouraged merchantmen to sail in convoys.

London-based ships therefore often assembled at Spithead (an area of the Solent off Hampshire in England, which is protected from strong winds by a 3-mile-long sandbank). These ships did not dare to venture out into the open sea, however, until they were fully under the protection of British warships. In fact, during the eighteenth and nineteenth centuries, more than 100 big East Indiamen could often be seen at Spithead – coming, going, loading, and unloading their cargos from all around the world – to be sent to customers all over the globe.

Closer to Britain itself in the Channel and in the North Sea, local trade and coastal shipping was always quite vulnerable smaller privateers, such as ketches and luggers based in the northern ports of France. In these congested waters, large-scale convoys were not feasible, so ship-to-ship fights, seizures, and narrow escapes happened almost daily.

Ship losses ran very high. During Napoleonic era, for example, over 5,000 British merchantmen were captured by privateers. In this process, more than 400 French privateers were captured or sunk. But, on balance, trade always tended to increase in the Channel and more ships were launched there.

British mercantile fortunes were on the up. The rich and the "middling people" ("middle class") fared very well indeed because they had both more money and a better education.

At the same time, however, lacking these assets and often trapped in dead-end jobs, the British poor grew poorer, eventually leading to what a later British statesman would correctly describe as the development of "two nations" (one quite rich, and the other quite poor) within England itself.

Making and Taking in Sail – How to Furl a Royal

For a hands-on nautical experience, below is a greatly condensed version of Richard Henry Dana, Jr.'s instructions to beginners on how to furl (how to fold up and to secure) one of the top-most sails on a big ship, which was known as a "royal".

As mentioned in earlier pages here, Dana wrote *Two Years Before the Mast* in 1840, which is probably the best book of its kind ever written. The excerpts that follow are from pages 59-60 of his other book, *The Seaman's Friend* (1879). It uses many nineteenth-century nautical phrases that are much too complicated to "translate" for the modern reader, so they are given here verbatim, just for local colour. This is what Dana tells the beginner:

When you have got aloft to the topgallant mast-head, see, in the first place, that the yard is well down by the lifts, and steadied by the braces; then see that both clews are hauled chock up to the blocks, and, if they are not, call out to the officer of the deck, and have it done. Then see your yard-arm gaskets clear. The best way is to cast them off from the tye, and lay them across, between the tye and the mast...

Having got all the sail upon the yard, make a skin of the upper part of the body of the sail, large enough to come down well abaft and cover the whole bunt when the sail is furled...

Now take your weather yard-arm gasket and pass it round the yard, three or four times, haul taut, and make it fast to the mast; then the lee one in the same manner. Never make a long gasket fast to its own part round the yard, for it may work loose and slip out to the yard-arm. Always pass a gasket *over* the yard and down abaft, which will help to bring the sail upon the yard.

Selected Bibliography

Allmond, Christopher. *The Hundred Years War: England and France at War, c. 1300-c. 1450*. Cambridge: Cambridge University Press, 1994.

American Battlefield Trust. "The Militia of the Sea: Privateering in the American Revolution and the War of 1812." htpps://www.battlefields, 2023. Accessed 12 February 2024.

__________. "David and Goliath: Privateers vs. the Mighty British Navy – When America turned to plunder to bolster its naval power during the "Second War of Independence". 10 June 2024. htpps://www.battlefieds, 2023. Accessed 17 August 2024.

American Merchant Marine at War. "Privateers and Mariners in the Revolutionary War." www.usmm.org. Accessed 28 January 2024.

Bailey, Roger A. "Commerce Raiders: Confederate Privateers and Cruisers in the Civil War". American Battlefield Trust, www.battlefieldtrust.org, 2024.

Bowen, H.V., John McAleer, and Robert J. Blythe. *Monsoon Traders: The Maritime World of the East India Company*. London: Scala Publishers, 2011.

British Library. "The American Revolution: A Timeline of the American Revolution from 1763-1787 – From the signing of the Treaty of Paris in 1763 to the Constitutional Convention in 1787.". London: 17 June 2016.

Chatterton, E. Kemble. *A World for the Taking: The Ships of the Honourable East India Company*. Tucson: Fireside Press, 2008.

Chapelle, Howard I. *The American Fishing Schooners, 1825-1935*. New York and London: Norton, 1994.

Cassard, Jean-Christophe. Rennes : *Les Bretons et la mer au Moyen Âge*. Rennes: Presses Universitaires de Rennes, 1998.

Chidsey, Donald Barr. *The American Privateers*. New York: Dodd, Mead & Company, 1962.

Cogliano, Francis D. and Kirsten E. Phimister (eds.). *Revolutionary America, 1763-1815: A Sourcebook*. New York and London: Routledge, 2011.

Chatterton, E. Keble. *A World for the Taking: The Ships of the Honourable East India Company*. Tucson: Fireship Press, 2008.

Cooper, Tim. "The One-Man Blockade of Great Britain – Thomas Boyle and the 'Pride of Baltimore'". 2023 War History Online. 15 August 2018. Accessed 22 November 2023.

Coker, P.C. III. *Charleston's Maritime Heritage 1670-1865*. Charleston: CokerCraft Press, 1987.

Claghorn, Charles E. "Maine Privateers during the Revolutionary War." *Maine History* 28,4(1989), pp. 210-212. https//digitalcommons.libray.umaine.edu/mainehistoryjournal/vol28/iss4/3. Accessed 10 February 2024.

Clodfelter, Michael. *Warfare and Armed Conflicts: A Statistical Reference to Casualty and Other Figures*. Jefferson: McFarland, 2002.

Cogliano, Francis D. and Kirsten E. Phimister (eds.). *Revolutionary America 1763-1815: A Sourcebook*. New York and London: Routledge, 2011.

Cushway, Graham. *Edward III and the War at Sea: The English Navy, 1327-1377*. Woodbridge: Boydell, 2011.

Dana, Richard Henry, Jr. *The Seaman's Friend: A Treatise on Practical Seamanship*. Mineola: Dover Publications, 1997.

Davis, William C. *The Pirates Lafitte: The Treacherous World of the Corsairs of the Gulf*. Boston and New York: HarperCollins, 2005.

Dolin, Eric Jay. *Rebels at Sea: Privateering in the American Revolution*. New York: Liveright, 2022.

__________. "Franklin's Privateers". National Maritime Historical Society, Sea History 180, Autumn 2022, pp. 18-21. Accessed December 2023.

Eastman, Ralph Mason. *Some Famous Privateers of New England*. Boston: Privately Printed by the State Street Trust Company in 1928.

Eddison, Jill. *Medieval Pirates: Pirates, Raiders and Privateers 1204-1453*. Stroud: The History Press, 2013.

Egerton, Douglas R. and Alison Games, Jane G. Landers, Kris Land, and Donald R. Wright. *The Atlantic World: A History, 1400-1888*. Wheeling: Harlan Davidson Inc., 2007.

Egloff, Florian. "Cybersecurity and the Age of Privateering". Carnegie Endowment for International Peace, "Understanding Cyberconflict". 16 October 2017. Accessed 23 November 2023.

Erikson, Emily. *Between Monopoly and Free Trade: The East India Company, 1600-1757*. Princeton and Oxford, 2014.

Friel, Ian. *Henry V's Navy: The Sea-Road to Agincourt and Conquest 1413-1422*. Stroud: The History Press, 2015.

Footner, Geoffrey M. *Tidewater Triumph: The Development and Worldwide Success of the Chesapeake Bay Pilot Schooner*. Centerville: Tidewater Publishers, 1998.

Frayler, John. "Privateers in the American Revolution". National Park Service Historian, Salem National Historic Site. No date or URL given online.

Fury, Cheryl A. (ed.). *The Social History of English Seamen 1485-1649*. Woodbridge: Boyell, 2012.

Garavelli, Dani. "Diary", an article on John Paul Jones. *London Review of Books*, Volume 46, Number 2, 25 January 2024, pp. 40-41.

González, Jennifer. "Pirates, Privateers, and Civil War Maritime Laws." Library of Congress Blogs: In Custodia Legis – Law Librarians of Congress, 28 May 2020, ISSN 2691-6592.

Greene, Jack P. *Negotiated Authorities: Essays in Colonial Political and Constitutional History.* Charlottesville and London: University Press of Virginia, 1994.

Hewittson, Jim. *Skull & Saltire: Stories of Scottish Piracy – Ancient and Modern.* Edinburgh: Black & White Publishing, 2005.

History.com Editors. "Alabama Claims". A&E Television Networks. 27 October 2009. Accessed 15 January 2024.

Heebøll-Holm, Thomas K. *Ports, Piracy and Maritime War: Piracy in the English Channel and the Atlantic, c. 1280-c. 1330.* Leiden and Boston: Brill, 2013.

Hewitson, Jim. *Skull & Saltire: Stories of Scottish Piracy – Ancient & Modern.* Edinburgh: Black & White Publishing, 2005.

Huggins, Stephen. "CSS Savannah". New Georgia Encyclopedia. 6 June 2017, pp. 1-3.

Hutchinson, Gillian. *Medieval Ships and Shipping.* London and Washington: Leicester University Press, 1997.

Jackson, Melvin H. Abstract of *Privateers in Charleston 1793-1796*. Smithsonian Studies in History and Technology, (1) 1-160. Accessed 23 April 2024.

Janin, Hunt with Ursula Carlson. *Mercenaries in Medieval and Renaissance Europe.* Jefferson and London: McFarland, 2013.

Johnson, Captain Charles. (Sam Willis ed.). *A General History of the Lives, Murders and Adventures of the Most Notorious Pirates.* London: British Library, 2020.

Kert, Faye M. "The Fortunes of War: Commercial Warfare and Maritime Risk in the War of 1812". *The Northern Mariner / Le Marin du Nord.* VIII. No. 4, October 1998, pp. 1-16. Accessed 7 January 2024.

__________. "'True, Publick and Notorious'": The Privateering War of 1812". London Journal of Canadian Studies. UCL Press, 20 August 2021, pp. 1-11.

__________. *Patriots and Profits in the War of 1812.* DailyHistory.org. "Privateering during the War of 1812: Interview with Faye M. Kert", accessed 30 May 2024.

Klein, Christopher. "How a Rogue Navy of Private Ships Helped Win the American Revolution". Original publishing date in *History*: 10 September 2020, https://www.history.com/news/american-privateers-revolutionary-war-private-navy. Accessed 11 November 2023.

Konstam, Angus. *Privateers & Pirates, 1730-1830*. Oxford: Osprey, 2001.

__________ and Roger Michael Kean. *Pirates: Predators of the Seas*. New York: Skyhorse Publishing, 2016.

Krawczynski, Keith. *William Henry Drayton: South Carolina Revolutionary Patriot*. Baton Rouge: Louisiana State University Press, 2001.

Langford, Paul. *A Polite and Commercial People: England 1727-1783*. Oxford: Clarendon Press, 1998. Lawson, Philip. *The East India Company: A History*. London and New York: Longman, 1993.

Lemisch, Jesse. "Privateering, the American Revolution, and the Rules of War: The United States was born in "Terrorism" and "Piracy." History News Network. Accessed 24 December 2023.

Lord Russell of Liverpool. *The French Corsairs*. London: Robert Hale, 1970.

Maclay, Edgar Stanton. *A History of American Privateers*. New York: D. Appleton & Company, 1899.

Magra, Christopher P. *"Guerre de Course* and the First American Naval Strategy" in *The Fisherman's Cause: Atlantic Commerce and Maritime Dimensions of the American Revolution*. New York: Cambridge University Press, 2009, pp. 27-39.

Maritimeheritage.org. "Ships, Captains, Seaports: Baltimore Clippers". The Maritime History Project. Accessed 6 January 2024.

Marshall, P.J. (ed.). *The Eighteenth Century*. Oxford. Oxford University Press, 2009.

McCullough, David. *John Adams*. New York, London, Toronto, Sydney, and Singapore: Simon & Schuster, 2001.

Middleton, Richard and Anne Lombard. *Colonial America: A History to 1763*. Fourth Edition. Chichester: Wiley-Blackwell, 2011.

Miller, Russell. *The East Indiamen*. Amsterdam: Time-Life Books, 1980.

Moody, T.W. and W.E. Vaughan (eds). *A New History of Ireland: Eighteenth-Century Ireland 1691-1800*. Oxford: Oxford University Press, 2009.

Musée Franco-Américain du Château de Blérancourt. The Guide. Ghent: Graphius, 2017.

National Park Service. "Star-Spangled Banner: National Historic Trail, DC, MD, VA – Joshua Barney". 10 February, 2021. Accessed 6 January 2024.

__________. "Jean Lafitte." National Historical Park and Preserve, Louisiana. Updated 22 September 2020. Accessed 7 February 2024.

__________. "George Roberts." 16 February 2022. https://touchpoints.app.cloud. gov. Accessed 26 February 2024.

__________. Copy of 1940 Guidebook, "Salem Maritime", covering the Salem Maritime National Historic Site in Salem, Massachusetts. 1940/sama/sec1.htm, 20 June 2010.

O'Shaughnessy, Andrew Jackson. *An Empire Divided: The American Revolution and the British Caribbean*. Philadelphia: University of Pennsylvania Press, 2000.

Paine, Lincoln. *The Sea and Civilization: A Maritime History of the World*. London: Atlantic Books, 2015.

Petrie, Donald A. *The Prize Game: Lawful Looting on the High Seas in the Days of Fighting Sail*. Annapolis: Naval Institute Press, 1999.

Porter, Roy. *English Society in the 18th Century*. Revised Edition. London: Penguin, 1990.

Rodger, N.A.M. *Safeguard of the Sea: A Naval History of Britain, 660–1649*. London: Penguin and National Maritime Museum, 1997.

Rogers, George C., Jr. *Charleston in the Age of the Pinckneys*. Columbia: University of South Carolina Press, 1980.

Rose, Susan. *Medieval Naval Warfare 1000–1500*. London and New York: Routledge, 2002.

__________. *England's Medieval Navy 1066–1509: Ships, Men & Warfare*. Barnsley: Seaforth, 2013.

__________. *The Wine Trade in Medieval Europe 1000–1500*. London, New Delhi, New York, Sydney: Bloomsbury, 2011.

Russon, Marc. *Les Côtes guerrières – Mer, guerre et pouvoirs au Moyen Âge. France – Façade océanique. Renn XIIIème au XVème siècles*. Presses Universitaires de Rennes, 2004.

Shannon Selin. "Imagining the Bounds of History: Pirate Consorts - Marie and Catherine Villard." Accessed February 2024.

Schultz, Marcel. "Prize Law and Contraband in Modern Naval Warfare". Springer Link excerpt from "Operational Law in International Studies and Current Maritime Security Challenges", pp. 211–243. 27 May 2018. Accessed 12 February 2024.

Sherburne, Andrew. *Memoirs of Andrew Sherburne: A Pensioner of the Navy of the Revolution, Written by Himself*. Utica: W. Williams, 1828, pp. 16–23.

Simon, Rebecca Alexandra. *Pirate Queens: The Lives of Anne Bonny & Mary Read*. Barnsley: Pen & Sword History, 2022.

__________. *The Pirates' Code: Laws and Life Aboard Ship*. Padstow: Reaktion Books, 2023.

Stevenson, Robert Louis. *Treasure Island*. Oxford: Oxford University Press, 1991.

Stern, Philip Van Doren. *The Confederate Navy: A Pictorial History*. New York: Da Capo Press, 1992.

Sutton, Jean. *Lords of the East: The East India Company and its Ships (1600-1784)*. London: Conway, 2000.

Swanson, Carl E. *Predators and Prizes: American Privateering and Imperial Warfare, 1739-1748*. Columbia: University of South Carolina Press, 1991.

Thomson, Janice E. *Mercenaries, Pirates, & Sovereigns: State-Building and Extraterritorial Violence in Early Modern Europe*. Princeton: Princeton University Press, 1994.

Waller, J. Michael. "Private ships of war and the American maritime tradition". PoliticalWarfare.org. Serviam, January-February 2008, pp. 1-2.

Wilbur, C. Keith. *Picture Book of the Revolution's Privateers*. Harrisburg: Stackpole, 1973.

Williamson, James Alexander. *The English Channel: A History*. Cleveland: World Publishing, 1959.

Willis, Kedon. "What role did the Caribbean play in the Revolutionary War?" A&E Television Networks. https://www.history.com/news/american-revolution-caribbean. Published 11 September 2023. Accessed 23 January 2024.

Wilson, Peter H. *Europe's Tragedy: A New History of the Thirty Years War*. London: Penguin, 2010.

Notes

1. Quoted by Konstam, "Privateers and Pirates", p. 19.

2. Dolin, "Rebels at Sea", p. 162.

3. See Dana, "Seaman's Friend", pp. xv–xx.

4. Quoted by Friel, "Henry V's Navy", p. 58.

5. Marshall, "Eighteenth Century", p. 178.

6. Coker, "Charleston's Maritime Heritage", p. 89.

7. Hutchinson, "Medieval Ships", pp. 73-75.

8. Lawson, "East India Company", p. 10.

9. Davis, "Pirates Lafitte", p. 29.

10. After Egerton, "Atlantic World", p. 131.

11. After a quotation in Heebøll-Holm, "Ports, Piracy and Maritime War", p. 12, citing Earle, *Pirate Wars*, pp. 21-22.

12. Cassard, "Les Bretons et la mer", p. 151.

13. Egerton et al, "Atlantic World", p. 116.

14. Konstam and Kean, "Privateers & Pirates", p. 93.

15. Coker, "Charleston's Maritime Heritage", p. 161.

16. Dolin, "Rebels at Sea", p. 219.

17. See Petrie, "The Prize Game", for an excellent discussion of this matter.

18. Kert, "Privateering War", p. 5.

19. Ibid, p. 6.

20. Ibid.

21. Ibid, p. 7.

22. Ibid.

23. Langford, "A Polite and Commercial People", p. 624.

24. Ibid.

25. Greene and Pole, "Companion", p. 9.

26. Marshall, "Eighteenth Century", p. 48.

27. American Battlefield Trust, "The Militia of the Sea", p. 1.

28. After Swanson, "Predators and Prizes", p. 66.

29. The unsourced quotes above all are after Rodger, "Safeguard", pp. 321-322.

30. Rodger, "Safeguard", p. 406.

31. Thomson, "Mercenaries, Pirates, and Sovereigns", p. 22.

32. Klein, "Rogue Navy", pp. 5-6.

33. Rodger, "Safeguard", p. 126.

34. Rose, "Medieval Navy", p. 159.

35. Thomson, "Mercenaries, Pirates, & Sovereigns", p. 22.

36. Fury, "English Seamen", p. 35.

37. Ibid, pp. 8-9.

38. Kert, "Privateering War of 1812", p. 2.
    Cushway, "Edward III", p. 110.

39. Rose, "Medieval Navy ", pp. 31-32.

40. These adventures are described by Janin and Carlson in "Mercenaries in Medieval and Renaissance Europe".

41. After Allmand, "Hundred Years War", p. 85.

42. Cushway, "Edward III", p. 110.

43. Friel, "Henry V's Navy", pp. 19-20.

44. Ibid, p. 16.

45. Rodger, "Safeguard", p. 182.

46. Williamson, "English Channel", p. 172.

47. Rodger, "Safeguard", p. 314.

48. Jackson, "Privateers in Charleston", p. 1.

49. Williamson, "English Channel", pp. 172-173.

50. Thomson, "Mercenaries, Pirates, and Sovereigns", p. 23.

51. Middleton and Lombard, "Colonial America", p. 39.

52. Fury, "English Seamen", p. 31.

53. Miller, "East Indiamen", p. 23.

54. Konstam and Kean, "Privateers & Pirates", p. 87.

55. Swanson, "Predators", p. 1.

56. Rodger, "Safeguard", pp. 294-295.

57. Quoted by Rodger, "Safeguard", p. 296.

58. Williamson, "English Channel", p. 214.

59. After Wilson, "Europe's Tragedy", p. 150.

60. Rodger, "Safeguard", p. 361.

61. Slaves arrived in British North America through a huge slave trade that brought about 3.4 million Africans from about 1662 and 1807, when the trade was at last abolished. (Source: Marshall, "Eighteenth Century", p. 2.)

62. Johnson, "Pirates", pp. 27-29.

63. Greene, "Negotiated Authorities", pp. 99-100.

64. Simon, 'Pirates' Code ", p. 28-29.

65. Coker, "Charleston", p. 53.

66. The gist of some of these points comes from Konstam, "Privateers & Pirates", pp. 1-8.

67. During the seventeenth century, there were even some privateers active along the coast of the Orkney Islands. At least one of them held a French commission for "taking and robbing all that he cann apprehend as ane common enemy". See Hewittson, "Skull & Saltire", p. 114.

68. Moody and Vaughan, "Ireland", p. 643.

69. Greene and Pole, "American Revolution", p. 507.

70. After Swanson, "Predators and Prizes", p. 223.

71. Swanson, "Predators and Prizes", p. 29.

72. Marshall, "Eighteenth Century", pp. 325-328.

73. Dolin, "Rebels at Sea", p. 3.

74. British Library, "Timeline", p. 2.

75. Greene and Pole, "Companion ", p. 171.

76. Williamson, "English Channel", p. 281.

77. Macay, "A History of American Privateers", p. xxiii.

78. Rose, "Medieval Naval Warfare", p. 1.

79. Ibid, p. 124.

80. Heebøll-Holm, "Ports, Piracy and Maritime War", p. 8.

81. After Rose, "Wine Trade", p. 79.

82. Rose, "Wine Trade", p. 79.

83. Quoted by Rodger, "Safeguard", p. 149.

84. Greene and Pole, "Companion", p. 327.

85. Rodger, "Safeguard", p. 199.

86. Langford, "A Polite and Commercial People", p. 624.

87. See Stevenson, "Treasure Island".

88. Cited in an 1863 reference book on maritime warfare, namely, Upton, *Maritime Warfare and Prize*, p. 23.

89. Kert, "Pioneering War", p. 4.

90. Fury, "Social History", pp. 8-9 and 31.

91. Rodger, "Safeguard", pp. 199-200.

92. Miller, "East Indiamen", p. 18.

93. American Battlefield Trust, "Militia of the Sea", p. 2.

94. Klein, "Rogue Navy", p. 3.

95. The 2,000 colonial privateers commissioned by the Continental Congress and by some stares are also discussed in Klein, "Rogue Navy", p. 1.

96. After Johnson, "Pirates", p. 29.

97. Fury, "English Seamen", pp. 196-197.

98. Ibid, p. 199.

99. Ibid, p. 201.

100. Swanson, "Predators and Prizes", p. 1.

101. All quotes in this section are from Konstam, "Privateers & Pirates", pp. 22-29.

102. This chapter draws from Swanson, "Predators and Prizes", pp. 222-225, and from Marshall, "Eighteenth Century", pp. 276-346.

103. Marshall, "Eighteenth Century", pp. 109-110.

104. Greene and Pole, "Companion", p. 8.

105. Langford, "A Polite and Commercial People", pp. 170-171.

106. O'Shaughnessy, "An Empire Divided", p. 58.

107. Konstam, "Pirates", p. 189.

108. After Langford, "A Polite and Commercial People", p. 702.

109. Maclay, "American Privateers", p. 506,

110. Magra, "The Fisherman's Cause", p. 31.

111. Drawn from Greene, "Companion", pp. 326-327.

112. Whaleboats were usually carried on the deck of a whaler and were lowered only during a hunt for a whale.

113. After Petrie, "The Prize Game", pp. 40-42.

114. Adapted from Wilbur, "Revolution's Privateers", pp. 91-92.

115. Klein, "Rogue Navy", pp. 3-4.

116. Konstam, "Privateers & Pirates", p. 52.

117. Dolin, "Rebels at Sea", pp. 147-148.

118. Ibid, pp. 149-150.

119. Waller, "Private ships of war", p. 1.

120. Cooper, *The One-Man Blockade of Great Britain – Thomas Boyle and the 'Pride of Baltimore'*", pp. 1-11.

121. Maclay, "History of American Privateers", p. 279.

122. Ibid, pp. 299-300.

123. After Maclay, "History of American Privateers", pp. 313-318.

124. Footner, "Tidewater Triumph", p. 112.

125. Maritimeheritage.org, "Ships, Captains, Seaports", p. 1.

126. This discussion is drawn in part from Petrie, "The Prize Game", pp. 2-3 and 9-10.

127. Paine, "The Sea", p. 338.

128. Faint copies of both these documents were reproduced in the Wikipedia article on "Letter of Marque".

129. After Wilbur, "Revolution's Pioneers", pp. 29-30.

130. National Park Service, "Privateers in the American Revolution", p. 1.

131. Ibid, p. 2.

132. Many of the facts and judgments in this chapter are drawn from Petrie, "The Prize Game", pp. 96 and 147-163.

133. Every ship of any size had its own boat, whether it was a small "cockboat" carried on deck or a "great boat" towed behind the ship because of its size.

134. Petrie, "The Prize Game", p. 163.

135. Cited by Dolin, "Rebels at Sea," p. 10.

136. After Dolin, "Rebels at Sea", p. 44.

137. Dolin, "Rebels at Sea", p. 231.

138. Petrie, "The Prize Game", p. 145.

139. The main source of information on the cargos is Konstam, "Pirates", pp. 182-192.

140. Cogliano and Phimister, "Revolutionary America", p. 40.

141. Magra, "The Fisherman's Cause", p. 27.

142. Swanson, "Predators and Prizes", p. 222.

143. American Merchant Marine at War, p. 1.

144. Ibid, p. 1, and Waller, "Private ships of war", p. 1.

145. After Langford, "A Polite and Commercial People", p. 624.

146. These comments are taken from Dolin, "Rebels at Sea", p. 45.

147. Maclay, "American Privateers", pp. 69-70.

148. A more technical definition of a "sharp-built hull" is given by Footner, "Tidewater Triumph", on p. 292. In such a hull, the bottom rises significantly from the keel to the point where the bilge or the bottom turns upward to form the vessel's topsides. That rise in the hull's bottom is called deadrise, and the greater the angle above the horizontal the sharper the vessel's hull.

149. Private communication from American boat expert Andy Sheehan.

150. Wilber, "Revolution's Privateers", p. 9.

151. Ibid.

152. Much of the information on early privateers used here is drawn from Dolin, "Rebels at Sea", pp. 29, 35-37, and 44-45.

153. Quoted by Chapelle, "American Fishing Schooners", p. 24.

154. Thomson, "Mercenaries, Pirates & Sovereigns", p. 24.

155. Konstam, "Privateers and Pirates", p. 8.

156. Ibid, p. 9.

157. The text of this document appears in Wilber, "Revolution's Privateers", p. 26, and in Konstam, "Privateers & Pirates", pp. 16–18.

158. Konstam, "Privateers & Pirates", pp. 9–10.

159. Greene and Pole, "American Revolution", p. 518.

160. The following two quotes are from Maclay, "American Privateers", pp. 206–207.

161. These tables are from Eastman, "Some Famous Privateers", p. viii.

162. Ibid, pp. 5–6.

163. Quoted by Eastman, "Some Famous Privateers", p. 81.

164. See Eastman, "Some Famous Privateers".

165. Eastman, "Some Famous Privateers", pp. 2, 6.

166. Ratlines, pronounced "ratlins", were lengths of thin rope tied between the shrouds of a sailing ship to form a ladder. Found on all square-rigged ships, whose crew had to go aloft to handle the sails, they were also used on some smaller fore-and-aft rigged vessels to make repairs easier or to get a better lookout from on high.

167. Eastman, "Some Famous Privateers", p. 20.

168. Dolin, "Rebels at Sea", p. 70.

169. Eastman, "Some Famous Privateers", p. 34.

170. These comments are drawn from Wilber, "Revolution's Privateers", p. 76.

171. Middleton and Lombard, "Colonial America", p. 39.

172. An excellent summary of early French contacts with America can be found in the Musée Franco-Américain's booklet "The Guide", especially the sections on "Transatlantic Ideals" and on "The Enlightenment Century", pp. 14–19.

173. The main source used here is the Musée Franco-Américain du Château de Blérancourt, "The Guide", pp. 50–51.

174. See Musée Franco-Américain, "The Guide", p. 12, for an illustration of a similar headdress.

175. Sources for our comments on William Bingham and on the French role in the Caribbean include Dolin, "Rebels at Sea", pp. 88–109.

176. Quoted by Dolin, "Rebels at Sea", p. 91. Emphasis added.

177. Quoted by Dolin, "Rebels at Sea", p. 92.

178. After Dolin, "Rebels at Sea", pp. 92–93.

179. O'Shaughnessy, "Empire Divided", p. 158.

180. Dolin, "Franklin's Privateers", pp. 1 and 21.

181. Davis, "Pirates Laffite", p. 12.

182. Ibid, pp. 52–53.

183. Ibid, p. 53.

184. Konstam, "Privateers & Pirates", p. 29.

185. See Maclay, "History of American Privateers", pp. 225-507.

186. Maclay, "History of American Privateers", p. xiv.

187. Kert, "Interview".

188. Maclay, "History of American Privateers", p. 225.

189. Ibid, pp. 12-13.

190. Kert, "Privateering War of 1812", p. 1.

191. This account is drawn from Maclay, "American Privateers", pp. 336-349.

192. Ship's biscuit was too hard to eat by itself, so it was broken up and mixed with stews or other food.

193. It is not clear whether Captain Coggeshall in fact had the right to give away the ship and its remaining cargo "as a present". The only alternative, however, would have been for him to staff the ship with a prize crew and then to have her sailed to a port where she could be legally condemned and sold. Given the local circumstances at that time, however, this does not seem to have been a feasible option.

194. The following comments are drawn from Maclay, "American Privateers", pp. 427-438.

195. The basic source for this section is Maclay, "American Privateers", pp. 462-472.

196. Maclay, "American Privateers", pp. 472.

197. Kert, "Privateering War of 1812", pp. 2 and 8.

198. Petrie, "Prize", p. 1.

199. Footner, "Tidewater Triumph", p. 121.

200. After Kert, "The Fortunes of War".

201. Konstam, "Privateers & Pirates", p. 11.

202. Maclay, "American Privateers", p. 335.

203. Eastman, "Some Famous Privateers", pp. 32-33.

204. Ibid, p. 37.

205. Konstam, "Pirates", pp. 188-189.

206. Ibid, p. 4.

207. Ibid, pp. 4-5.

208. See Petrie, "The Prize Game", pp. 1 and 165. Petrie is one of the shortest and clearest sources on the ships active in the War of 1812. Also very good on the War of 1812 is Konstam, "Privateers & Pirates", pp. 10-13. Note that, in a related private communication of 7 January 2024, Canadian Professor Carl Benn in Toronto warned the authors about what he called the prevalent "bad history" regarding the War of 1812. For example, he said, American comments on the war have often focused chiefly on specific frigate actions, in which the

Americans handled quite well, but tend to avoid any discussion of the broader picture of the war which, fundamentally, the Americans lost.

209. The comments of Niles are quoted in Dolin, "Rebels at Sea", pp. 240-241.

210. National Park Service, "Joshua Barney", p. 1.

211. There were two major kinds of landsmen on privateer ships. The first consisted of men who through social or financial connections came abord as officers, even though they had no nautical experience or training whatsoever. Such men lined up for voyages only because they hoped that they would bring them honour or profit. They were not welcomed either by the "real" officers or by the crews, the latter disliking them because of their lax discipline and their scramble for plunder. Sir Walter Raleigh expressed his hostility toward landsmen who were made officers only "by virtue of the purse" and by the "special favour of Princes". (See Fury, "Social History", p. 135).

212. Adapted from part of a 2023 article published by the U.S. Naval Institute.

213. Waller, "Private ships of war", pp. 1-2.

214. Eastman, "Some Famous Privateers", pp. 43-47.

215. Maclay, "History of American Privateers", p. 507.

216. Information on the Baltimore armed schooner *Patapsco* comes from Footner, "Tidewater Triumph", pp. 112- 119.

217. Thomson, "Mercenaries, Pirates, & Sovereigns", pp. 69-70.

218. Sources for the Declaration of Paris include Thomson, "Mercenaries, Pirates & Sovereigns", pp. 70-76.

219. Egloff, "Cybersecurity and the Age of Privateering", p. 3.

220. Thomson, "Mercenaries, Pirates, & Sovereigns", p. 72.

221. Ibid, pp. 72-73.

222. This chapter draws from, "The Sea and Civilization", pp. 549-553, and on History.com Editors, "Alabama Claims", pp. 1-2.

223. Bailey, "Confederate Raiders", p. 1.

224. The information on the Confederate raider *Sumter* used here is from Stern, "Confederate Navy", pp. 30-31.

225. Stern, "Confederate Navy", p. 27.

226. Paine, "The Sea and Civilization", p. 551.

227. Dolin, "Rebels at Sea", p. 244.

228. Maclay, "History of American Privateers", p. 505.

229. An excellent source for Charleston and its privateers is P.C. Coker, *Charleston's Maritime Heritage, 1670-1865*, published in 1987, which has fine illustrations and a good text.

230. This account follows Coker, "Charleton's Maritime Heritage", pp. 13-16.

231. Coker, "Charleston's Maritime Heritage", p. 48.

232. After Rogers, "Charleston", pp. 3-4.

233. Some of the points made in this chapter are drawn from Coker, "Charleston's Maritime Heritage", pp. 11, 61, 88-92, 131-135, 160-169, and 300-301.

234. Coker, "Charleston's Maritime Heritage", p. 61.

235. Krawczynski, "William Henry Drayton", p. 213.

236. Coker, "Charleston's Maritime Heritage", p. 135.

237. After Coker, "Charleston's Maritime Heritage", pp. 49-52.

238. After Maclay, "American Privateers", p. 325.

239. These examples are cited by Coker, "Charleston's Maritime Heritage", pp. 88-92.

240. The American schooner *Vixen*, launched in 1803, carried 14 guns and became the first in a series of small warships designed to protect American commercial commerce from attacks by enemy privateers. These schooners were later upgraded into brigs, which let them carry much heavier guns but also slowed them down. (Source: Konstam, "Privateers & Pirates", p. 10.)

241. After Coker, "Charleston's Maritime Heritage", p. 133.

242. Coker, "Charleston's Maritime Heritage", p. 135.

243. Middleton and Lombard, "Colonial America", p. 128-129.

244. After Marshall, "Eighteenth Century", p. 398.

245. Marshall, "Eighteenth Century", p. 394.

246. Ibid, pp. 394-395, 418.

247. O'Shaughnessy, "An Empire Divided", p. 3.

248. Greene, "Companion", p. 518.

249. O'Shaughnessy, "An Empire Divided", pp. 163-164.

250. Davis, "Pirates Lafitte", p. 30.

251. Ibid, p. 31.

252. Some of the points in this chapter are drawn from Willis, "What role did the Caribbean play in the Revolutionary War?", pp. 1-8. Also very useful is O'Shaughnessy, "An Empire Divided", especially on the roles of the privateers in the Caribbean.

253. Dolin, "Rebels at Sea", pp. 163-164.

254. Coker, "Charleston's Maritime Heritage", p. 91.

255. Information on these two privateers is drawn from Dolin, "Rebels at Sea", pp. 43, 44, 57, 153-154, and 231.

256. Some of the points made in the following discussion are drawn from Dolin, "Rebels at Sea", pp. 43-45.

257. Quoted by Dolin, "Rebels at Sea", p. 45.

258. This information comes from O'Shaughnessy "An Empire Divided", as cited by Willis, on p. 2 of his "What role did the Caribbean play in the Revolutionary War"?

259. Cited by Willis in "What role did the Caribbean play in the Revolutionary War?", p. 4.

260. O'Shaughnessy, "An Empire Divided", p. 155.

261. After O'Shaughnessy, "An Empire Divided", p. 167.

262. Packet ships were medium-sized vessels designed chiefly for domestic mail, passenger, and freight transportation in Europe and in North America during the eighteenth and nineteenth centuries.

263. Konstam, "Privateers & Pirates", p. 26

264. Cited by McCullough, "John Adams", p. 99.

265. Quoted by Klein, "Rogue Navy", p. 3.

266. McCullough, "John Adams", p, 100.

267. Quoted by McCullough, "John Adams", p. 105.

268. McCullough, "John Adams", p. 204.

269. Sources for this section include Dolin, "Rebels at Sea", p. 58, and Wilbur, "Revolution's Privateers", p. 71.

270. Konstam, "Privateers & Pirates", p. 20.

271. National Park Service, Guidebook on Salem Maritime National Historic Site, full text of 1940 Guidebook.

272. The accounts used here on the two privateers both named *Grand Turk* are chiefly drawn from Eastman, "Some Famous Privateers", pp. 38-47.

273. Konstam "Privateers & Pirates", p. 44.

274. Eastman, "Famous Privateers", p. 17.

275. Wilber, "Picture Book of the Revolution's Privateers", p. 27.

276. Eastman, "Some Famous Privateers", p. 10.

277. Dolin, "Rebels at Sea", p. 227.

278. The best source on the Laffites is Davis, "The Pirates Laffite", which is used here. The National Park Service piece on Jean Lafitte is also very good.

279. Davis, "The Pirates Lafitte", p. 179.

280. Sherburne, "Experiences on a Privateer", pp. 16-23.

281. Quoted by Dolin, "Rebels at Sea", p. 197.

282. Quoted by Eastman, "Some Famous Privateers", p. 48.

283. Petrie, "The Prize Game", full text.

284. After Petrie, "The Prize Game", pp. 20-21.

285. After Konstam, "Privateers & Pirates", p. 3.

286. After Petrie, "The Prize Game", p. 105.

287. McCormack et al, "Black Sailors", p. 9.

288. Ibid.

289. National Park Service, "George Roberts", pp. 1-2.

290. Quoted by Dolin, "Rebels at Sea", p. 57.

291. The source of many of the comments in this chapter is Fury, "English Seamen", Chapter 9.

292. This account is drawn from the texts of Selin, "Pirate Consorts" and from Davis, "Pirates Laffite".

293. Shannon Selin, "Pirate Consorts", p. 2.

294. In 1834, the English East India Company withdrew from all its commercial operations in India and restricted itself to administering the Indian territories it possessed. The company's final charter from the British government expired in 1874.

295. This picture appears in Dolin's "*Rebels at Sea*" after p. 164 (see Bibliography).

296. Cited in Rodger, "Safeguard", p. 407.

297. One of the best studies of the rise and fall of the East India Company is Jean Sutton's *Lords of the East: The East India Company and its Ships* (see Bibliography).

298. After Bowen, McAleer, and Blyth, "Monsoon Traders", p. 13.

299. Erikson, "Between Monopoly and Free Trade", p. 57.

300. This statement and its explanation below come from Miller, "East Indiamen", p. 125.

301. See Erikson, "Between Monopoly and Free Trade: The East India Company, 1600-1757", pp. 56-57- 62, and 174.

302. Erikson, "Between Monopoly and Free Trade", p. 61.

303. Quoted by Erikson, "Between Monopoly and Free Trade", p. 62.

304. After Chatterton, "World for the Taking", pp. 168-169.

305. These quotations from Drowne and Franklin come from Dolin, "Rebels at Sea", pp. 238-239.

306. Swanson, "Predators and Prizes", p. 22.

307. Some of the following observations in this section are drawn from Konstam and Keen, "Pirates", pp. 182-191.

308. Miller, "East Indiamen", p. 78.

309. Swanson, "Predators and Prizes", p. 151.

310. Quoted by Swanson, "Predators and Prizes", p. 179.

311. Konstam and Kean, "Pirates", p. 191.

312. After Clodfelter, "Warfare and Armed Conflicts".

313. Quoted by Wilbur, "Revolution's Privateers", p. 53.

314. See Williamson, "Channel Coast".

Index